Multidimensional Evidence-Based Practice

Synthesizing Knowledge, Research, and Values

Edited by
Christopher G. Petr

Routledge
Taylor & Francis Group

NEW YORK AND LONDON

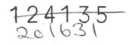

First published 2009
by Routledge
270 Madison Ave, New York, NY 10016

Simultaneously published in the UK
by Routledge
2 Park Square, Milton Park, Abingdon, Oxon OX14 4RN

Routledge is an imprint of the Taylor & Francis Group, an informa business

Typeset in Times by
Keystroke, 28 High Street, Tettenhall, Wolverhampton
Printed and bound in the United States of America on acid-free paper by
Edwards Brothers, Inc.

Library of Congress Cataloging in Publication Data
Multidimensional evidence-based practice: synthesizing knowledge, research, and values /
Christopher G. Petr editor.
p.cm.
1. Social service. 2. Public welfare. I. Petr, Christopher G.
HV40.M847 2007
361.0068—dc22
2007051758

ISBN 10: 0–7890–3676–2 (hbk)
ISBN 10: 0–7890–3677–0 (pbk)
ISBN 10: 0–203–88372–1 (ebk)

ISBN 13: 978–0–7890–3676–6 (hbk)
ISBN 13: 978–0–7890–3677–3 (pbk)
ISBN 13: 978–0–203–88372–3 (ebk)

Multidimensional Evidence-Based Practice

Multidimensional Evidence-Based Practice (*MEBP*) is a new and comprehensive approach to determining best practices in social services.

MEBP improves upon traditional evidence-based approaches by incorporating the views of consumers and professionals, qualitative research, and values. The book begins with a review of the context of best practice enquiry and goes on to present the seven steps of the MEBP model, discussing each step in detail. The model is appraised and explains how questions are formed, how various forms of knowledge and evidence are summarized and evaluated, and how values are used to both critique current best practices and point toward needed improvements. The final seven chapters illustrate the MEBP process at work specific to a range of topics, including best practices in the prevention of child abuse and best practices in restorative justice.

This book will be of interest to social workers and other professionals involved in the delivery of human services. It is also suitable for students and researchers of evidence-based practice.

Christopher G. Petr is Professor of the School of Social Welfare at the University of Kansas, USA. He is also a licensed clinical social worker in Kansas and practiced for a number of years at the local Community Mental Health Center.

Social Work Practice in Action
Edited by Marvin D. Feit
The University of Akron in Ohio, USA

Also available in the series:

Contents

Illustrations

Figures

Tables

Foreword

Irwin Epstein

Over the past decade in social work and the other helping professions, academic champions of the *evidence-based practice (EBP) movement* have promoted a narrowly positivist, empirically oriented, contextually stripped and, ultimately, reductionist prescription for choosing practice interventions. Elevating "gold standard" experimental studies and meta-analyses based on these experiments to the highest rung of knowledge generation, some EBP advocates have gone so far as to suggest that social workers who do not follow their prescribed mandates are professionally irresponsible and even guilty of malpractice. To such doctrinaire proponents of EBP any alternative source of professional knowledge and practice wisdom is deemed "authority-based," devoid of critical thinking.

Not surprisingly, the vast majority of practicing social workers with whom I have spoken about EBP here and in several other countries find this perspective and its accompanying accusations hard to swallow. But practitioners the world over are used to being disparaged by academics. Harder for them to stomach however is the potential loss of professional autonomy associated with the promotion of "manualized" practice guidelines based on reviews of empirical studies conducted and synthesized by non-practitioners.

Worse still is the implicit assumption of a division of labor between academics who create knowledge and practitioners who implement it. In the EBP world, gone is the place for the "reflective practitioner" (Schon, 1983) who generates and shares knowledge from within practice.

At a recent social work conference dominated by academics, where the air was heavy with self-righteous assertions of their EBP superiority, Chris Petr and I found ourselves in need of personal escape. Introduced to each other by a mutual friend, I had recently read Dr. Petr's co-authored article on teaching doctoral students to extract, critique and distill best practices (Petr & Walter, 2005) and found it to offer a heuristic guide to best practice synthesis that was refreshingly balanced, practical and even-handed. He called it *Multidimensional Evidence-Based Practice* (MEBP).

Although our work was quite different, at some level Dr. Petr and I were engaged in parallel efforts to integrate social work research and practice. Over the past decade, my approach was to seek ways that practitioners could contribute to their own knowledge of best practices via *practice-based research* (PBR) studies that they themselves could conduct in their own practice settings but did not require research designs that denied consumers the services they wanted or posed value conflicts for practitioners (see, for example, Epstein, 1995, 1996, 2001; Peake, Epstein & Medeiros, 2005). These studies could be qualitative, quantitative or employ mixed methods. They might rely on available clinical information or on original data collection. Either way, PBR studies were grounded in an authentic agency context rather than an aspiration to a research laboratory. Moreover, they were explicitly intended to promote practice decision-making.

Dr. Petr's strategy for arriving at best practices was to broaden the scope of review and assessment of *existing* literature including but not limited to intervention research studies. Similar to mine, his approach gave comparable credence to qualitative as well as to quantitative research findings rather than locating them on a hierarchy in which the former were treated as methodologically inferior to the latter. He extended his range of inquiry beyond mine by giving attention to the voices of consumers and the values of professionals.

I encouraged him to do a book on the subject, fully illustrating his methodology with exemplars in multiple practice contexts. And he and his doctoral students did it extremely well—providing exemplars in practice contexts as diverse as child abuse and teen pregnancy prevention, increasing access to health care for poor children, increasing parental involvement in child mental health services and therapeutic foster care, improving provider communication with parents whose children are in care, structuring effective restorative justice programs for crime victims and enhancing spirituality among the seriously mentally ill.

Predictably and gratifyingly, since Dr. Petr teaches at the University of Kansas School of Social Welfare, the book is infused with a commitment to consumer empowerment, the strengths perspective and a family focus—values for which his school is widely known and justifiably admired. Thus, the book's contribution goes beyond simply explicating a new methodology for arriving at best practices. Instead it views the synthesis of current best practices as only a first step in a dynamic, thoughtful, and creative process whereby future evaluation studies, values-based criticism and consumer involvement will add to the depth of our understanding and selection of best practices. The MEBP process can be profitably employed by students, practitioners, and academics alike.

For this more intellectually open, value-embracing, and consumer-inclusive model, we owe Dr. Petr and his fellow contributors a considerable debt. In a congratulatory spirit, let's raise a glass.

Irwin Epstein, Ph.D.
H. Rehr Professor of Applied Social Work Research
(Health & Mental Health)
Hunter College School of Social Work
New York, N.Y.

References

Epstein, I. (1995). Promoting reflective social work practice: Research strategies and consulting principles. In P. Hess & E. Mullens (Eds.), *Practitioner-researcher partnerships: Building knowledge from, in, and for practice* (pp. 83–102). Washington, DC: NASW Press.

Epstein, I. (1996). In quest of a research-based model for clinical practice: Or, why can't a social worker be more like a researcher? *Social Work Research, 20*, 97–100.

Epstein, I. (2001). Using available information in practice-based research: Mining for silver while dreaming of gold. In I. Epstein & S. Blumenfield (Eds.), *Clinical data-mining in practice-based research: Social work in hospital settings* (pp. 15–32). Binghamton, NY: Haworth Press.

Peake, K., Epstein, I., & Medeiros, D. (Eds.), (2005). *Clinical and research uses of an adolescent intake questionnaire: What kids need to talk about*. Binghampton, NY: Haworth Press.

Petr, C.G., & Walter, U. (2005). Best practices inquiry: A multi-dimensional, value-critical framework. *Journal of Social Work Education, 41*(2), 251–268.

Schon, D. (1983). *The reflective practitioner: How professionals think in action*. New York: Basic Books.

Preface

Despite its economic prosperity and high standard of living, the United States is confronted with a myriad number of social problems and issues. Homelessness, child abuse, mental illness, adult and juvenile crime, and substance abuse are just a few of the issues that plague the nation. Millions of citizens experience these problems and their attendant human suffering. Millions, even billions, of dollars are spent on prevention and treatment programs. In this context, it is vital that "best practices" be employed by professionals so that the dollars are well spent and the problems are addressed and resolved.

This book presents a comprehensive (multidimensional, evidence-based, value-critical) approach to determining best practices that was developed in a doctoral-level social work course at a major Midwestern university.[1] Conventional best practices approaches focus on thorough and systematic reviews of quantitative research studies, identifying empirically validated interventions for a given target population and problem. Clearly, this empirical approach to identifying best practices is an important and indispensable component of any best practices inquiry.

The principal contribution of this book centers on broadening and deepening the method and knowledge base of what is considered best practices, providing an expanded and more comprehensive foundation of information to guide professionals, policymakers, and funders. In this multidimensional evidence-based practice (MEBP) approach, it is not enough to report on the empirical research; instead, it is incumbent on the investigator to augment the empirical data with knowledge from consumer and professional sources, to utilize value criteria to identify gaps in current best practices, and to put forward recommendations regarding how to elevate current best practices by addressing those gaps. In addition to quantitative research, the MEBP approach incorporates diverse perspectives on best practices that warrant inclusion: qualitative research, professional practice wisdom, and consumer values and experiences. The MEBP method also includes a blueprint for conducting a value-based critique of the best practices themselves, then utilizing that critique to make recommendations about how best practices in a particular field can be improved.

Chapter 1 presents the intellectual context of best practices inquiry, in all of its considerable complexity. It defines and discusses several key, interrelated, and often confusing concepts: best practices, practice-based research, empirically based practice, evidence-based practice, and knowledge-based practice. This overview chapter concludes with an outline of the MEBP approach that is the subject of this book.

Chapter 2 presents the specific, seven-step MEBP model for determining current state-of-the-art best practices relative to a particular population and problem. These seven steps are:

- STEP 1: Identify the MEBP question.
- STEPS 2–4: Identify multiple sources of knowledge and evidence pertaining to the MEBP question:
  - STEP 2: Identify sources and summarize consumer perspective.
  - STEP 3: Identify sources and summarize professional perspective.
  - STEP 4: Identify sources and summarize research perspective, including both quantitative and qualitative studies.
- STEP 5: Summarize findings of best practices across three perspectives.
- STEPS 6 and 7: Critique current best practices:
  - STEP 6: Assess the potency of the identified best practices.
  - STEP 7: Use value criteria to critique and improve current best practices.

Chapters 3–9 are exemplars of the MEBP method, focused on a variety of social issues, and written by former students who attended the doctoral class in which this approach was developed and refined. These chapters fulfill two purposes: they illustrate the process of MEBP, and they contribute content that greatly enriches our understanding of best practices in each topic area. Chapter 3, written by Jacqueline Counts, addresses a major social problem: child abuse. Taking a prevention approach, the author identifies six key best practice components of prevention programs. She concludes that best practices in this area are very well developed and researched, but could be improved by establishing practice/policy feedback loops, strengthening parent leadership, and disseminating the results of research toward wider adoption of best practices. Emily McCave, in Chapter 4, identifies five best practices to prevent teen pregnancy, none of which included abstinence-only programs: sex education, access to contraceptives, youth leadership and development, parent involvement, and community alliances. One recommended improvement is to target research at what works for marginalized youth. In Chapter 5, Karen Stipp addresses the issue of health care access for poor children, identifying best practices as administrative appointment-keeping supports; non-medical supports including referrals, parent education and outreach; provider–parent relationships built upon effective communication; and usual sources of care maintained by continuity of care and a primary provider. To improve best practices, she recommends that providers work more collaboratively to reduce costly emergency visits. Chapter 6, by Tara McLendon, explores the timely issue of parent involvement in mental health services for their children. The two most commonly cited best practices across all three perspectives are the provision of culturally competent services and showing respect and concern to families. Better incorporation of the strengths perspective during initial contacts is one recommendation for improvement. Uta Walter's review of therapeutic foster care identifies two sets of best practices in Chapter 7. The first set revolves around connecting to, involving, and supporting biological families; the second set focuses on the provider families communicating clearly with agency staff and families, and receiving systematic support and training. She concludes that best practices can be improved by more fully operationalizing the value of family-centered practice. Jung Jin Choi, in Chapter 8, identifies three types of restorative justice programs and the best practices components that they share. Noting that programs are under-utilized by persons of color, the gap that he identifies is the lack of attention to cultural competence. In Chapter 9, Vincent Starnino focuses on ways to enhance spirituality among the seriously mentally ill. Although research on this topic is sparse, he identifies eight current best practices, and recommends improvements based on ensuring safety and enhancing practitioner competence and self-awareness.

Note

1   Some sections of the Preface and first two chapters are adaptations of previously published work by Petr and Walter (2005).

References

Petr, C.G., & Walter, U. (2005). Best practices inquiry: A multi-dimensional, value-critical framework. *Journal of Social Work Education, 41*(2), 251–268.

1 Best Practices Context

Christopher G. Petr

The context for best practices is fraught with conceptual confusion and controversy. Interrelated and overlapping terms such as "practice-based research," "empirically based practice," "evidence-based practice," and "knowledge-based practice" contribute to the untidiness and disarray. Meanwhile, funding agencies and the general public demand that programs be accountable and produce results. An effective and systematic method for determining best practices is vital to respond to this mandate and to ensure the well being of needy and vulnerable clients. This chapter assesses the intellectual context of best practices inquiry and concludes with a blueprint for conducting of a multidimensional inquiry that integrates various types of knowledge, research, and values.

Social workers, psychologists, and other helping professionals undertake a variety of work roles and responsibilities that require them to maintain high levels of competence in order to ensure the success of their clients and of their service agencies. These roles and responsibilities include providing direct service to clients, program development, administration, scholarship, grant writing, consultation, and research. In order to develop and sustain competence in these activities, helping professionals need to know about current state-of-the-art programs and practices.

For example, a new therapist at a Veteran's Administration Hospital may want and need to incorporate the most promising approaches for the treatment of adults with Post Traumatic Stress Disorder (PTSD). A foster care administrator, responding to requirements of new federal legislation, may ask staff to research and develop a state-of-the-art program to reunify children with their biological families. At a university, a student may be asked to write a paper on the most effective interventions to combat homelessness. At a family service agency, an administrator may seek the help of a university professor in writing a grant to secure funding for a new initiative to prevent domestic violence. A state legislator, seeking to create legislation to fund the treatment of drug addiction as an alternative to incarceration, may call upon expert professionals to serve as consultants to identify treatment programs that are cost effective.

These are but a few examples. Common to all of the scenarios is a focus on "best practices." That is, common to the above situations is the desire to ascertain or discover the current best practices in the given arena of concern. Although the term *best practices* may mean different things to different people in different contexts, generally speaking, best practices are those behaviors, methods, interventions, attitudes, and knowledge which represent the state of the art in a particular area or field of practice. Not confined to the human services, the term *best practices* is used extensively in business and other fields as well. For example, the British Columbia Ministry of Economic Development has defined best practices as the programs, initiatives, or activities which are considered leading edge, or exceptional models for others to follow (retrieved from www.sbed.gov.bc.ca, April 17, 2007).

Interest in best practices spans the globe. In the United States, the National Governor's Association for Best Practices (www.nga.org) produces reports for governors and their staff in five categories: education; health; homeland security and technology; environment, energy, and natural resources; and social, economic, and workforce programs. In the latter category alone, 68 publications were produced between January 2004 and June 2007, on topics such as prisoner re-entry, transition from foster care, and senior involvement in volunteerism. At www.best practices.org, the United Nations Habitat organization co-sponsors an international database of best practices programs that improve life in cities and communities worldwide. Countries may submit model programs for a three-stage assessment and review process, potentially resulting in a $30,000 cash prize. Over 2,000 practices from 137 countries are contained in the database, including topics such as housing, poverty reduction, and empowerment of women.

As mentioned above, a uniform definition of best practices remains elusive: there are many assorted ways to define and determine what best practices are including practice wisdom, use of expert advice, professional standards and guidelines, and evidence-based practice (Kessler, Gira, & Poertner, 2005). There is wider consensus about what is meant by *practices*, which are the direct service, program level, professional actions that are undertaken to ameliorate or prevent problems and symptoms among a target population of clients, or consumers. Practices are distinguished from policies, which are the broader guidelines that are embedded in legislation and organizations, that spawn and guide programs and practices at the direct service level.

More problematic is the term *best*. What makes a practice best? Who decides? What criteria are employed? Are the best practices those endorsed by expert professionals? By clients, the users of services? Are best practices those that have been proven by science to work? Are they the practices determined in a local setting to meet the needs of local clients? What levels of empirical support and general consensus is necessary to be a *best* practice?

In determining what practices are best, Multidimensional Evidence Based Practice (MEBP) is one method among many. Depending on one's point of view, best practices can also be conceptualized as *practice-based research, empirically based practice, evidence-based practice, or knowledge-based practice.* Yet, there are no firm and distinct boundaries around these categories, as will be discussed in the following sections.

Practice-Based Research

Practice-based research asserts that, in order to improve local performance and enhance accountability, it is important for practitioners and agencies to study their own practices and clients (Epstein & Blumenfield, 2001). This view of best practices posits that practitioners must continually monitor and reflect on their own practice approaches as part of a continuous quality improvement effort. In practice-based research, practitioners define the issues and practices that they want to improve upon, and may or may not seek help from researchers to help with study design and data analysis. One form of practice-based research is clinical data mining (Epstein & Bloomenfield, 2001). Typically, because of limited time and budgets, the practitioners retrospectively analyze data that are readily available and routinely collected in the agency, such as case records. This retrospective analysis of data and case records can help providers understand service trends and make better decisions regarding staff assignments and changes in service delivery.

For example, Nilsson (2001) reported on a practice-based study in a children's hospital aimed at identifying psychosocial factors common to frequently readmitted pediatric diabetes patients. These frequent readmissions were frustrating to medical personnel and required the expenditure of considerable resources. The study hoped to gain insight into how to serve the population better. A social worker analyzed the case records, including medical histories, social work records, and mental health files of those 18 patients most frequently readmitted. Content analysis of these records identified psychosocial issues that were common to the group. Recommendations from the study included focusing parent and family work on gender issues because results indicated a preponderance of teenage females in the sample, who were affected more by parenting problems of over-involvement than boys, who were more affected more by under-involvement. Other recommendations included early screening for psychiatric symptoms and the initiation of a new family therapy program to respond to the predominance of family-related psychosocial factors.

A recent iteration of practice-based research has been advanced by Scott Miller and colleagues (www.talkingcure.com). This group of mental health clinicians and researchers have developed two simple measurement scales that service providers can use to assess, from the client perspective, both client outcomes (Miller, Duncan, Brown, Sparks, & Claud, 2003) and the therapeutic alliance between the worker and the client (Duncan, Miller, Sparks, Claud, Reynolds, Brown, & Johnson, 2003). Irrespective of theoretical orientation or technique, these tools provide immediate practice-level data to keep the work focused on achieving individual client-directed goals while monitoring the quality of the helping relationship.

Empirically Based Practice

In contrast to practice-based research in which the practitioner focuses on local, internally generated data to improve service, another view of best practices holds that the role and responsibility of the practitioner is to behave in accordance with *externally* generated and validated interventions and methods. In this way of thinking, the practitioner imports best practices that have been endorsed by experts and/or validated by rigorous research. This broad, external locus of best practices encompasses the remaining categories of best practices for discussion in this chapter, including MEBP. It is important to note that practice-based research, with its internal locus of emphasis, is not antithetical to these external views; that is, best practices can be generated both from within and from without a particular practice setting. Practice-based research is a means to verify the applicability of externally generated practices to individual situations.

To many, best practices are those that have been proven to work. That is, best practices are those treatments or interventions that have been shown to be effective through rigorous scientific research. This approach to best practices is termed *empirically based practice*. Calls for empirically based practice have been issued from policymakers and other authorities, who stress the need for performance-based accountability in social programs. Years ago, Lisbeth Schorr, in the highly influential book *Within Our Reach: Breaking the Cycle of Disadvantage* (1988), stated that "reliable evidence about interventions that work has become more important than ever" (p. 268).

Since then, a plethora of professional organizations and government agencies have endorsed and promoted an empirically based approach to best practices. The American Psychological Association (APA), Division of Clinical Psychology commissioned reviews of the literature to ascertain the scientific evidence for the efficacy of various treatments, resulting in *A Guide to Treatments that Work* (Nathan & Gorman, 1998). The President's New Freedom Commission on Mental Health (2003) identified the need for more research-based interventions, and recommended strategies to bridge the gap between science and service.

Government-sponsored initiatives and private institutions support a variety of online clearinghouses and collaborations that conduct and disseminate systematic reviews of empirical studies for various fields of practice. These include the Campbell Collaboration (www.campbellcollaboration.org) focusing on education and social welfare; Cochrane Collaboration (www.cochrane.org) for health care issues, the "What Works Clearinghouse" (www.whatworks.ed.gov) established in 2002 by the U.S. Department of Education, and National Registry of Evidence-based Programs and Practices (www.nrepp.samhsa.gov) sponsored by the U.S. government's Substance Abuse and Mental Health Services Administration (SAMHSA). Other international centers of this type include the Nordic Campbell Center in Denmark, the Institute for Evidence-Based Social Work Practice in Sweden, the Australian Centre for Evidence-Based Clinical Practice (Morego, 2006), and the Belgian Center for Evidence-Based Medicine (Hannes & Laurence, 2007).

Empirically based practice in social work is exemplified by *The Handbook of Empirical Social Work Practice Volume 1: Mental Disorders* (Thyer & Wodarski, 1998), and *Volume 2: Social Problems and Practice Issues* (Wodarski & Thyer, 1998). In these volumes, the editors have organized materials by chapters which summarize research articles on various diagnoses and topics, and provide guidelines for effective practice based on that research. For example, for Post Traumatic Stress Disorder (PTSD), the conclusions are that "effective treatments of PTSD maintain a focus on the trauma and related memories, thoughts, and feelings; avoid blaming or stigmatizing the victim; provide information about responses to trauma; attempt to strengthen client's internal resources, such as work, family, and social support; and instill hope about the chances for improvement" (Vonk & Yegedis, 1998, p. 371). For effective psychosocial treatments of Attention Deficit Hyperactivity Disorder (ADHD), conclusions indicated that short-term behavioral interventions were effective with children who are unmotivated and lack insight, while long-term cognitive treatments were recommended for insightful adults and adolescents (Markward, 1998).

The empirical approach to best practices inquiry is driven not only by concerns about performance and accountability, but also by ethical considerations. The statement of *Ethical Principles of Psychologists and Code of Conduct* of the American Psychological Association (2002) states that "Psychologists' work is based upon established scientific and professional knowledge of the discipline" (2.04). The *Code of Ethics* of the National Association of Social Workers (1996) states that "Social workers should critically examine and keep current with emerging knowledge relevant to social work and fully use evaluation and research evidence in their professional practice" (5.02 (c)). This guideline also pertains to the ethical mandate of informed consent, because professionals need to know the evidentiary basis for alternative practices and policies in order to fully honor the informed consent principle (Gambrill, 2003).

Clearly, there is a strong rationale to support the idea of empirically based practice. Basing practice decisions on empirical evidence is an attempt to assure quality of services and accountability. It also honors the ethical mandate of informed consent and protects professionals from liability for using untested procedures. Ideally, basing decisions on established evidence is more effective and efficient in achieving outcomes, because time, energy, and dollars are not wasted on ineffective attempts to remedy the problems. Finally, empirically based practice may be more objective and scientific, forcing professionals to tether their own more subjective and emotional responses.

However, criticisms of empirically based practice are also widespread, calling attention to important issues (Beutler, 2000; Denzin & Lincoln, 2005; Ferguson, 2003; Friedman, 2003; Gould, 2006; Hoagwood, Burns, Kiser, Ringeisen, & Schoenwald, 2001; Hurlburt & Knapp, 2003; Krill, 1990; Schön, 1983, 1987; Webb, 2001; Witkin, 1998, 2001). Objections to the traditional empirically based practice approach center on difficulties and costs in applying research results to real-world routine practice situations, the subversion of clinical judgment and individualized care, disagreements about what constitutes evidence, and the exclusive use of quantitative approaches.

The scientific process of developing rigorous, valid empirical support for a particular model of intervention is a laborious, complex, costly, and time-consuming process in the real world. Then, after the development and validation phases, dissemination and adoption of the empirically based models are hindered by cost and resistance from providers (Beutler, 2000; Schoenwald & Hoagwood, 2001). The typical stages of the validation process are to first establish *efficacy* through strict research protocols and randomized trials, next establish the *effectiveness* of the model in real-world situations, then *disseminate* and *transport* the model to a wide, often skeptical professional audience. Concerned about the principle of individualized care, many professionals note that even the best randomized controlled studies only establish differences between groups of clients, and that many individual clients are not helped by the so-called proven methodology.

A principal criticism of empirically based practice centers on the issue of what constitutes evidence. Within the empirical camp itself, evidence generally means quantitative data, but even here, there is disagreement about what level of research quality is required to certify that an intervention is in fact empirically based. Researchers can agree that best practice is what has been proven to work, but what level of scientific "proof" is required to certify that a certain set of practices actually works? For example, the Promising Practices Network (www.promisingpractices. net), an influential consortium of private and government organizations including the RAND Corporation and the New York State Office of Children and Families, lists a variety of programs that have been categorized as "proven" or "promising." To be listed as "proven," the program needs to document only one experimental or quasi-experimental study with a sample of at least 30 in both the treatment and the comparison groups, demonstrating that at least one outcome is changed by 20%. These criteria are much less rigorous than those of the U.S. Office of Management and Budget (OMB) (www.whitehouse.gov/omb/part/2004_program _eval.pdf), which emphasizes that strong evidence of program impact requires more than one randomized controlled trial, preferably conducted by an independent party, in typical real-world settings.

Even when experts agree on the standards, deciding whether or not those research standards have been met can spur heated, even acrimonious, debate about the quality of evidence produced by empirical studies. This situation was extant in the recent published controversy over the effectiveness of Multisystemic Therapy (MST). For years, MST has been widely recognized as an empirically based practice for youth with severe behavior problems, with apparently strong evidence of effectiveness derived from several randomized, controlled studies. Yet, a thorough systematic review of the scientific evidence originally conducted for the Cochrane Collaboration (Littell, Popa, & Forsythe, 2005), and later summarized in *Children and Youth Services Review*, (Littell, 2005) concluded that the evidence indicated that MST was not consistently more effective than other alternatives for youth with social, emotional, or behavioral problems.

Scott Henggeler, the principal founder of MST, and his colleagues responded with an emotionally charged defense of MST and intense criticism of Littell's methods, conclusions, and motives (Henggeler, Schoenwald, Bourdin, & Swenson, 2006). Their defense encompassed not only methodological issues, but also attacked Littell's motivations, suggesting that she was defending the status quo because of some unspecified self-interest. In the same issue, Littell responded to those comments (Littell, 2006). Littell reiterated and defended her critique, including among other things, the flawed method of random assignment in MST studies, the questionable validity of fidelity measures, the inconsistent reporting of sample sizes, and the paucity of independent trials of the MST model. She particularly noted the potential conflict of interest inherent when the developers of models evaluate, promote, and financially benefit from the success of their models. Even though government and professional organizations endorse a model's empirical foundation, Littell cautioned that these endorsements can be influenced by political necessity. Promoting programs with some evidence of effectiveness, she asserted, is different from waiting to disseminate and transport programs until they have been subjected to rigorous independent evaluations of their effectiveness.

Perhaps the overarching lesson in this controversy is that there are always limitations and methodological flaws in the conduct of scientific research investigating the effectiveness of complex intervention strategies in the complex world of health and social systems. That is, to some extent, empirical findings of the effectiveness of human services programs are always suspect. Thus, it behooves us not to rely exclusively on empirical data to uncover best practices, but to incorporate other, also admittedly less than perfect, sources of evidence or knowledge, such as professional experience and consumer wisdom (Ferguson, 2003).

What is "best" should not be defined simply as "what works" in a narrow, quantitative way, but should be established via a range of sources and opinions, including qualitative research, which can be particularly useful in systematically documenting consumer and professional experiences. Because it disparages the basic assumptions of empirically based practice, a particularly damaging criticism is that leveled by qualitative researchers (Denzin & Lincoln, 2005). According to these authors, knowledge to guide practice should not be limited to that knowledge derived from a positivist, conservative paradigm that values quantitative methods of inquiry. In contrast to quantitative research which seeks, through the scientific method, to quantify data and analyze causal relationships between variables, qualitative research seeks to find individual meaning, focusing on the processes of social experience. Thus, knowledge is defined more broadly by qualitative researchers, to include voices of those otherwise not heard in the traditional, quantitative approach. Despite its long history and recent resurgence in many academic disciplines, qualitative research is marginalized in the world of empirically based practice. The resulting narrow view of science and evidence is seen to serve the interests of a conservative political agenda by maintaining the status and power of a Eurocentric, patriarchal world view (Lincoln, 2005).

Evidence-Based Practice

In recent years in the United States and much of Europe, the discourse about best practices has been dominated by evidence-based practice (EBP). EBP is an outgrowth of evidence-based medicine, which is defined as the use of current best evidence in making decisions about individuals (Sackett, Strauss, & Richardson, 1997).

In considering the intellectual context of best practices, one of the most confusing semantic issues is the close affiliation of the terms *empirically based practice* and *evidence-based practice*. Although these two terms are sometimes used interchangeably, recent proponents (Cournoyer, 2004; Gambrill, 2003) of evidence-based practice (EBP) assert a clear distinction. These authorities frame evidence-based practice as an outgrowth and improvement on empirically based practice. For our purposes it will remain fruitful to distinguish between empirically based practice and EBP, but the reader is forewarned that this distinction is not always made in other texts and sources.

Departing from a strict and narrow focus on empirical studies, evidence-based practice is a broader term than empirically based practice in that it considers three important factors: external research findings in the context of the appropriateness of their application to an individual situation; ethical issues such as informed consent; and client values and expectations (Gambrill, 2003). Franklin (2001) states "the basic principle for evidence-based practice is to choose interventions based on the best empirical evidence that are also appropriate for the client and situation" (p. 131). The experts in deciding whether and how to apply an empirically based practice guideline to a given client situation are the clients and providers themselves. Thus, evidence-based practice is viewed by its proponents as extending and enriching empirically based practice toward integrating practice and research. The broader definition acknowledges that empirical data should not dictate action, but should be considered in context.

Gilgun (2005), after reviewing evidence-based medicine, evidence-based nursing, and evidence-based social work, concluded that there are four "cornerstones" of EBP in social work. These are 1) what we know from research and theory; 2) professional wisdom and professional values; 3) what we have learned from personal experience; and 4) what clients bring to practice situations. Social workers should not blindly apply or impose research findings to every individual client, but instead use their own experience as well as the client's preferences to honor client self-determination.

Still, despite the acknowledgment of factors other than research findings, it is the empirical evidence that is central to evidence-based practice, as its name denotes (MacDonald, 2000; McNeill, 2006). Perhaps because of this, the broad definition of evidence-based practice cited above is not universally endorsed. Gilgun's review (2005) of evidence-based social work in the United Kingdom, for example, noted the lack of recognition of clinical expertise and client's perspectives at the point of application of evidence. *Evidence-based Practice Manual: Research and Outcome Measures in Health and Human Services* (Roberts & Yeager, 2004a) is a 1,050 page, 104 chapter book with wide interdisciplinary scope published by Oxford University Press. It is perhaps the most comprehensive and thorough examination of evidence-based practice to date. In the introductory chapter (Roberts & Yeager, 2004b), the editors define evidence-based practice as "the conscientious, explicit, and judicious use of the best available scientific evidence in professional decision making" (p. 5), and "the use of treatments for which there is sufficiently persuasive evidence to support their effectiveness in attaining the desired outcomes" (p. 5).

A second important, and related, semantic issue and point of clarification relative to EBP is the distinction between EBP as a *process* or verb, and EBP as a validated *intervention* (Regehr, Stern, & Shlonsky, 2007), or put another way, EBP as a verb versus EBP as a noun (Proctor, 2007). As a process, EBP centers on the inquiry process of finding and applying empirically based strategies to address specific client problems. Questions are posed, evidence is searched for and evaluated, and the available evidence is applied within the client, agency, and policy context. The five steps of evidence-based practice as directly quoted from Gambrill (2003, p. 7) are:

1. "Converting information needs related to practice decisions into answerable questions.
2. Tracking down, with maximum efficiency, the best evidence with which to answer them.
3. Critically appraising that evidence for its validity, impact (size of effect), and applicability (usefulness in practice).
4. Applying the results of this appraisal to practice and policy decisions. This involves deciding whether evidence found (if any) applies to the decision at hand (e.g., Is a client similar to those studied?) and considering client values and preferences in making decisions as well as other applicability concerns.
5. Evaluating our effectiveness and efficiency in carrying out steps and seeking ways to improve them in the future (Sackett et al., 2000, pp. 3–4)."

As a noun, especially its plural form *evidence-based practices* (EBPs), EBP refers to programs and interventions which have been empirically validated (Regehr, Stern, & Shlonsky, 2007). This meaning of the term is very similar to empirically based practice, in the sense that EBPs are approaches to prevention or treatment that have been validated by empirical studies. It is this second, intervention sense of the term that is used by the aforementioned private and government websites. Systematic reviews of the empirical research are conducted and a judgment is made about the level and quality of empirical support for a model, which may or may not then be designated as an EBP. Unlike EBP as a process, which considers consumer and professional viewpoints in the context of implementation decisions, the systematic reviews to uncover EBPs as interventions generally do not consider consumer and professional perspectives. Thus, the distinction between empirically based and evidence-based practice is not so clear when considering EBPs as interventions, because the systematic reviews do not contextualize their findings in the same way. So the evidence-based practices might more accurately be termed empirically based practices. The statement "We need to adopt evidence-based practices in our agency" means that staff should be trained in those interventions which have been empirically validated. It does not usually mean that staff should become expert in the EBP inquiry process identified in the five steps above.

Proponents of EBP sometimes seek to both promote EBP as a process and encourage research and adoption of EBPs as interventions. The Institute for Evidence-based Social Work at the University of Toronto has developed EBP partnerships with direct service organizations in the community. These partnerships include training for agency staff in EBP as a process, disseminating information about EBPs as interventions, and conducting collaborative research projects (Regehr et al., 2007).

Judging from the proliferation of books, articles, and websites sponsored by government and private organizations, EBP is clearly the predominant way to define best practices at the present time. The impact and influence of EBP has extended to the policy level, so that *evidence-based policy* is now advocated as a way to promulgate EBPs through legislation and executive action. Evidence-based policy is particularly popular and well established in Britain (Davies, 2004). In the United States, The Coalition for Evidence-Based Policy was established in 2001 by the Council for Excellence in Government (www.excelgov.org). Examples of evidence-based policy include the Substance Abuse and Mental Health Services Administration (SAMHSA), which has developed six evidence-based practice toolkits that many states have utilized to improve services, and The Education Sciences Reform Act of 2002, which established the Institute of Education Sciences, whose mission is to improve the empirical base for educational practices.

Knowledge-Based Practice

The broad definition of EBP as a process takes a large step in the direction of putting empirical evidence in context. Empirical evidence is not blindly implemented at the local level; instead, the client and the professional decide if and how it will be implemented. However, it is still empirical evidence that is contextualized, not other sources of knowledge. Evidence is research evidence, not other forms of evidence. Professional and client experiences are important at the application phase, but they are not themselves considered part of the body of evidence to be collected and reviewed. As a counterpoint to this view, some authors advocate a broader definition of evidence (Gould, 2006; Upshur, VandenKerkhof, & Goel, 2001), and the Social Care Institute for Excellence (SCIE) has been established to conduct systematic reviews that validate other sources of knowledge in the search for best practices, toward *knowledge-based practice.*

SCIE (www.scie.org.uk) was established in the United Kingdom in 2001. This organization produces reports and other resources on best practices in social care, with a focus on providing guidelines that are useful to consumers of services. SCIE sponsors systematic research reviews which they call knowledge reviews. Knowledge reviews combine research knowledge with practitioner and consumer knowledge, within an organizational and policy context. Practitioners and consumers are involved in all stages of the review process, from formation and modification of the question to summary of findings.

Five types of knowledge are explicitly sought: policy knowledge, organizational knowledge, practitioner knowledge, user knowledge, and research knowledge (Coren & Fisher, 2006). *Policy knowledge* constitutes legislative and policy information that is included as part of the context in the introductory sections of a review. *Organizational knowledge* encompasses issues at the agency level that may facilitate or hinder implementation of best practices. This information may be available in research reports about the implementation of services. Often this information is gathered using a practice survey, an element of knowledge reviews which is highly encouraged. Practice surveys are designed to obtain information from direct line providers of service about practices and tacit knowledge that may not be included in formal reviews. They also identify how widespread is the utilization of research knowledge in the field. Thus, they are also a main source of the *practice knowledge*, the third form of knowledge that is actively sought in the review. *User knowledge* is derived from consumers who serve on the review team, from published sources of the experiences and testimonials of the users of services, and from practice surveys. Finally, *research knowledge* from both qualitative and quantitative studies is systematically searched, assessed for quality, and summarized.

A recent example is the SCIE knowledge review on the topic "Outcome-focused services for older people" (Glendinning et al., 2006). The purpose of this report was to review the research evidence on the outcomes that older people value and the factors that inhibit or facilitate achievement of those outcomes. Outcomes were separated into outcomes involving change, such as physical symptoms; outcomes involving maintenance or prevention, such as keeping alert and active; and service process outcomes, such as feeling valued and respected. The review of published research concluded that there was a lack of research on the effectiveness of various initiatives to achieve these outcomes; instead, research has focused on organizational barriers and supports for delivering various services. Barriers identified included assessment measures that did not offer choice and overlooked emotional needs, lack of connections between health care and social care service systems, and difficulty in recruiting and retaining staff. Supports included care reviews that were conceived as continuous processes rather than discrete events and flexible, individualized assessments based on client needs and preferences. The practice survey part of the knowledge encompassed both a postal survey and in-depth case studies, the latter incorporating interviews with both professionals and users of services. Findings from the two-part practice survey indicated that outcomes were most readily achieved via strong interprofessional teams who had maximal control over resources.

Multidimensional Evidence-Based Practice

Thus far, this chapter has traced an evolutionary progression of intellectual thought about notions of externally derived best practices. Empirically based practice emphasized the importance and ethical requirement of basing practice decisions on empirically validated treatments and approaches. In part because of criticisms of this approach, later thinking about best practices have sought, in various ways, to contextualize empirical findings. EBP stresses the importance of thoughtful and reflective application of research within the context of the specific setting and clients' values. From knowledge-based practice we glean the importance of honoring and validating sources of wisdom other than only empirical studies into the best practices inquiry itself. This helps decision-makers take into account more than just local professional and consumer viewpoints. Also, the research evidence is positioned within a wider context of policy and broad professional and consumer voice.

But even after honoring and mobilizing knowledge from qualitative research, consumer experiences, and professional wisdom, the best practices inquiry process is still lacking one crucial component: a value critical analysis that juxtaposes the best practices findings against the preferred values and principles that guide service delivery. In other words, values help determine how good a practice is, whether it is indeed *best*. A systematic review of best practices must ideally synthesize knowledge, research, and values; thus, the need for the MEBP approach to best practices. The step that is remaining is a systematic way to incorporate values into the inquiry, specifically the analysis of current best practices. *Value-critical analysis* is a term and method of analysis elucidated by Donald Chambers (2000), who based much of his thinking on the ideas of policy analyst Martin Rein (1976). An examination of the key principles of value-critical analysis will demonstrate its utility in MEBP.

According to Rein and Chambers, there are two distinct types of policy and program analysis. One is an *analytic–descriptive* method in which the policy analyst essentially reports on how the policies and programs function—the focus is on describing how things *are*. The second type of analysis, the value-critical approach, builds on the analytic–descriptive approach by considering also how things *could be*. It makes judgments about the current state of affairs. The value-critical approach uses evaluative criteria to identify gaps and shortcomings in policies and programs, but it does not stop there. The value critique inherently includes implications for action, ideas about how the current state of affairs can be improved. Thus, the intent and purpose of a value-critical analysis is to create an outline or blueprint for something that might work better than the existing policy. Clearly, the approach seeks to move toward a more ideal state of affairs—it is not content with the status quo, because the status quo is always flawed in some way or ways.

Readers may be anticipating that the critical question with this approach is "Which values?" For Chambers, key values in a policy analysis include *adequacy*, *equity*, and *efficiency*. How adequate is the policy with respect to meeting the need of the population it is intended to benefit? How equitable are access to services and distribution of resources? How efficiently does the program or policy achieve its ends? These values represent the general principles or goals that cross all programs and policies. Each specific policy has its own goals, objectives, eligibility rules, and financing mechanisms, but across all of these are the standards or ideal characteristics that we want all programs and policies to strive for.

This value-critical approach is highly relevant and transferable to MEBP. The findings of a best practices inquiry represent a sort of composite program. That is, the findings identify those practices, behaviors, approaches, and model programs that are deemed the most likely to succeed. Thus, the composite program can be analyzed according to a set of evaluative criteria that judge how the best practices measure up against generally preferred outcomes and processes, and ultimately then, how they can be can be improved.

Both evidence-based practice and knowledge-based practice tend to parallel the analytic–descriptive approach described above; that is, both approaches present what best practices are, not what they could be. The analysis or critique centers on the quality of the research and, in knowledge-based practice, on barriers to implementation of best practices. Values are not an explicit or overt component of the critique, although values do come into play with respect to the values of the consumer and professional at the point of implementation. But this limited role for values is quite disparate from the value-critical approach whose core purpose and function is to advance the state of the art. In MEBP, the last step of the process is the most important, because it moves beyond methodological critique and description of barriers toward a view of a better world.

Selection of the evaluative criteria in MEBP are somewhat dependent on the topic, but there also are some universal values that apply across populations and problems. This topic will be discussed more fully in Chapter 2, but an example here will help illustrate the point. The principle or value "respect for diversity and difference" is widely acknowledged. Regardless of population and problem, professionals and society as a whole believe that services should be provided with respect and consideration for a client's own race, culture, age, sexual orientation, and gender. This value is widely endorsed not so much because we believe (or have data to support) that outcomes will be improved if a program respects diversity and difference, but because we simply believe that people deserve to be treated with respect. We would believe that whether or not there was empirical support for the assertion.

This general value has specific relevance dependent on the population and problem. For example, in working with children, the general call to respect diversity and difference might focus on the issue of age difference, especially with young children. Just as persons can be egocentric or ethnocentric, adults can be "adultcentric" toward young children, for example, by asking them to communicate verbally, in the adult's preferred mode of communication, when young children are not that proficient or comfortable at verbal communication (Petr, 1992). Adultcentric professionals may view children as young adults and have little patience or acceptance of their developmental needs and issues. So when applying a value-critical stance to best practices with young children, the MEBP approach could judge whether the identified best practices are free of adultcentrism. Are methods other than talking used to communicate with the young children? Are waiting rooms and offices child friendly, complete with furniture and materials that are appropriate for young children? Are the best practices based on an individual assessment of the child's developmental needs?

This example also demonstrates how the value critique generates ideas about how to improve current state of the art. Where the best practices are not consistent with the preferred values, improvements can be made. The current state-of-the-art practices are not discarded, they are supplemented. In the above example, staff can be trained on methods of nonverbal communication with children, waiting rooms can be made more child friendly, and individual assessments can become part of the routine. These changes would be made not because they would necessarily improve outcomes, although this could well be the case, but because the preferred values mandate that certain processes are important, in and of themselves.

Conclusion

This chapter has explored the concept of best practices, revealing a complex intellectual context. Practice-based research, empirically based practice, evidence-based practice, knowledge-based practice, and multidimensional evidence-based practice are related methods for determining best practices.

Practice-based research focuses on internal agency issues and data, answering local questions that are relevant to consumers, professionals, and administrators. Best practices are those which are based on locally generated research. The other methods listed above seek to import externally derived best practices. Evidence-based practice broadens and improves upon empirically based practice in important and helpful ways. The expanded notion of evidence-based practice recognizes the importance of the professional and the consumer in determining the relevance of the evidence to the situation at hand.

If, as evidence-based practice asserts, the multiple perspectives and experiences of consumers and professionals are vital in implementing research at the clinical decision-making level, at the point where the best practices inquiry is put to use, might not they also be vital to the best practices inquiry itself? Would not such an expanded inquiry, that integrates empirical knowledge with consumer and professional viewpoints, help the administrator, practitioner and consumer at the practice, program, and policy levels, know better how to, or whether to, follow the empirical guidelines? This is the basic proposition of knowledge-based practice, which seeks to honor and validate knowledge of various kinds, especially that of professional practitioners and consumers of services.

Research knowledge and other sources of knowledge need not be thought of as mutually exclusive, dichotomous, nor inherently incompatible. In a fashion similar to evidence-based practice's incorporation of professional and consumer wisdom at the implementation stage, the wisdom of professionals and consumers, as well as results of qualitative research, can be incorporated into the inquiry itself. Bereft of these perspectives, inquiry into best practices is incomplete and therefore less useful to professionals and clients. The incorporation of qualitative research and of consumer and practitioner perspectives into the best practices inquiry is important because new information is added to deepen the understanding of best practices. New information can take the form of constructive consumer or professional ideas about program components that have not been quantitatively evaluated. New information can also be gained from individual insights that are not captured in the aggregate data. Additionally, consumer and professional perspectives provide critiques of current best practices, guide the development of future research, and offer direction for the modification and improvement of best practices.

But this expansion of the knowledge base is only one step toward a multi-dimensional approach. The other step involves a value appraisal, in which the relevant best practices are measured and judged against evaluative criteria that help point the way to improved practices and outcomes for clients. So, the MEBP model presented in this book expands on the inquiry process for evidence-based practice in two ways: first, the inquiry searches for relevant information from qualitative studies, consumer perspective, and practice wisdom; second, the inquiry incorporates a value-critical analysis of the results to identify the strengths and weaknesses of current best practices.

MEBP includes the following seven steps, which are elaborated upon in the next chapter:

- STEP 1: Identify the MEBP question.
- STEPS 2–4: Identify multiple sources of knowledge and evidence pertaining to the MEBP question:

  - STEP 2: Identify sources and summarize consumer perspective.
  - STEP 3: Identify sources and summarize professional perspective.
  - STEP 4: Identify sources and summarize research perspective, including both quantitative and qualitative studies.

- STEP 5: Summarize findings of best practices across three perspectives.
- STEPS 6 and 7: Critique current best practices.

  - STEP 6: Assess the potency of the identified best practices.
  - STEP 7: Use value criteria to critique and improve current best practices.

References

American Psychological Association. (2002). *Ethical principles of psychologists and code of conduct*. Retrieved July 12, 2007, from www.apa.org/ethic/code2002html.

Beutler, L.E. (2000). David and Goliath: When empirical and clinical standards of practice meet. *American Psychologist*, 55(9), 997–1007.

Chambers, D.E. (2000). *Social policy and social programs: A method for the practical public policy analyst* (3rd ed.). Boston: Allyn and Bacon.

Coren, E., & Fisher, M. (2006). *The conduct of systematic research reviews for SCIE knowledge reviews*. London: Social Care Institute for Excellence.

Cournoyer, B.R. (2004). *The evidence-based social work skills book*. Boston: Pearson Education.

Davies, P. (February, 2004). Is evidence-based government possible? Paper presented at the Fourth Annual Campbell Collaboration Colloquium, Washington, DC.

Denzin, D.K., & Lincoln, Y.S. (Eds.) (2005). *The Sage handbook of qualitative research* (3rd ed.). Thousand Oaks, CA: Sage.

Duncan, B.L., Miller, S.D., Sparks, J.A., Claud, D.A., Reynolds, L.R., Brown, J., & Johnson, L.D. (2003). The session rating scale: Preliminary psychometric properties of a "working" alliance measure. *Journal of Brief Therapy, 3*(1), 3–12.

Epstein, I., & Blumenfield, S. (Eds.) (2001). *Clinical data-mining in practice-based research: Social work in hospital settings.* Binghamton, NY: Haworth Press.

Ferguson, H. (2003). Outline of a critical best practice perspective on social work and social care. *British Journal of Social Work, 33*, 1005–1024.

Franklin, C. (2001). Onward to evidence practice for schools (Editorial). *Children and Schools, 23*(3), 131–134.

Friedman, R. (2003). Presentation at the 16th Annual Research Conference Systems of Care for Children's Mental Health, March 2–5, 2003, Tampa, FL, retrieved May 3, 2003, from http://rtckids.fmhi.usf.edu/rtcpresents/mentalhealthpolicy/RobertFriedman plastic.htm

Gambrill, E. (2003). Evidence-based practice: Sea change or the emperor's new clothes? *Journal of Social Work Education, 39*(1), 3–23.

Gilgun, J. (2005). The four cornerstones of evidence-based practice in social work. *Research on Social Work Practice, 15*(1), 52–61.

Glendinning, C., Clarke, S., Hare, P., Kotchetkova, I., Maddison, J., & Newbronner, L. (2006). *Outcome-focused services for older people.* London: Social Care Institute for Excellence.

Gould, N. (2006). An inclusive approach to knowledge for mental health social work practice and policy, *The British Journal of Social Work, 36*(1), 109–125.

Hannes, K., & Laurence, C. (2007). Learn to read and write systemic reviews: The Belgian Campbell group. *Research on Social Work Practice, 17*(6), 748–753.

Henggeler, S.W., Schoenwald, S.K., Bourdin, C.M., & Swenson, C.C. (2006). Methodological critique and metaanalysis as Trojan horse. *Children and Youth Services Review, 28*, 447–457.

Hoagwood, K., Burns, B.J., Kiser, L., Ringeisen, H., & Schoenwald, S.K. (2001). Evidence-based practice in child and adolescent mental health services. *Psychiatric Services, 52*(9), 1179–1189.

Hurlburt, M., & Knapp, P. (Spring/Summer, 2003). The new consumers of evidence-based practices: Reflections of providers and families. *Data Matters: An Evaluation Newsletter of the National Technical Assistance Center for Children's Mental Health*, Special Issue #6, 21–23.

Kessler, M.L., Gira, E., & Poertner, J. (2005). Moving best practice to evidence-based practice in child welfare. *Families in Society, 86*(2), 244–250.

Krill, D.F. (1990). *Practice wisdom.* Newbury Park, CA: Sage.

Lincoln, Y.S. (2005). Institutional review boards and methodological conservatism: The challenge to and from phenomenological paradigms. In D.K. Denzin & Y.S. Lincoln (Eds.), *The Sage handbook of qualitative research* (3rd ed.) (pp.165–182). Thousand Oaks, CA: Sage.

Littell, J.H. (2005). Lessons learned from a systematic review of Multisystemic Therapy. *Children and Youth Services Review, 27*, 445–463.

Littell, J.H. (2006). The case for Multisystemic Therapy: Evidence or orthodoxy? *Children and Youth Services Review, 28*, 458–472.

Littell, J.H., Popa, M., & Forsythe, B. (2005). Multisystemic therapy for social, emotional, and behavior problems in youth age 10–17. *Cochrane library, issue 3, 2005.* Chichester, UK: John Wiley & Sons, Ltd.

MacDonald, G. (2000). Evidence-based practice. In M. Davies (Ed.), *The Blackwell encyclopedia of social work* (pp. 123, 124). Oxford, UK: Blackwell.

Markward, M.J. (1998). Attention deficit hyperactivity disorder. In B.A. Thyer & J.S. Wodarski (Eds.), *Handbook of empirical social work practice: Volume 1 mental disorders* (pp. 55–74). Hoboken, NJ: John Wiley & Sons.

McNeill, T. (2006). Evidence-based practice in an age of relativism: Toward a model for practice. *Social Work, 51*(2), 147–156.

Miller, S.D., Duncan, B.L., Brown, J., Sparks, J.A., & Claud, D.A. (2003). The outcome rating scale: A preliminary study of the reliability, validity, and feasibility of a brief visual analog measure. *Journal of Brief Therapy, 2*(3), 91–100.

Morego, P. (2006). Evidence-based practice: From medicine to social work. *European Journal of Social Work, 9*(4), 461–477.

Nathan, P.E., & Gorman, J.M. (Eds.) (1998). *A guide to treatments that work.* New York: Oxford University Press.

National Association of Social Workers. (1996). *Code of ethics.* Alexandria, VA: NASW Press.

New Freedom Commission on Mental Health. (2003). *Achieving the promise: Transforming mental health care in America: Final report.* DHHS Pub. No. SMA-03-3832. Rockville, MD.

Nilsson, D. (2001). Psycho-social problems faced by "frequent flyers" in pediatric diabetes unit. In I. Epstein & S. Blumenfield (Eds.), *Clinical data-mining in practice-based research: Social work in hospital settings* (pp. 53–70). Binghamton, NY: Haworth Press.

Petr, C.G. (1992). Adultcentrism in practice with children. *Families in Society, 73*(7), 408–416.

Proctor, E.K. (2007). Implementing evidence-based practice in social work education: Principles, strategies, and partnerships. *Research on Social Work Practice, 17*, 583–591.

Regehr, C., Stern, S., & Shlonsky, A. (2007). Operationalizing evidence-based practice: The development of an institute for evidence-based social work. *Research on Social Work Practice, 17*(3), 408–416.

Rein, M. (1976). *Social science and public policy.* New York: Penguin Books.

Roberts, A.R., & Yeager, K.R. (Eds.) (2004a). *Evidence-based practice manual.* New York: Oxford University Press.

Roberts, A.R., & Yeager, K.R. (2004b). Systematic reviews of evidence-based studies and practice-based research: How to search for, develop, and use them. In A.R. Roberts and K.R. Yeager (Eds.), *Evidence-based practice manual* (pp. 3–14). New York: Oxford University Press.

Sackett, D.L., Straus, S.E., & Richardson, W.S. (1997). *Evidence-based medicine. How to practice and teach EBM.* New York: Churchill Livingston.

Sackett, D.L., Straus, S.E., Richardson, W.C., Rosenberg, W., & Haynes, R.M. (2000). *Evidence-based medicine: How to practice and teach* (2nd ed.). New York: Churchill Livingston.

Schoenwald, S.K., & Hoagwood, K. (2001). Effectiveness, transportability, and dissemination of interventions: What matters when? *Psychiatric Services, 52*(9), 1190–1197.

Schön, D. (1983). *The reflective practitioner.* New York: Basic Books.

Schön, D. (1987). *Educating the reflective practitioner.* San Francisco, CA: Jossey-Bass.

Schorr, L. (1988). *Within our reach: Breaking the cycle of disadvantage*. New York: Doubleday.

Thyer, B.A., & Wodarski, J.S. (Eds.) (1998). *Handbook of empirical social work practice: Volume 1 mental disorders*. Hoboken, NJ: John Wiley & Sons.

Upshur, R., VandenKerkhof, E., & Goel, V. (2001). Meaning and measurement: An inclusive model of evidence in health care. *Journal of Evaluation in Clinical Practice, 7*(2), 91–96.

Vonk, M.E., & Yegedis, B.L. (1998). Post traumatic stress disorder. In B.A. Thyer & J.S. Wodarski (Eds.), *Handbook of empirical social work practice: Volume 1 mental disorders* (pp. 365–384). Hoboken, NJ: John Wiley & Sons.

Webb, S.A. (2001). Some considerations on the validity of evidence-based practice in social work. *British Journal of Social Work, 31*, 57–79.

Witkin, S.L. (1998). The right to effective treatment and the effective treatment of rights: Rhetorical empiricism and the politics of research. *Social Work, 43*(1), 75–80.

Witkin, S.L. (2001). Whose evidence and for what purpose? *Social Work, 46*(4), 293–296.

Wodarski, J.S., & Thyer, B.A. (Eds.) (1998). *Handbook of empirical social work practice: Volume 2 social problems and practice issues*. Hoboken, NJ: John Wiley & Sons.

2 Multidimensional Evidence-Based Practice

Christopher G. Petr

The extensive review of the context of best practices presented in Chapter 1 has revealed that the predominant, empirical approach to best practices inquiry is a necessary, but not sufficient, component of seeking state-of-the-art knowledge to guide practice. A best practices inquiry is improved when it is broadened to include experiences and preferences of consumers, the wisdom of professionals in a given field, and a critical appraisal of the values inherent in best practices interventions themselves. Chapter 2 presents the seven steps of Multidimensional Evidence-Based Practice, an approach that integrates various types of knowledge, qualitative and quantitative research, and values.

To this point, the reader has been presented with the case for an approach to best practices that honors various forms of knowledge and evidence, that recognizes the crucial role of values, and that presumes that best practices are dynamic processes. Chapter 2 presents Multidimensional Evidence-Based Practice (MEBP), which is a seven-step framework for identifying best practices that incorporates fundamental principles of evidence-based practice (EBP) and knowledge-based practice. Simply defined, MEBP is a method of best practices inquiry that integrates knowledge, research, and values. To be considered a "best" practice under MEBP, the process or activity must be endorsed by various sources and be consistent with the values that undergird the human services system. MEBP enriches the best practices inquiry process by explicitly and systematically including 1) qualitative research, 2) the perspectives of both the consumers and the professional practitioners, and 3) a critique of current best practices in the given topic area. This critique is twofold: first, the critique considers the potency of the current best practices, including factors such as the strength of the evidence, the quality of sources, and the level of agreement among sources; second, the critique exams the best practices against the preferred values and principles that guide service delivery. MEBP is a seven-step systematic review process for identifying current best practices and recommending ways to improve them. In contrast with the EBP process which focuses on an individual practitioner responding to the clinical situation of an individual client, MEBP tends to focus more on broader client populations and the programs that are designed to address their needs.

The seven steps of the MEBP model are listed below and are illustrated in Figure 2.1.

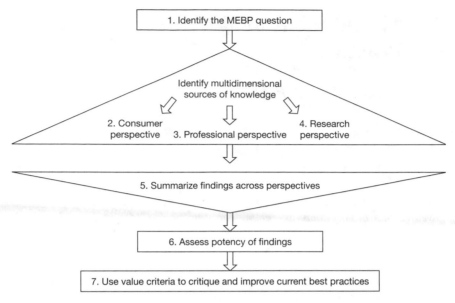

Figure 2.1 Multidimensional Evidence-Based Practice (MEBP) Seven Steps

- STEP 1: Identify the MEBP question.
- STEPS 2–4: Identify multiple sources of knowledge and evidence pertaining to the MEBP question:
  - STEP 2: Identify sources and summarize consumer perspective.
  - STEP 3: Identify sources and summarize professional perspective.
  - STEP 4: Identify sources and summarize research perspective, including both quantitative and qualitative studies.
- STEP 5: Summarize findings of best practices across three perspectives.
- STEPS 6 and 7: Critique current best practices:
  - STEP 6: Assess the potency of the identified best practices.
  - STEP 7: Use value criteria to critique and improve current best practices.

Formulate the Question

STEP 1: Identify the MEBP Question

The MEBP process begins with a careful construction of the question. What is the target population, the problem(s), and the desired outcomes that are the focus of the inquiry? The question can be in regards to treatment/intervention for either an existing problem or the prevention of that problem. The template for the intervention question is: *What are the best practices for X population/problem to achieve Y outcome(s)?* For prevention, the template is: *What are the best practices for X population/problem to prevent Y outcome(s)?*

For example, what are best practices to treat men who engage in domestic violence to reduce or eliminate violent episodes? . . . for treatment of attention-deficit hyperactivity disorder in teenagers to improve school performance? . . . for young teenage girls to prevent pregnancy? This question–formation process differs from the first step in the EBP process (see previous chapter) in that it is focused less on a practice level decision of a direct service provider regarding an individual client situation, and more on questions that might be generated by an administrator or researcher who is interested in a program-level response to a broader population. The process involves identifying a particular population who has identifiable needs/problems that involve costs and consequences for themselves and for society. Of course, an individual client's situation is relevant to the extent that the client's situation reflects those of a larger population.

The question structure in MEBP is different than asking whether a particular approach or set of practices work. This latter approach is often utilized by those interested in documenting evidence-based practices (EBPs). For example, the Substance Abuse and Mental Health Services Administration (SAMHSA) sponsors a National Registry of Evidence-based Programs and Practices (NREPP) (www.nrepp.samhsa.gov) that accepts and reviews submissions from intervention models. The question for the reviewers is "Is this particular model effective in achieving specified outcomes for a specified population?" Examples of models listed on the NREPP registry are Cognitive Behavioral Therapy for Late Life Depression and The United States Air Force Suicide Prevention Program. Similarly, the reviews at the Cochrane Database of Systematic Reviews (www.cochrane.org/reviews) and the Campbell Collaboration (www.campbellcollaboration.org) tend to focus on the effectiveness of specific models or types of approaches. For example, recent titles on the Cochrane website include "Scared Straight And Other Juvenile Awareness Programs For Preventing Juvenile Delinquency" and "Marital Therapy for Depression." From the Campbell Collaboration website are "Exercise to Improve Self Esteem in Children and Young People" and "Cognitive-behavioral Interventions for Children Who Have Been Sexually Abused."

There are several factors to be considered in formulating the question in the MEBP approach. First, it is important to note that the question itself is centered on achieving one or more desirable outcomes for a given population. It is essential to specify the desired outcomes because the best practices to achieve one outcome with a given population/problem may be different from practices aimed to achieve another outcome with the same population/problem. For example, in the area of spousal abuse, if the desired outcome is reduction/cessation of physical abuse on the part of the perpetrator, the best practices to achieve that goal could be different (more targeted at the individual perpetrator) than the best practices which lead to the desired outcome of preserving the marriage (targeted at both the perpetrator and the couple), or the best practices for assisting the abused spouse to maintain safety, to overcome dependence, and to leave the relationship altogether (targeted more at the spouse).

A second consideration is that the question itself must be structured in such a way that an answer can be readily obtained. That is, the question cannot be too broad and general, nor too narrow and circumscribed. If the question is too broad, the inquiry will uncover more information than can be assimilated. If it is too narrow, the investigator will have difficulty locating sufficient sources with adequate information to answer the question.

An example of a question that is too general is: "What are the best practices for helping abused and neglected children become successful adults?" In this example, both the population and the outcome encompass vast territories. Abused and neglected children, as a population of concern, come in many subtypes or subpopulations, such as age, type of abuse, and severity of abuse. The best practices for a three year old who has been severely sexually abused by a parent over a period of several months are most probably different than the best practices for a teenager who was fondled by her brother on one occasion, or who was slapped by her parents. Moreover, the outcome to "become successful adults" is problematic because it is a goal that is both difficult to measure and very long term, or distant, in nature. Yet, in an attempt to limit the scope of the question, it is possible to phrase it too narrowly. For example, it could be futile to attempt to answer the question, "What are the best practices to help Native American girls aged 3–5 who have been sexually abused by their mothers to become successful in school?"

In order to appropriately structure the question, it is useful to explore and understand the context of the topic of concern. Thus, the third vital consideration in MEBP question construction is to examine the needs, strengths, and desired outcomes for the population and problem at hand. This overview can clarify important issues at both the program and the policy levels that impact the population and problem of concern. What is the scope and incidence of the problem? Who is affected? What are the costs and consequences of the problem? What are the subgroups or subpopulations of the population of concern, and how might their needs differ for the group as a whole? Why is this problem and population of concern to society? What outcomes are the most important?

With respect to the question about child abuse and neglect above, suppose that a review of the basic facts about child abuse and neglect would reveal that physical neglect of young children, spurred by parent substance abuse, is a major aspect of the problem. Furthermore, African American children experiencing the problem are disproportionately represented in foster care. Thus, to focus on the needs of the population, the original question "What are the best practices for helping abused and neglected children become successful adults?" might be reframed in a more focused way as "What are the best practices to achieve successful reunification of African American children placed in foster care for physical neglect related to parent substance abuse?" If this question proves to be too narrow, perhaps because it is found that most programs do not work only with African American foster children, it can again be restructured, perhaps to read, "What are the best practices to achieve successful reunification of children placed in foster care for physical neglect related to parent substance abuse?"

Thus, in practice, the question itself may be re-worded and restructured several times. If too general, the question can be narrowed by reconsideration of the population, subpopulations, and preferred outcomes. Conversely, if it is too narrow, the question can be expanded by broadening the scope of either the population or the outcomes (see Chapters 3–9 for examples of MEBP questions).

Identify and Summarize Knowledge (Evidence) Pertaining to the Question from Multiple Perspectives

This multidimensional review of best practices broadens and enriches the traditional empirical approach to best practices by including, as evidence, additional sources of knowledge. Whereas traditional EBP involves a systematic review of the quantitative research, MEBP involves a systematic review of both qualitative and quantitative research as well as other legitimate sources of knowledge. The three knowledge perspectives are categorized as consumer, professional, and research. Consumers are the users, or recipients of services, the persons whom the best practices are targeted to help. Professionals are those persons from a variety of disciplines who use the best practices to help the targeted population. The research perspective consists of the systematic collection and analysis of data relevant to the question, including both qualitative and quantitative approaches. Although the search for best practices can be conducted in any order, and may in reality be more circular than linear, it is suggested that the consumer perspective be initiated first in order to validate the perspective and to combat the traditional tendency to reify knowledge that derives from the research perspective.

Search strategies typically involve extensive databases such as PsycINFO, Social Services Abstracts, Social Work Abstracts, ERIC, Expanded Academic ASAP, Google Scholar, and ProQuest Nursing Journals. Although theoretically these computer data bases should contain all journal articles and studies related to the topic, practical experience shows that many important sources are found not through these databases, but through search of reference lists in both journal articles and books (see, for example, Chapter 9). Government websites related to the topic often contain best practices information, as do the websites of the SCIE and the Cochran and Campbell collaborations. The search for consumer and professional sources is aided by Google and other search engines which can help identify consumer and professional organizations and testimonials.

For each perspective, the best practices investigator decides upon quality criteria for selection and inclusion into the report. It is impossible to read and summarize everything that is available on a topic, especially in the internet age. Thus, the investigator establishes guidelines or criteria for the selection of sources within each perspective.

Criteria for rating quantitative research, and to a lesser extent for qualitative research, are well established, and will be discussed in Step 4. Not so for consumer and professional sources. Clear criteria for the evaluation of the quality of the consumer and professional sources and information have not been developed to date in the literature. What constitutes a credible, quality consumer or professional source that is worthy of inclusion in a best practices inquiry? Conversely, which sources should be ignored? The *credibility* of the source is important, so that the best practices inquiry would value endorsements of practices from large organizations or renowned individuals. A source which has been widely quoted and is noted for its *wide influence* on changing practices is generally better than a source whose opinions have not been recognized or noticed by others. Ideally, a source would be *representative* of the larger group; even if written by an individual, the insights must resonate with the experiences of others. Finally, and perhaps most importantly, it is essential to *consider the vested interests* of the source for potential bias and conflict of interest. For example, an individual or organization affiliated with the psychiatric residential treatment of children may be inclined to endorse the benefits of residential treatment, based in part on legitimate experiences and in part on self-interest and self-preservation.

STEP 2: Identify Sources and Summarize the Consumer Perspective

In the steps of the traditional EBP process discussed in Chapter 1, the individual consumer, or recipient of services, whose circumstances generated the practice-level decision question, is consulted after the literature review relative to implementation of the research results. Here, in MEBP, the consumer perspective on the question is sought in the literature and from other sources at the beginning of the search process, so that a broad base of consumer voice can be incorporated into the findings.

One prime source of consumer wisdom is qualitative research studies that explore consumer experiences in a focused and structured manner. Examples of topics for this type of study include barriers to pediatric health care (Sobo, Seid, & Gelhard, 2006), "reasonable efforts" to prevent placement of children with disabilities (Petr & Barney, 1993), and experiences of family caregivers of the chronically ill (Berg-Weger, Rubio, & Tebb, 2001).

Consumer and family organizations are another important source for consumer wisdom, especially when they are national organizations, such as the National Alliance for the Mentally Ill (NAMI), that represent the views of constituents to law-makers and other decision-makers. These groups often distribute position statements on a variety of issues affecting their membership, including their views on current best practices.

A third vital source for the consumer viewpoint is first-person accounts of consumers or ex-consumers. Although these testimonials depict only one person's experiences, they can be powerful and influential when they resonate with experiences of others. For example, in her reflections on the experience of child abuse and subsequent recovery, Weaver (2007) discusses such factors as assurance of safety, a reliable support system, involvement in activities, and therapy as important factors in her recovery from the trauma of abuse. Books, articles, and even motion pictures can provide powerful insights into consumers' experiences regarding a wide variety of topics including child abuse (Elridge, 1994; Pelzer, 1995), autism (Grandin, 1995), mental illness (Grazer & Howard, 2001[film]; Lundin, 1998; Phillips, 1995), and suicide (Walen, 2002).

A practical issue here (and to a lesser extent with the professional perspective) is that consumer testimonials often encompass a wide range of topics and experiences, so that sometimes best practices about a specific MEBP question are implied rather than explicit (see, for example, Chapter 9). Also, it is often difficult to distinguish between those practices that consumers *have experienced* as helpful or not helpful, and those which they *think would be* helpful. Consumers can endorse practices that they have experienced, or, just as often, identify practices that they think are needed. Thus, when conducting the inquiry, it is important to note this distinction when reporting the results (see, for example, Chapter 3).

STEP 3: Identify Sources and Summarize the Professional Perspective

In the conventional EBP inquiry process, professional wisdom is important in deciding whether and how to implement the research results in the particular client situation. In MEBP, sources for professional wisdom are sought in the literature and other sources, similar to the process in Step 2 for the consumer perspective. Just as this wisdom is valuable at the individual client level, it is also crucial at the time of the inquiry itself. Professional practice wisdom is the wisdom of experienced professionals and practitioners who operate in the real practice world, a world that is quite different from the research-about-practice world. Professionals "put it all together," all of the multitude of contextual and individual factors which produce knowledge about best practices that is unique. For Krill (1990) practice wisdom is the unique process in which a worker creatively integrates knowledge about self, the client, and the interpersonal situation. For Klein and Bloom (1995), practice wisdom is a personal system of knowledge that is value-driven and that is derived from the both the experience of the client situation and the use of empirical information.

Sources of professional practice wisdom include at least five different types or categories. One is *program descriptions*, especially of new programs and approaches that have not yet been fully evaluated, but that are based on sound theory, experience, and values (see for example, Biegel, Tracy, & Corvo, 1994; Hodge & Williams, 2002; Indyk, Belville, Lachapelle, Gordon, & Dewart, 1993; Valentine & Gray, 2006). Another source is *professional organizations* such as the Child Welfare League of America that issue position papers or standards of practice in a given area. A third source is *single first-person accounts* of the experiences of learned practitioners over time and in particular situations. Yalom (2002), for instance, published what he called an "open letter to a new generation of therapists and their patients" filled with advise and wisdom accumulated over 45 years of therapeutic practice. Similarly, Armstrong (2001) shares his insights gained over the course of 25 years as a school social worker. A fourth source is *professional commentaries* on existing practices which expand thinking and programming in innovative directions; for example, in the area of domestic violence (van Wormer & Bednar, 2002) or interventions for female youth identified as having serious emotional and behavioral disorders (Walter & Peterson, 2002). A final source is *interviews or surveys of professional experts' opinions* about best practices, such as the systematic involvement of an expert panel in identifying key elements of community-based "wraparound" services in children's mental health (Walker & Bruns, 2006), and interviews with professional foster parents (Wells, Farmer, Richards, & Burns, 2004).

STEP 4: Identify Sources and Summarize the Research Perspective

In MEBP, both quantitative and qualitative research is valued. As discussed earlier, the importance of determining the quantitative empirical evidence relative to the question is unquestioned, and various methods to do so are well established (Cournoyer, 2004; Crane, 1998; Gibbs & Gambrill, 1999; Gorey & Thyer, 1998; MacLeod & Nelson, 2000; Shadish, Ragsdale, Glaser, & Montgomery, 1995; Sprague & Thyer, 2002). Generally, quantitative studies are rated on these criteria: research design, with the gold standard being experimental designs in which the sample is randomly assigned to a treatment and control group; sample size, methods of selection, representativeness, and diversity; data collection procedures; validity and reliability of measurement instruments; data analysis techniques; significance of findings; relevance to the question at hand; and independence of the researchers.

In addition to quantitative evidence, a best practices inquiry is enriched through incorporation of the dimension of relevant qualitative research. Qualitative studies aim at an in-depth understanding of phenomena or experiences that takes into account the relationships, meanings, biases, and ambiguities of the context in which they occur (Creswell, 1998; Denzin & Lincoln, 2005). Qualitative research traditions include ethnography, grounded theory, narrative, case study, and evaluation research (Padgett, 2004a). Although highly variegated, all qualitative approaches view knowledge as tied to the meaning people attribute to events. Thus knowledge evolves and emerges from its situational and cultural context (Creswell, 1998). The utility of qualitative designs is exemplified in mixed-method research, in which the findings from the two methods can be compared and contrasted, enhancing the capacity of the study to generate and test theory (Gioia, 2004; Padgett, 2004b).

Standards for the rigor of qualitative inquiries differ from those used in quantitative research, and vary according to the academic tradition upon which they draw. Social work frequently uses Lincoln and Guba's (1985) criteria of "trustworthiness," that is, the need for the research to be believable to an audience, to evaluate qualitative studies as to their credibility, transferability, dependability, and confirmability. Briefly stated, findings should "ring true" to those who provided the data, and thick descriptions (Geertz, 1973) should provide enough contextual information about participants, researcher, environments, and actions to judge the consistency of insights and their informative value for different situations. Unlike quantitative inquiries, qualitative approaches are thus not focused on statistical likelihood but on lifelikeness, or verisimilitude, that allows for a deepened understanding of a given phenomenon. Anastas (2004) identified these dimensions of quality in qualitative evaluation research: clarity of the research question, identifying the epistemological framework, using theory and prior knowledge effectively, addressing ethical issues, documenting all aspects of the study method, ensuring trustworthiness of the data, and communicating findings effectively.

For both quantitative and qualitative research, an invaluable source for the research perspective are *systematic reviews of research* which have been published in journals or on websites that specialize in these reviews, such as the Cochran Collaboration, Campbell Collaboration, and SCIE. The span of topics examined by these reports extends from what works in adult correctional settings (Golder et al., 2005) to the effects of intercessory prayer (Hodge, 2007). In quantitative research, one particularly valuable type of systematic review is the *meta-analysis*, in which statistical analyses are performed on the results of numerous studies to arrive at an overall effect size. Excellent examples of these include the work of Lundahl, Nimer, and Parsons (2006) and MacLeod and Nelson (2000) in the area of child abuse prevention (see Chapter 3).

Although methods for synthesizing qualitative research are less developed than those for meta-analysis of quantitative research, metasynthesis of individual qualitative studies can be very useful to knowledge development and to practice, yielding new insights and understandings that are not apparent from the individual studies (Bondas & Hall, 2007; Drisko, 2007). Examples of systematic reviews of qualitative research include Attree's (2004) review of studies of children's experiences growing up in poverty and Kearney's (2001) synthesis of studies of the experience of domestic violence.

Because of their utility, the search for best practices should begin by searching for systematic reviews of both the quantitative and the qualitative variety. Since stringent criteria are used and the systematic reviews are conducted by experts with peer review, this type of source not only saves time, but also lends credibility to the findings. The professional or program administrator who conducts the best practices review can trust that rigor has been maintained in the evaluation of the individual studies included in the systematic review. On the other hand, these systematic reviews may not contain detailed information about the specific best practices on the topic. Rather, they may just report the effectiveness of various general approaches or models, without information about the specific components or interventions of the model. In this case it would be necessary to locate other sources about the models that describe the specific components.

STEP 5: Summarize Current Best Practices Across Three Perspectives

In this step, MEBP focuses on what is common across all three perspectives. In order to be state of the art, or a "best" practice, an intervention or program component needs to be endorsed by more than one of the three perspectives, preferably by all three. So in MEBP, "best" is defined in part by agreement within and across perspectives. A specific practice must appear in a majority of sources within each perspective to be included in best practice summary of any one of the three perspectives. In order to make the final list of best practices in the overall summary, a specific practice must also be included in the summary list of other perspectives. Thus, each perspective's summary of best practices is juxtaposed with the summaries of the other two perspectives to identify the commonalities.

This process entails identifying similarities and differences among the consumer, professional, and research perspectives. Are there areas of agreement, even consensus, between and across the perspectives; that is, are there practices that are deemed exemplary by more than one perspective or by all three—research, consumers, and professionals? Conversely, are there areas of disagreement, in which the ideas about best practices in one perspective are contradicted by notions from another perspective? Given these comparisons, what can be said about the preferred activities, approaches, structures, and interventions for achieving positive outcomes relative to the question? What are the overall best practices to achieve outcomes for the population and problem?

Critique of Current Best Practices

The critique of current best practices involves two parts. First, the "potency" factor is assessed. Here, potency refers to the strength of the best practices, or how much support exists for them. If an agency or practitioner were to implement the best practices, how confident could they be that they would achieve success? What needs to happen to improve the potency of current best practices? The second part of the critique is a value-critical analysis of the best practices. It is not enough to describe and report what the best practices are, one needs also to analyze their strengths and weaknesses, and recommend how they could be improved.

STEP 6: Assess the Potency of the Identified Best Practices

What is the strength of the support for the best practices described in Step 5? In EBP, the empirical evidence is critically appraised; in MEBP, the critical appraisal applies to the quantitative evidence as well as to the qualitative research, consumer perspective, and practice wisdom.

The potency analysis provides one way to assess what "best" means. Best is a relative concept. The best practices for one topic may be highly developed and supported by extensive research and widespread support from consumers and professionals. For another topic, the current best practices may actually not be very good, in the sense that there is little empirical research or consensus among consumers and professionals. Still, the identified best practices are the best that currently exist. So, the reader needs to be informed about exactly what level of support exists for current best practices, so that informed decisions can be made about their use. For this potency critique, the three criteria to be assessed and discussed are the quality of sources for each perspective, the level of agreement within each perspective, and the level of agreement across perspectives.

The quality of sources is judged by appraising the sources against the criteria for selection established in Steps 2–4. For the consumer and professional perspectives, just how credible and influential were the sources? Did national or state organizations contribute? Were there recent, high-quality qualitative studies and surveys of consumers and professionals, or were the studies quite dated and poorly designed? For the research perspective, how did the studies fare overall when judged against the quality criteria? Were there numerous, recent, well-designed quantitative studies or were there in fact only a few, dated studies with poor designs? Was the research perspective dominated by quantitative studies to the exclusion of more in-depth qualitative studies?

Assessing the level of agreement within and across perspectives is a way to assess the level of support for best practices. If there is strong agreement, confidence is enhanced. Of interest is the situation wherein two perspectives are in agreement but a third perspective is not. This often can reflect the different world views and values that consumers, professionals, and researchers bring. If there is little agreement, within and across sources, then it should be acknowledged that best practices are in their fledgling stage.

After the quality of individual sources has been assessed, and the level of agreement within and across perspectives has been ascertained, the writer assesses the overall strength of the support for the current best practices, across all the perspectives. The potency of the best practices are greater when the quantitative and qualitative research is extensive and rigorous; when consumer and professional sources are credible, influential, and free of potential conflicts of interest; and when there is consensus, or at least extensive common ground, among all the perspectives. Recommendations for how to improve the potency of best practices are born from this potency analysis.

STEP 7: Use Value Criteria to Critique and Improve Current Best Practices

In EBP, it is enough for the inquiry to determine the empirical support for practice; it is then up to the practitioner and consumer and to apply the results of that inquiry as warranted by the situation. Yet, scholars, doctoral level students, and many creative and innovative administrators are expected both to critique and to advance the state of the art. Best practices should not be viewed as immutable, but as starting points for improving services and agency practices (Manela & Moxley, 2002). Conducting a methodical, multidimensional review that summarizes current best practices is only one part in a full inquiry. The other part is to apply evaluative criteria to identify the gaps or problems that exist in current practices and then to make specific recommendations for improvement. Otherwise, current best practices are mistakenly accepted as the end point.

As discussed in Chapter 1, criteria for judging the overall quality of policies and practices are ultimately value criteria (Chambers, 2000). Just as there is an ethical mandate for practitioners to hold and provide knowledge about the extent to which interventions are empirically validated, so it is ethically necessary for professionals to consider and evaluate the merits of all perspectives on "state-of-the-art" practices against the values and ethical standards endorsed by the professional organizations and society as a whole. For example, even though we value empirical support, professionals would be unlikely to endorse a program that physically or emotionally abused clients, no matter how much the research validated its success in achieving desired outcomes, because it would violate professional ethics. The ethical mandate to ensure safety and well being of clients would "trump" the empirical data about outcome effectiveness. The professional code of ethics is the first set of value criteria to be considered, but additional, broader values that are not explicit in the code are also essential.

Consider "least restrictive environment" (LRE), the legal and practice principle that is widely (though not universally) endorsed. It holds that services should be delivered in the environment that is least restrictive of a client's personal liberties. This principle, or value, was instrumental in the deinstitutionalization of patients from mental hospitals (Foley & Sharfstein, 1983) and in the inclusion of children with disabilities in regular classrooms (Turnbull, Turnbull, Shank, & Leal, 1995). Employing this principle in Step 7, the value-critical analysis, a comprehensive best practices inquiry asks, "How do these best practices measure up to the standard of services in the least restrictive environment? Even if current best practices are effective, could they be just as effective, or even more so, in a less restrictive environment?"

This value-critical analysis can involve a wide range of ethics, values, principles, and standards that are explicitly or implicitly endorsed by the professional organizations, policymakers, practitioners, the legal system, and the society at large. For example, in addition to LRE, general value criteria for best practices include respect for diversity and difference (or cultural competence), honoring and utilizing client strengths (Saleebey, 2006), ethical treatment of clients including informed consent, safety for all participants and staff, empirical support for interventions, sound theoretical base, and client empowerment. We also believe that services should be accessible, affordable, accountable, and linked to others in the community.

Most of these value criteria apply across all realms of human services, but others may be specific to the population and problem of concern. For example, "family-centered practice" (Petr, 2004) is a value principle that is highly relevant to services to children and their families, but perhaps not to other populations. Thus, selection of the value criteria that are relevant to a given best practices inquiry depends in part on the question being investigated.

To illustrate how value criteria apply to the improvement of current best practices, speaking hypothetically, a review of the empirical literature might reveal that inpatient programs with certain standard interventions such as group therapy and psychoeducational groups have been shown to be effective in the treatment of adolescent substance abusers. Suppose further that qualitative research about the consumer and professional perspectives concur with those best practices identified in the research. In a value-critical approach, focusing on the LRE principle as an evaluative criterion, one could ask whether the same results, or better, could be achieved in a shorter program, or in a day treatment program in the community. It is not assumed that current best practices should be accepted or implemented unconditionally. Further, consider this same example but change the focus of the value-critical analysis to the value of cultural competence. Perhaps the program's effectiveness has only been established with white, middle-class males. In this case, the best practices inquiry, using the value criteria "respect for diversity and difference," would identify this weakness in the current state of the art and seek to target this area for improvement. Recommendations could focus on replicating the program with more diverse groups or modifying the program for females and persons of color, based upon what we know about culturally competent services to these populations.

The relevance of a value frame of reference is evident when one considers that even empirically based practice is value laden. When empiricists assert that empirical evidence is paramount in determining what practices are best, they are making a value assertion. Such persons value empirical research. They believe that empirical support is the most important evaluative criteria by which to judge programs and policies. Empiricists may claim to be value free, because they look at "objective" evidence, but values are inherent in what people believe is important: there is no escaping the conclusion that empiricists value empirical evidence.

Determining which values to include as evaluative criteria is not always a simple and tidy process. Values may not be universally endorsed, as in the aforementioned value of LRE. Often, one value may conflict with another. For example, the value of LRE may conflict with the value of client safety and well being. That is, clients with mental illness may be safer and better fed in hospitals than when they are in the community, especially if they are homeless and not involved in active treatment. But in hospitals, their rights to freedoms and self-determination may be curtailed more than they are in the community.

Given this situation, the intent of a value-critical best practices analysis is not to identify the "correct" or "best" values to be utilized in the analysis. Values are indeed subjective, and there may be no "best" values to use in the analysis. As Chambers (2000) points out, a value-critical approach forces one to make hard choices among multiple and competing values. What is incumbent on the investigator is to be transparent about the process, to provide an explanation, or justification, for the application of particular values.

Since values are subjective, this justification can be personal, based on personal experiences and personal belief systems. An example of this would be in the field of child welfare, where the values of child safety are sometimes at odds with the value of preserving families (Petr, 2004). Here, the best practices investigator who believes strongly in child safety as the top priority could acknowledge that personal bias in the selection of child safety as the main evaluative criteria. It would be important to acknowledge that the recommendations for improvement in best practices based on this value of child safety would likely differ from those based on the value of preserving families.

This example also demonstrates that the priorities of legislation and the values endorsed by organizations can also serve as the rationale or justification to select certain values. Since both child safety and preservation of families are values embedded in the main enabling federal legislation, both could be used to critique best practices in child welfare. Other examples of values embedded in federal legislation or programs include the Child Abuse Prevention and Treatment Act in which community-based programs are encouraged to support family-centered, holistic, prevention services (see Chapter 3), and the children's mental health system of care initiative which promotes the values of family involvement, inter-agency collaboration, and least restrictive environment (see Chapter 6).

The value-critical analysis places the summary of best practices in its proper context, allows for strengths and weaknesses to be identified, and facilitates improvements being made. Practitioners, consumers, and program developers then have the information they need on how to understand, interpret, implement, and improve upon current state of the art.

Utilization of MEBP

MEBP is designed to be used by helping professionals with at least a bachelor's degree in a human services field. One must have a working understanding of how to search for, collect, and organize information using library and internet sources. These skills, together with the ability to judge the quality of information sources—be they consumer, professional, or research sources—are crucial. The quality of the conclusions of the best practices inquiry are dependent on the quality of the sources used, as demonstrated by the MEBP emphasis on assessing the potency of best practices with respect to the quality of sources and the level of agreement among them (Step 6). For consumers and professional perspectives, this means finding sources that are credible, influential, and representative of the experiences of the respective group.

For the research perspective, it is helpful to have a basic understanding of criteria to rate research design, as well as the ability to judge whether or not study conclusions are based on relevant data. However, one must also trust the experts who conduct the peer-review process for major journals and EBP organizations such as the Cochran Collaboration, whose endorsement means that a certain level of quality can almost be assumed. It can also be almost assumed that the empirical support is weak when the only sources of empirical evidence are studies in minor journals and non-refereed book chapters. The point, again, is that a person conduct-ing the MEBP inquiry can rely on others to have assessed the quality of the research sources. It is not imperative that MEBP be conducted by persons with advanced knowledge of statistics and research design, but one does need to be able to accurately read, comprehend, and summarize these studies and reviews.

The MEBP approach to best practices inquiry is well suited to the education of social workers and other helping professionals at all educational levels. In the spirit of critical thinking, it provides a concrete framework with which students can appraise not only the quality of available research, but also the values that guide the research, policies, and practices in a particular field. As aforementioned, the framework has been piloted in a doctoral-level class in which students spend most of the semester immersing themselves in the literature about best practices in their chosen topic area, and following the complete steps outlined above to produce a comprehensive paper on best practices in their chosen topic area.

One student, writing about best practices in the psychosocial realm with the terminally ill, concluded that current best practices in that arena (hospice and related programs) were based largely on professional wisdom about what was effective, with little empirical support. Using the value-critical framework, the student also concluded that the current best practices were designed without experience with or sensitivity to the needs of diverse persons of color. In her recommendations for improvement, the student suggested both more outcome research and solicitation of the opinions of consumers of color regarding needed changes that would increase the model's sensitivity to diversity and difference.

Another student found general empirical support for certain practices relative to adults with the dual diagnosis of substance abuse and a major psychiatric diagnosis. Then, using a value-based critique inspired by the perspectives of female consumers and professionals, the student opined that outcomes for women could be enhanced by sensitivity to gender-specific issues such as many female consumers' identity as mothers and to their frequent histories of sexual abuse.

A third student explored best practices for working with street children, and published a concise, abbreviated version of the class assignment (Dybicz, 2005). This example will be discussed at some length in order to provide a more extensive illustration of the process and product.

In his article, Dybicz attempted to build on previously published studies which had described the mental health functioning and needs of street children in Columbia, South America. These quantitative studies had great historical impact in that they had dispelled the myth of the street child as delinquent, thus encouraging a move away from correctional methods and interventions, which had previously been considered best practices. These descriptive studies also helped programs see that the factors leading children into street life were rooted in extreme poverty.

Despite an extensive search of the research literature, the author was unable to uncover any quantitative research focusing on the efficacy of any particular approach. Because of the paucity of intervention research, qualitative research articles focusing on best practices, conducted in Africa, Latin America, and Mexico were the primary sources for the research perspective. The main sources for professional wisdom were a UNICEF report and information from the websites of two organizations focusing on the problem, one with an international membership and focus, and one based in Brazil. These sources gave detailed information about practice methods, yet the experience and voice of actual practitioners was notably absent. With respect to the consumer perspective, the author was able to find two credible sources. Both were studies focusing on qualitative interviews, and both were conducted in Africa.

Several aspects of best practices were common to all three perspectives. These included communicating respect to the street children for their strength and resiliency, emphasizing voluntary participation, rejecting residential care, and working to prevent the problem through community development. In addition, consumer and research perspectives emphasized meeting basic needs over the long term (job training) rather than in the short term (providing food, clothing, and shelter). In this regard, the author noted that it was interesting that micro-enterprise interventions were seen as short-term measures to meet immediate needs, rather than building skills that could be taken into adulthood. The research and professional wisdom sources emphasized engagement skills and a broad approach.

There were, as well, messages that were distinct to each perspective. Consumers, the youth themselves, strongly supported formal education at regular school, rather than classes provided by agencies. Professionals emphasized job creation and skill development that would lead to income. Unique to the research perspective was an emphasis on the need to track outcomes related to political consciousness-raising, especially about legal and human rights.

Finally, the author used the values of empiricism, least restrictive environment, respect for diversity, and accessibility to recommend that improvements in current best practices should focus on enhancing intervention research, continuing the movement away from residential care, initiating gender-sensitive programming, and increasing the percentage of street children who receive services.

In this doctoral class, the best practices inquiry assignment forms the basis for a follow-up assignment that asks the student to use their first paper to design an innovative program for their target population. In effect, they are asked to translate their conclusions about best practices and recommendations for improvement into a specific program design. Before submitting the written product, the students invite a consumer and a professional to class to hear an oral presentation of the program design. These guests give their feedback and ideas, which the students incorporate into the final written paper.

At the bachelor's and master's levels, MEBP can be modified to suit the purposes and objectives of the course and overall curriculum. Students in research classes can use the framework to position research in its proper value context, and assess the applicability of research to practice situations. In foundation- and advanced-level clinical classes, the framework can help prepare students for internships, as they research the best practices for the populations they serve. In program design and program development courses, MEBP can be included to emphasize that new programs need to be based on the very best available knowledge about current best practices. At all educational levels, the process reinforces that students, in their future positions as practitioners, administrators, researchers and scholars, must view current best practices as transitory and dynamic, not as immutable.

To reinforce the importance of multiple perspectives, students can be assigned to obtain direct data about the consumer and professional perspectives by conducting interviews of consumers and professionals, then synthesizing this with the empirical data on best practices in their chosen area. This first-hand experience can enrich the literature review, demonstrate concretely the intelligence and insight of consumers and professionals, and solidify the student's commitment to obtaining multiple perspectives in their future work.

Summary and Conclusion

This book asserts that MEBP improves upon the conventional evidence-based approach to best practices inquiry in two fundamental ways. First, following the lead of current thinking embodied in knowledge-based practice, best practices inquiry can itself incorporate a systematic review of consumer and expert professional opinions and perspectives. This, together with available qualitative research, provides a richer context for consideration of the empirical evidence and allows the user of the best practices information to make more fully informed decisions. Second, MEBP enriches best practices inquiry by incorporation of a value-based critique of current best practices that moves beyond description of current state of the art to identify areas in which improvements are warranted. More than a critique of the empirical base and study methodology, this comprehensive critique utilizes the combined consumer and professional perspectives as well a value-critical analysis to suggest areas for innovation and improvement. In learning how to conduct this expanded MEBP approach to investigating best practices, professionals and students will be prepared to synthesize, analyze, and apply knowledge in a given field to the benefit of client populations.

In Chapters 3–9, seven exemplars of the MEBP approach in action are presented. The topics that are explored are prevention of child abuse, prevention of teenage pregnancy, health care access for poor children, family involvement in children's mental health services, therapeutic foster care, restorative justice, and enhancing spirituality in recovery for the seriously mentally ill.

References

Anastas, J.W. (2004). Quality in qualitative evaluation: Issues and possible answers. *Research on Social Work Practice, 14*(1), 57–65.

Armstrong, R.P. (2001). Reflections of twenty-five years as a school social worker: Joys and lessons from the long haul. *Journal of School Social Work, 11*(2), 36–49.

Attree, P. (2004). Growing up in disadvantage: A systematic review of the qualitative evidence. *Child: Care, Health, and Development, 30*(6), 679–689.

Berg-Weger, M., Rubio, D.M. & Tebb, S.T. (2001). Strengths-based practice with family caregivers of the chronically ill: Qualitative insights. *Families in Society, 82*(3), 263–272.

Biegel, D.E, Tracy, E.M., & Corvo, K.N. (1994). Strengthening social networks: Intervention strategies for mental health case managers. *Health and Social Work, 19*(3), 206–216.

Bondas, T., & Hall, E.O.C. (2007). Challenges in approaching metasynthesis research. *Qualitative Health Research, 17*, 113–121.

Chambers, D.E. (2000). *Social policy and social programs: A method for the practical public policy analyst* (3rd ed.). Boston: Allyn and Bacon.

Cournoyer, B.R. (2004). *The evidence-based social work skills book*. Boston: Pearson Education.

Crane, J. (Ed.) (1998). *Social programs that work*. New York: Russell Sage Foundation.

Creswell, J.W. (1998). *Qualitative inquiry and research design choosing among five traditions*. Thousands Oaks, CA: Sage.

Denzin, D.K., & Lincoln, Y.S. (Eds.) (2005). *The Sage handbook of qualitative research* (3rd ed.). Thousand Oaks, CA: Sage.

Drisko, J.W. (2007, January). Synthesizing qualitative research: Affirming and critical perspectives; practical challenges. Paper presented at Annual Conference of Society for Social Work Research (SSWR), San Francisco, California.

Dybicz, P. (2005). Interventions with street children: An analysis of current best practices. *International Social Work, 48*(6), 763–771.

Elridge, H. (1994). Barbara's story—a mother who sexually abused. In M. Elliot (Ed.), *Female sexual abuse of children* (pp. 74–88). New York: Guilford.

Foley, H.A., & Sharfstein, S.S. (1983). *Madness and government: Who cares for the mentally ill?* Washington, DC: American Psychiatric Press.

Geertz, C. (1973). *The interpretation of cultures: Selected essays*. New York: Basic Books.

Gibbs, L., & Gambrill, E. (1999). *Critical thinking for social workers: Exercises for the helping professions* (2nd ed.). Thousand Oaks, CA: Pine Forge Press.

Gioia, D. (2004). Mixed methods in a dissertation study. In D.K. Padgett (Ed.), *The qualitative research experience* (pp. 122–151). Belmont, CA: Wadsworth/Thomson Learning.

Golder, S., Ivanoff, A., Cloud, R.N., Besel, K.L., McKierman, P., Bratt, E., & Bledsoe, L.K. (2005). Evidence-based practice with adults in jails and prisons: Strategies, practices, and future directions. *Best Practices in Mental Health, 1*(2), 100–132.

Gorey, K.M., & Thyer, B. (1998). Differential effectiveness of prevalent social work practice models: A meta-analysis. *Social Work, 43*(3), 269–278.

Grandin, T. (1995). *Thinking in pictures and other reports from my life with autism*. New York: Doubleday.

Grazer, B., & Howard, R. (producers), & Howard, R. (director) (2001). *A Beautiful Mind* [motion picture] Distribution: Universal Pictures.

Hodge, D.R. (2007). A systematic review of the empirical literature on intercessory prayer. *Research on Social Work Practice, 17*(2), 174–187.

Hodge, D.R., & Williams, T.R. (2002). Assessing African American spirituality with spiritual ecomaps. *Families in Society, 83*(5/6): 585–595.

Indyk, D., Belville, R., Lachapelle, S., Gordon, G., & Dewart, T. (1993). A community-based approach to HIV case management: Systematizing the unmanageable. *Social Work, 38*(4): 380–387.

Kearney, M.H. (2001). Enduring love: A grounded formal theory of women's experience of domestic violence. *Research in Nursing and Health, 24*(4), 270–282.

Klein, W.C., & Bloom, M. (1995). Practice wisdom. *Social Work, 40*(6), 799–807.

Krill, D.F. (1990). *Practice wisdom*. Newbury Park, CA: Sage.

Lincoln, Y.S., & Guba, E.G. (1985). *Naturalistic inquiry*. Newbury Park, CA: Sage.

Lundahl, B., Nimer, J., & Parsons, B. (2006). Preventing child abuse: A meta-analysis of Parenting Training Programs. *Research on Social Work Practice, 16*, 251–262.

Lundin, R.K. (1998) Living with mental illness: A personal experience. *Cognitive and Behavioral Practice, 5*(2), 223–230.

MacLeod, J., & Nelson, G. (2000). Programs for the promotion of family wellness and the prevention of child maltreatment. *Child Abuse and Neglect, 24*(9), 1127–1149.

Manela, R.W., & Moxley, D.P. (2002). Best practices as agency-based knowledge in social welfare. *Administration in Social Work, 26*(4), 1–24.

Padgett, D.K. (Ed.) (2004a). *The qualitative research experience*. Belmont, CA: Wadsworth/Thomson Learning.

Padgett, D.K. (2004b). Mixed methods, serendipity, and concatenation. In D.K. Padgett

(Ed.), *The qualitative research experience* (pp. 273–288). Belmont, CA: Wadsworth/ Thomson Learning.

Pelzer, D.J. (1995). *A child called "It": one child's courage to survive.* Deerfield Beach, FL: Health Communications.

Petr, C.G. (2004). *Social work with children and their families: Pragmatic foundations* (2nd ed.). New York: Oxford University Press.

Petr, C.G., & Barney, D.D. (1993). Reasonable efforts for children with disabilities: the parents' perspective. *Social Work, 38*(3), 247–255.

Phillips, J. (1995). *The magic daughter: A memoir of living with multiple personality disorder.* New York: Viking.

Saleebey, D. (2006) (Ed.). *The strengths perspective in social work practice* (4th ed.). Boston, MA: Allyn & Bacon.

Shadish, W.R., Ragsdale, K., Glaser, R.R., & Montgomery, L.M. (1995). The efficacy and effectiveness of marital and family therapy: a perspective from meta-analysis. *Journal of Marital and Family Therapy, 21*(4), 345–360.

Sobo, E., Seid, M., & Gelhard, L. (2006). Parent-identified barriers to pediatric health care: A process-oriented model. *Health Services Research (41)*1, 148–172.

Sprague, A., & Thyer, B.A. (2002). Psychosocial treatment of oppositional defiant disorder: A review of empirical outcome studies. *Social Work in Mental Health, 1*(1), 63–72.

Turnbull, A.P., Turnbull, H.R., Shank, M., & Leal, D. (1995). *Exceptional lives: Special education in today's schools.* Englewood Cliffs, NJ: Prentice Hall.

Valentine, V., & Gray, M. (2006). Keeping them home: Aboriginal out-of-home care in Australia. *Families in Society, 87*(4), 537–545.

Van Wormer, K., & Bednar, S.G. (2002). Working with male batterers: A restorative-strengths perspective. *Families in Society, 83*(5/6), 557–566.

Walen, S. (2002). It's a funny thing about suicide: A personal experience. *British Journal of Guidance and Counseling, 30*(4), 415–430.

Walker, J.S., & Bruns, E.J. (2006). Building on practice-based evidence: Using expert perspectives to define the wraparound process. *Psychiatric Services, 57*(11), 1579–1586.

Walter, U.M., & Peterson, K.J. (2002). Gendered differences: Postmodern feminist perspectives and young women identified as "emotionally disabled." *Families in Society, 83*(5/6), 596–603.

Weaver, A. (2007). A real mother's embrace: Reflections on abuse and recovery. *Focal Point, 21*(1), 9–11.

Wells, K., Farmer, E.M.Z., Richards, J.T., & Burns, B.J. (2004). The experience of being a treatment foster mother, *Qualitative Social Work, 3*(2), 117–138.

Yalom, I. (2002). *The gift of therapy—An open letter to a new generation of therapists and their patients.* New York: Harper Collins.

3 Best Practices for Preventing Maltreatment of Children Ages Birth to Five

Jacqueline M. Counts

Child abuse and neglect continues to be a societal problem that has long-term consequences for the victims and poses significant costs to society. Using the Multidimensional Evidence-Based Practice (MEBP) approach, the author reviewed the quality of sources across perspectives and developed a quality equation that quantifies the quality of all sources. Consumer and professional perspectives tend to provide the how-to for the delivery of services, while the research perspective provides the justification and rationale for funding. A value-critical analysis yields recommendations for future improvements to prevention efforts. A policy/practice feedback loop is essential to connect the wisdom and improve the utility of the three perspectives.

Overview of the Population and Problem of Concern

Despite being recognized as a societal problem for the last 40 years, there has not been a significant reduction in the occurrence of child maltreatment (Center for Study of Social Policy, 2004). The trauma these children experience can have significant and long-term adverse effects on them throughout their lifespan. Because of the extraordinary human and financial costs of child abuse, it behooves society to develop and sustain prevention efforts so that the incidence and prevalence of child abuse can be reduced.

Child abuse is defined as "an act or failure to act which results in significant harm or risk of harm to a minor" (North Carolina Institute of Medicine, 2005, p. 2). The four types of child maltreatment are physical abuse, neglect, sexual abuse, and emotional/psychological abuse. According to the ecological model, child maltreatment is a result of complex interactions of protective and risk factors at the child, family, community, and societal levels. Risk factors increase the likelihood of abuse, and protective factors insulate individuals and families from stress and mitigate negative influences (National Research Council: Panel on Research and Child Abuse and Neglect, 1993).

In 2004, some 872,000 children were maltreated (National Child Abuse and Neglect Data System, 2004). Child maltreatment slowly decreased from 12.5 children per 1,000 (2001) to 11.9 children per 1,000 (2004). Children under the age of four are the most vulnerable and account for 79% of child maltreatment fatalities, with infants under one year accounting for 44% of deaths (Department of Health and Human Services, 2005). In a survey conducted in North Carolina, mothers reported using harsh punishment 43 times higher than the child abuse rate (Runyan, Wattam, Ikeda, Hassan, & Ramiro, 2002).

Adverse consequences for maltreated children are well documented and include minor injuries, permanent injuries such as burns, brain injuries, developmental delays, psychiatric disorders, and in the most severe cases—death (Runyan et al., 2002). As adults, maltreated children are at greater risk for adverse health effects and behaviors, including smoking, alcoholism, drug abuse, eating disorders, obesity, depression, suicide, sexual promiscuity, and certain chronic diseases (Felitti et al., 1998).

Direct costs to society in 2001 were estimated at $24 billion per year (Fromm, 2001). These costs include associated costs of maintaining a child welfare system such as judicial, law enforcement, health, and mental health services. Indirect costs to society are those associated with the long-term adverse effects of child maltreatment such as juvenile and adult criminal activity, mental illness, substance abuse, and domestic violence. Other consequences include loss of productivity because of unemployment and underemployment, costs for special education services, and increased use of health care. These other costs are estimated to be more than $69 billion per year (Fromm, 2001). These are the financial consequences of child maltreatment. The emotional consequences of maltreatment cannot be quantified. Compared to these billions of dollars, the direct costs of prevention programs are minor. In the fiscal year 2005, the federal appropriation was $40.1 million with state matches of $8 million (National Resource Center for Community Based Child Abuse Prevention, n.d.). Because child abuse prevention generates approximately a 19 to one return on investment for taxpayers (Colorado Children's Trust Fund, 1992), it is important to identify and promulgate those programs and practices which achieve outcomes.

The principal desired outcome of prevention efforts is a sustained reduction in child maltreatment cases as measured by substantiated child maltreatment rates. However, a reduction in reported and substantiated cases does not necessarily mean there is a reduction in the prevalence of maltreatment. Many programs measure intermediate or proxy variables such as reductions in abusive behaviors and reports to child protective services. Other programs focus on increases in protective factors, as measured by psychometric measures, to demonstrate program effectiveness. Tomison (2000) asserts that many issues impede the rigorous evaluation of prevention programs. These include fear of an external evaluation and negative findings, perception of evaluation as a diversion of resources, and lack of evaluation capacity and expertise. In addition to such infrastructure and capacity issues, the nature of the services themselves pose evaluation challenges. Prevention programs address complex social problems that are typically difficult to control in research designs. Historically, governments have placed low priority on prevention programs and have not provided funding and research dollars to conduct long-term projects and evaluations. In response, Tomison (2000) recommends that outcomes should not be selected based on the availability of measurement instruments. Rather, outcomes should reflect program goals. Program effectiveness should be determined using a framework that is flexible to real-world people and programs.

The focus of this chapter is: *what are best practices for preventing maltreatment of children ages birth to five?* Using the multidimensional evidence-based practice (MEBP) method described in Chapter 2, the author explores best practices from consumer, professional, and research perspectives, then offers a value-critical analysis that yields recommendations for future improvements to prevention efforts. Perspectives are denoted by a C for consumer, P for professional, and R for researcher followed by a source number. The references are provided in parentheses.

Best Practices Inquiry: MEBP Process and Results

Consumer Perspective: Selection Method

Library, database, and Google Scholar searches were conducted using the terms, "consumer, parents, and at-risk" in combination with "child abuse and neglect prevention programs." Four criteria guided selection for this model: 1) outcomes were consumer-defined, 2) implications for the field were provided, 3) consumer perspectives were based on experience with a prevention program, and 4) sources were published after 1997. Sources meeting criteria number one were limited. Most consumer articles reported outcomes that were determined by evaluators, researchers, and program designers.

Consumer Perspective: Sources

C1 (DeMay, 2003) is a qualitative study exploring the perceptions of 62 clients' experiences in a public nurse home visiting program for the prevention of child abuse and neglect. Participants were divided into two groups: intensive and usual services. Mothers in the intensive group received services based on theoretical concepts, including the following: maternal and child outcomes are the result of complex interactions between psychosocial, economic, and physical factors; a trusting nurse/client relationship is crucial; and prenatal to age three is a crucial time for establishing a parent–child bond. Families in the usual group received services ranging in the number of visits and intensity. Research questions included how clients experience home visiting, similarities and differences between the groups' experiences, congruency of client and practitioner experiences, and how client experiences can inform public health nursing practice. Groups were given a blank piece of paper and asked for comments about their experience by responding to the title, "My experience in the (intervention or current practice) study."

C2 (Oynskiw, Harrison, Spady, & McConnan, 1999) is a formative evaluation of a collaborative community-based, and multidisciplinary project to prevent child abuse and neglect through family support and programming. The project, *Together for Kids*, occurred in two mid-size Canadian cities with a high prevalence of family violence, child welfare, and social services involvement. Participants were referred to the program by schools, child welfare agencies, community agencies, and police. Multidisciplinary teams from health, social services, and law enforcement agencies provided integrated services to children and families. The qualitative study used in-person interviews with 17 clients and 10 team members to assess program operations and progress toward goal attainment. The formative evaluation focused on program accessibility, seamless service delivery, and suggestions for project improvement. Client and team member results were reported separately. Results in these three areas provided collaboration teams with input on what was working well for parents and what programmatic elements needed attention.

C3 (Toban & Lutzker, 2001) evaluated parental satisfaction and acceptability of Project SafeCare, an ecobehavioral program that addresses home safety, infant and child health care, and bonding and stimulation. The program serves families with children birth to five. Families at-risk for abuse were referred by a hospital maternity center or child welfare agency. The study used social validity question-naires to determine if consumers were satisfied with the procedures and outcomes of the program. The premise of social validity questionnaires is that if parents are not connected with staff and satisfied with treatment, they will not access services. A questionnaire evaluated parental satisfaction with outcomes. Open-ended questions enabled parents to provide additional information about the quality of services.

C4 (Minnesota Department of Children, Families and Learning and the Children's Trust Fund, 2000) summarized the results of three organizations in Minnesota that posed the following question to parents: "What, if any, is the impact of parent involvement in the lives of children and families?" The organizations worked with families to prevent child abuse and neglect and identified positive impacts for parents, children and families, parents as employees, schools, commu-nities, and family support organizations. Although the direct relationship between this question and the inquiry question may not be apparent, parent involvement and development of parent leaders is a strategy of parent organizations such as Circle of Parents to decrease child maltreatment. Implications for the field to involve parents and develop leadership capacity were provided.

Consumer Perspective: Results

Six best practices were identified as common to at least two of the four sources as shown in Table 3.1

Building strong and positive relations between parents and practitioners was emphasized as an essential component among the four sources. Regardless of the discipline, a trusting relationship with nonthreatening and accepting practitioners was critical. Without it, clients were less likely to access services or be receptive of the information practitioners had to give. Having the same practitioner or consistency was mentioned as an important factor in the development of a trusting relationship. This was the only practice mentioned by all four sources.

Five other practices were mentioned by two of the four sources. C1 and C2 shared several common practices. A support system, both informal and formal,

Table 3.1 Consumer Best Practices

Best Practices	C1	C2	C3	C4
1. Strong, positive relationships between parents and practitioners are essential.	X	X	X	X
2. Provide a support system for parents (both formal and informal for parents when under stress).	X	X		
3. Provide nonjudgmental services that respect the client and their values and validate their parenting skills.	X	X		
4. Services must be accessible: flexible hours, location.	X	X		
5. Be sensitive about too much paper work and testing.	X	X		
6. Services should maintain privacy and prevent stigma.		X	X	
7. Provide concrete support for day-to-day crisis, either through referral or case management.		X		
8. Teams should be multidisciplinary to address the complex needs of families.		X		
9. Involve fathers in the program.		X		
10. Training and support should be provided to nurture parent leadership. A ladder of opportunities should allow parents to grow as leaders.				X

Note: Best practices for the consumer perspective are shaded.

was indicated as a best practice by C1 and C2. In C1, clients with limited social connections valued the support provided by the nurse practitioners. In C2, clients said they appreciated the informal support of team members when they were under stress. Clients said that they knew about appropriate parenting skills but did not always practice them. That is, they were able to "lean on" team members outside of sessions. C2 participants valued parent support groups and the emotional support they received from others with similar problems. They requested groups to be formed around common concerns, such as for wives whose children were sexually abused by spouses. They also asked for skill groups for cooking, sewing, budgeting, and cutting hair.

C1 and C2 also emphasized the importance of providing nonjudgmental services that respect clients and their values. Clients do not like to feel under scrutiny and appreciate it when practitioners validate their parenting skills. According to C1 and C2, accessibility is a key factor. Services must be available to clients at times that meet their needs. C1 clients said that home visits and the length of them can sometimes be too much for a new mother. Some C2 clients felt that home visits were intrusive. Both sources concluded that services must be flexible to meet individual needs and desired levels of intensity. That is, intensity of services should be adapted based on the level of involvement that the client wants, rather than what the practitioner wants. If clients are traveling to the site, the location must be easily accessible, either within walking distance or by public transportation. C1 and C2 noted that practitioners should be sensitive about too much paperwork and testing.

Coordinated communication between providers lessens the burden on clients to be subjected to several interviews from multiple agencies. Finally, C2 and C3 identified privacy as a critical factor. Services must be nonstigmatizing. Otherwise, clients are too embarrassed to access services and may be resistant to treatment.

Professional Perspective: Selection Method

Database and Google Scholar searches were conducted using the terms "best practices," "child abuse and neglect prevention," and/or "social work." Several states are moving toward a set of practice standards to develop a comprehensive and coordinated system for prevention. Four selection criteria were applied for this inquiry: 1) focused on practice standards rather than program-specific practices because these can be widely applied, 2) focused on birth to five, 3) limited to the past ten years, although many of the practice standards were based on the collective wisdom of what has worked in prevention programs over the past 30 years, and 4) endorsed by national or state advisory panels or task forces.

Professional Perspective: Sources

P1 is a new initiative sponsored by the Center for the Study of Social Policy (CSSP, 2004) to reduce child abuse and neglect by embedding practice strategies into existing systems. Nationally, 12.9 million children are enrolled in some type of early care and/or education programs (CSSP, 2004). Therefore, these strategies can be implemented in early care and education programs as a systematic and affordable way to reach parents of children birth to five. This framework focuses on increasing protective factors for all families, rather than targeting at-risk families. The protective factors were identified by reviewing research that focused on factors that buffer or protect families who might be at risk for abuse. A national advisory panel of multidisciplinary researchers and practitioners from early childhood, child abuse and neglect prevention, and family support reviewed the literature and selected factors that promote strengths, rather than address deficits. The protective factors are: parental resilience, social connections, knowledge of parenting and child development, concrete support in times of need, and social and emotional competence of children. Several strategies were provided to address these five protective factors and are embedded in Table 3.2.

P2 (Family Support America & New Jersey Task Force on Child Abuse and Neglect, 2003) is the result of a New Jersey task force to determine standards for prevention programs. The standards are based on the family support approach, which builds on families' strengths, are community-based, and provide comprehensive supports as selected by the Standards Working Group of the task force. The group limited the standards to prevention programs, reviewed research and analytic studies, and focused on effective program elements. The report provides conceptual, practice, and administrative standards. Tools are also provided for programs to determine how well they are meeting the criteria for effective programs.

P3 (Faver, Crawford, & Combs-Orme, 1999) discussed help-seeking and under-utilization of prevention and treatment. Authors reviewed studies to determine why at-risk families under investigation by child welfare agencies do not receive the services they need. The article mentioned three types of families who underutilize prevention programs: consumer families who acknowledge limited skills, dependent families who are unaware of services and their need for them, and resistant families who have not been reached by prevention efforts.

In P4 (Daro & Donnely, 2002), leading child abuse prevention advocates summarized accomplishments and challenges in child abuse prevention over the last 30 years. The article identified four causal theories of maltreatment: psychodynamic, learning, environmental, and ecological. Prevention strategies and their impact were also discussed. Emerging ideas for researchers, practitioners, and policymakers were presented and noted in Table 3.2 as "needed."

Professional Perspective: Results

Professional perspectives were fairly consistent across the four sources. To be a best practice among professionals, three of the four sources had to list the practice. Seven best practices were identified by the professional sources as shown in Table 3.2.

Linking families to opportunities such as job training, education, health providers, and mental health consultants was mentioned by every professional source. P3 suggested that such linkages would reach clients who might not typically utilize prevention programs. P1, P2, and P4 promoted friendship and mutual support among families. Programs should encourage connections with other parents via support groups, leadership opportunities, potlucks, "bring-a-dish" dinners, and classes among others. These three sources also advocated for interventions that strengthen parenting skills. Home visiting, parent education classes, and resource lending libraries provide parents with child development and discipline information. Home visiting programs also focus on the secure and positive attachment between parent and child.

P1, P2, and P4 argued that services must be voluntary and universal. P4 stated that targeted programs will never engage the large numbers of individuals necessary to significantly reduce child abuse and neglect. Therefore, universal systems must provide varying levels of service based on a family's level of need. P1 suggested that promoting resilience in all families through early education is not only attractive to parents but also reaches large numbers of children.

P2, P3, and P4 noted that programs should provide community-based comprehensive and integrated services to address families with multiple problems. This approach is based on the ecological theory of maltreatment. Prevention programs need to share a common vision for prevention and operate in a coordinated manner. These same sources stressed the importance of flexible services that can be adapted to the needs and levels of intensity desired by the family. Services should be of sufficient duration and intensity as suggested in P1, P2, and P4. The sources cautioned that one-shot approaches are not effective. Rather, P2 emphasized the

Table 3.2 Professional Best Practices

Best Practices	P1	P2	P3	P4
1. Facilitate friendships and mutual support between families.	X	X		X
2. Strengthen parenting through education, home visits, family support workers, etc.	X	X		X
3. Respond to family crises by offering extra support to parents when facing illness, job loss, housing problems, and so on.	X			
4. Link families to services and opportunities such as job training, education, health providers, and mental health consultants.	X	X	X	X
5. Facilitate children's social and emotional development by helping children describe their feelings and get along with others.	X			
6. Observe and respond to early warning signs of child abuse or neglect.	X	X		
7. Provide strengths-based services that value and support parents.	X	X		
8. Be universally available and voluntary.	X	X		N
9. Provide community-based comprehensive and integrated services that are available on a continuum.		X	X	N
10. Accessibility: flexible and responsive.		X	X	X
11. Services should be long term and of adequate intensity.	X	X		X
12. Provide culturally competent services that match clients' stated needs and interests.		X	X	

Note: X=Present, N=Needed; Best practices for the professional perspective are shaded.

need for research on short-term and long-term approaches that vary in length, intensity, and type of skills.

Research Perspective: Selection Method

Over the last 30 years, hundreds of studies have been conducted to determine what works to prevent child maltreatment. Three meta-analyses with rigorous inclusion standards and two sources using randomized trials were selected for this review. Each meta-analysis included a rigorous selection process for inclusion in the analysis. The author of this chapter selected sources to reflect the spectrum of maltreatment prevention programs. Overlap between studies was minimal. Following is a description of the standards and rationale for including three meta-analyses and two randomized trials.

The rationale for including meta-analysis R1 (Lundahl, Nimer, and Parsons, 2006) in this inquiry was that it focused on parent training and education programs. Six criteria were used to select studies from the 186 studies retrieved through computer searches: focused on parent training programs, involved actual parental training, treated parents and children with no developmental or cognitive delays, reported pre–post treatment on at least five participants, were published in English in a peer-reviewed journal, and provided enough data to calculate an effect size. An eight-point scale was used to rate the rigor of each study. Studies received one point for each of the following: a control group, blind coders, observational data, a treatment manual, assessment of fidelity, a minimum of three descriptions of the sample, and standardized measures of the outcomes. Studies were coded by two raters to demonstrate reliability of the coding criteria. Alphas were above .90, indicating consistency amongst raters.

To overcome sampling and publication bias (the tendency of journals to publish statistically significant results over less significant results), fail-safe n's were conducted to determine the stability of meta-analytic results. The fail-safe n calculates the approximate number of unpublished studies with an effect size of 0.00 needed to reduce the obtained effect size to a certain level (Lipsey & Wilson, 2000). Fail-safe n's were parental attitude (22), emotional adjustment (21), and child-rearing behavior outcomes classes (20). The fail-safe n for documented abuse outcomes was 3.75.

R2 (MacLeod and Nelson, 2000) was included in this study because it provided a range of prevention programs to promote wellness factors (protective factors) and decrease maltreating behaviors. Authors applied a three-step model testing process to assess the effectiveness of 56 prevention programs to promote family wellness and decrease child maltreatment. Eight criteria were applied to determine inclusion in the meta-analysis. Studies were included if children under the age of 12 were the target population, all types of prevention (universal, selective, and indicated) programs were included, it did not focus on sexual abuse, it used a prospective and controlled design, and it employed measures related to child maltreatment or family wellness. Additionally, journal articles, book chapters, books, published reports, and dissertations were included. The review covered the time span 1979–1998.

Selected studies were coded based on participant, intervention, methodological characteristics, and study context characteristics. Inter-coder reliability was reported to be .87. Effect sizes were coded within each study and were pooled for each outcome measured (out-of-home placement rates, maltreatment, parent attitudes, and parent behaviors) and also by time of assessment (pre or post). Non-significant effect sizes were reported as "0." Effect sizes were reported for maltreatment, parent attitude, parent behavior and home environment. The three-step analysis included an overall estimate of effective magnitude, testing of moderator variables, and examination of confidence intervals. A fail-safe n of 59 was calculated, and the authors concluded that there were not sufficient missing studies to challenge the meta-analysis results.

R3 (Geeraert, Noortgate, Grietens, & Onghenta, 2004) was selected because of its international review of child abuse and prevention studies. Authors reviewed international databases to create an inventory of prevention programs. The searches were conducted in English, French, German, and Dutch. For inclusion, studies had to be conducted between 1975 and 2002, focused on prevention of child abuse for families at risk, based on early intervention before a child's third birthday, and occur before any physical abuse or neglect had taken place. The meta-analysis examined a reduction in maltreatment risk by increasing child, parent, and family functioning. Authors used a multilevel process to analyze data from 43 programs that were structured at different levels. Only studies that used independent groups or a pre-test/post-test design were selected for inclusion. Studies focused on sexual abuse were excluded.

In most of the studies, several criteria were used to determine program effectiveness. As a result, 587 effect sizes were calculated for the 43 studies. The effect sizes between the studies varied considerably, so authors explored potential explanations. Variations could be explained by sampling variance, the use of many different criteria to determine effectiveness, and program characteristics. Parameters of the three variations were established using specialized software (RIGLS algorithm of MLwiN). Moderator effects and confidence interval estimates were considered during interpretation of the effect sizes.

The two other (DuMont et al., 2006; Olds, 2002) studies selected for this chapter had to score a minimum of 75 points out of 100 on a Quality of Study Rating Form devised by the author for inclusion in this inquiry. Table 3.3 shows the selection criteria and the assigned point value for the two selected studies. Two additional studies were reviewed but not included in this inquiry (Daro & Harding, 1999; McGuigan, Katzev, & Pratt, 2003). One explored the multilevel determinants of retention in a home-visiting program. The study had significance for the field but was not relevant for this inquiry. Another study provided a useful summary of various Healthy Families America program evaluations. However, evaluation details and the process for selection in the summary were not provided.

Research Perspective: Sources

R1 (Lundahl et al., 2006) was a meta-analysis of 23 studies to determine the effectiveness of parent training programs to reduce the risk of child maltreatment. The dependent measures or outcomes were parents' emotional adjustment, child-rearing attitudes, child-rearing behaviors, and documented abuse. Standardized

Table 3.3 Quality Standards and Selected Studies

Area	R4	R5
Research design	10	10
Theory of change	10	7
Data collection/Sample size	10	10
Outcome measures are valid and reliable	8	8
Program effectiveness	7	15
Replication/Fidelity	9	8
Significance	9	10
Relevance	10	10
Cost-benefit relationship	8	0
TOTAL	81	78

measures were used in each of these areas. Researchers explored six moderators to determine if these factors influenced outcomes. The moderators were location of parent training, use of a home visitor, mode of parent training delivery, length of treatment, use of a control group, theoretical underpinnings of the intervention, and methodological rigor. Overall, parenting program results showed moderate effects (d=.45–0.60) and significant and positive gains in all areas. Concerning the moderator effects, there was a negative correlation between rigor and outcomes, suggesting that the impact of parental training may be overstated and more rigorous studies would show smaller effect sizes. Authors concluded that parent training programs were effective in reducing maltreatment. Applications for research and practice were provided.

R2 (MacLeod & Nelson, 2000) was a meta-analysis to determine program effectiveness of 56 programs to promote family wellness and prevent child maltreatment. Authors used a broad definition of child maltreatment. Family wellness was defined as the "presence of supportive, affectionate and gratifying parent–child relationships and a stimulating home environment that is conducive to positive child development" (MacLeod & Nelson, 2000, p. 1129). Authors identified a continuum of programs, ranging from promotion of wellness at one end to intervention for reoccurrence at the other. Along this continuum, programs can be universal, selective, or indicated. Universal and selective programs were labeled as proactive and indicated approaches reactive. Proactive approaches included home visiting, multicomponent, social support, and media interventions. Reactive approaches included family preservation services, multicomponent, social support/mutual aid, and parent training. The overall effect size was .41, suggesting that the treatment group showed better outcomes than 66% of the control/comparison groups. Only proactive or preventive approaches are included in this prevention inquiry.

R3 (Geeraert et al., 2004) conducted an international database search of primary, selective prevention programs conducted between 1975 and 2002 to decrease maltreatment by having a positive effect on the child's function, parent–child interaction, parent's functioning, family functioning, and the family context (socioeconomic situation and the social network). Authors reviewed 43 studies for several characteristics: theoretical framework, screening procedures, mode of intervention, start of intervention, length of intervention, staff, and goals for intervention. To be included, programs had to provide services to the family of the targeted child. The overall effect size was estimated to be .29. Authors concluded that there was strong evidence that prevention programs to reduce maltreatment generally have a positive effect. To be considered a best practice for this inquiry, a practice had to be a characteristic of a majority of programs or mentioned in the discussion section.

R4 (Olds, 2002) summarized 25 years of research on randomized trials of the Nurse Home Visiting Program with low-income, unmarried, adolescent, and first-time mothers and their children. While focusing on mothers, father involvement was strongly encouraged. Study sites included Elmira, New York (N=400), Memphis, Tennessee (N=1135), and Denver, Colorado (N=735). The target populations and program content were based on the author's research and grounded in epidemiology, child development and behavioral theory. A conceptual model of influences on child and maternal and child development guided the research. Influences included prenatal health behaviors, sensitive and competent care of the child, early parental life course, and early life course modifiable risks for early onset anti-social behavior. The same program design was used at the three sites (frequency and length of visits was not reported for Denver). The frequency of home visits was based on the parents' needs. Enrollment of mothers occurred during the second trimester of pregnancy. The average number of visits during pregnancy was nine in Elmira and seven in Memphis. The average number of visits from birth to two was 23 in Elmira and 25 in Memphis. Visits lasted approximately 75 to 90 minutes. Positive outcomes were reported for prenatal health behaviors, birth outcomes, sensitive and competent care of the child, maltreatment and injuries, child neurodevelopmental impairment, early parental life course, later parental life course, and child/adolescent function (Elmira). Elmira results were provided for children at 2 and 15 years. Home visiting demonstrated the best results for mothers at the greatest risk (smokers, low income, and unmarried) and their children. Memphis results were provided at 6, 12, 24, and 54 months and showed similar outcomes to the Elmira study. Results were not presented for Denver, but the author reported similar outcomes. Although implementation standards and strict fidelity to the model were alluded to, best practices and guidelines were not delineated in this review. Therefore, guidelines were found at the Center for Substance Abuse Prevention (2003) and referenced Olds' (2002) research.

R5 (DuMont et al., 2006) explored the effectiveness of Healthy Families New York, a home-visiting model. Authors proposed a framework to explain the discrepant findings of other Healthy Families America randomized trials that found little or no evidence on the reduction of child maltreatment. The goals of the program are to promote positive parenting skills and parent–child interaction, prevent maltreatment, promote prenatal care and healthy child development, and improve parents' self-sufficiency. This study was a randomized trial of 1,173 families who were offered home visitation services after being determined to be at risk. Interviews and scores on a stress checklist determined risk. Family Support Workers (FSW) are specially trained paraprofessionals, speak the same language as participants, and are of the same culture. Program fidelity and quality assurance is achieved through a standardized core-training, ongoing supervision, and systematic observation. Home visits occurred bi-weekly throughout pregnancy and increased to every week from birth to six months. Thereafter, visits were based on the family's need and progressively decreased until the child was five years old. Visits included activities to improve the parent–child relationship, promote child development, assist with access to health care, address family challenges such as substance abuse and mental health issues, and develop Family Support Plans to increase self-sufficiency and family functioning.

After year one, the treatment group reported significantly fewer acts of very serious physical abuse, minor physical or psychological aggression, and harsh parenting behaviors. After year two, parents in the treatment group self-reported having committed one-third fewer acts of serious physical abuse (e.g., hitting child with fist, kicking child, slapping on face) than in the past year. Treatment effects were significant at year two for a prevention subgroup (first-time mothers younger than 19 years). These mothers were less likely to self-report minor physical aggression and harsh parenting behaviors. Psychologically vulnerable women were one-third less likely to self-report serious maltreatment than their control counterparts.

Research Perspective: Results

Although there were 126 studies reviewed in the three meta-analyses and the randomized controls, several best practices were consistently gleaned from the five reviewed articles. Because articles varied in the reporting of best practices or implications for practice, a mention by three of the five sources was deemed sufficient for inclusion in this inquiry. Eight best practices emerged and are shown in Table 3.4.

Home visiting was mentioned by all five articles as an effective approach. Some articles provided more detail than others regarding the content of home-visiting models. Most articles stressed the importance of providing information on child development, child socialization strategies, and roles of children and parents. The same sources also suggested providing interventions that focus on negative affect, such as anger, stress, or lack of parental confidence. Such interventions are related to child, parent, and family functioning. Specifically, parents' emotional well-being acts as a buffer to maltreatment. Targeting these negative affective experiences is thought to increase emotional stability and encourage adaptive child management practices.

R3, R4, and R5 stressed the importance of comprehensive approaches that met the various needs of families. R2 suggested the importance of providing services that are multicomponent, however, they did not find conclusive evidence in the programs reviewed. Most of the programs in these three sources emphasized the importance of addressing the multiple problems of parents. Frequency and duration of the intervention was noted as an important factor in program effectiveness. The most effective treatment was found to last a minimum of six months and included a minimum of 12 visits.

Sources R3, R4, and R5 stressed the importance of targeting mothers and families most at risk for maltreatment. Specifically, young (under 19), first-time, unmarried, low income mothers showed the most significant results, suggesting that prioritizing services can increase protective factors in these mothers and reduce the occurrence and subsequent long-term adverse affects of maltreatment. These programs do not suggest limiting services to at-risk mothers with these characteristics. Rather, an at-risk population yields the greatest treatment effects.

These same sources (R3, R4, and R5) recommended that services begin during pregnancy and continue afterwards. R5 suggested that services continue until age five and R4 until age two. R3 was not as specific, but over 80% of the programs

Table 3.4 Research Best Practices

Best Practices	R1	R2	R3	R4	R5
1. Provide information on child development, child socialization strategies, and roles of children and parents.	X		X	X	X
2. Provide interventions that focus on negative affect, such as anger, stress, or parental confidence.	X		X	X	X
3. Provide home visiting that provides emotional support for parents and helps them individualize/apply information learned during parent training.	X	X	X	X	X
4. Interventions should be a mixture of home visits and in the office.	X				
5. Provide parent training in group and individual settings.	X				
6. Interventions should include behavior and nonbehavioral programs.	X				
7. Promote policies that address poverty, a primary component of maltreatment.		N			
8. Provide comprehensive (multicomponent) approaches.		P	X	X	X
9. Interventions should last a minimum of six months and include a minimum of 12 visits.		P	X	X	X
10. Interventions need to have community input and support to succeed.				X	
11. Target families at greatest risk for abuse.			X	X	X
12. Staff must be well-trained and of professional status (nurses or social workers).			X	X	
13. Services should begin during pregnancy and continue afterwards.			X	X	X
14. Services should promote the development of a support system.			X	X	X
15. Limit caseloads and provide supervision.				X	X
16. A tracking system should be used to ensure that services match family needs and characteristics.				X	
17. Match the culture and language of participants to home visitors.					X

Note: X=Present, N=Needed, P=Promising; Best practices for the research perspective are shaded.

reviewed provided services ranging from six months to five years. Almost 40% of the programs continued for three to five years.

Finally, these three sources (R3, R4, and R5) promoted the development of a support system to decrease social isolation or ensure that mothers get the health and human services needed. For example, the Nurse-Partnership Program stressed the involvement of friends and fathers where appropriate. R3 noted both formal and informal networks as buffers to social isolation.

In summary, conclusions about effective prevention programs remain limited. Consistently, the sources reported home visiting as a successful model to improve positive child, parent, and family outcomes and to decrease negative, risk behaviors and occurrences of abuse. Most other best practices are elements of programs that can be applied in a variety of settings and interventions.

Best Practices Summary

Six best practices were identified by the consumer perspective, seven by the professional best practices, and eight by the research perspective. The consumer best practices tended to focus on how services were perceived by consumers and had transparent connections to social work values. The professional best practices centered on guidelines or standards with apparent links to social work values. The research perspective, on the other hand, focused on programmatic elements. Of the eight research perspective best practices, three were removed at this stage because of the lack of agreement with the consumer and professional perspectives. These were: *provide interventions that focus on negative affect, such as anger, stress, or parental confidence; target families at greatest risk for abuse; and services should begin during pregnancy and continue afterwards.* These practices tend toward intervention content, targeted approaches, and time of intervention.

In summary, the consumer perspective focused on best practices that worked or facilitated services from a client perspective. The professional perspective provided general guidelines or standards that could be adapted across various intervention approaches. The professional best practices seem to mediate the client–consumer perspective with research evidence regarding what is effective. The research perspective isolated effective programmatic elements. The 124 articles–programs reviewed by the sources suggest that home visiting, as a model, is an evidence-based practice. Although parent education and parent training programs show promise, exactly what elements are essential to successful education or training are not as clearly identified.

Six best practices that cut across consumer, professional, and researcher perspectives consistently emerged as essential elements to reduce child maltreatment. Table 3.5 shows the best practices and the endorsement by perspectives.

Critique of Current Best Practices and Recommendations for Improvement

Just how "good" or "potent" are the current best practices reported previously? How confident can we be that the implementation of these best practices will result in successful outcomes? How well do current best practices measure up against value criteria that are relevant to this topic?

This section critiques current best practices along two dimensions: 1) potency— an assessment of the quality of sources and level of agreement within and across perspectives; and 2) a value-critical assessment.

Table 3.5 Summary Table of Best Practices

Best Practices	Consumer	Professional	Research
1. Provide and promote a support system for parents (both formal and informal).	#2 (C1, C2, C3, C4)	#1 (P1, P2, P4)	#14 (R1, R3, R4, R5)
2. Provide services that strengthen parenting through education on child development, socialization strategies, and roles of children and parents.	#3 (C1, C2)	#2 (P1, P2, P4)	#1 (R1, R3, R4, R5)
3. Services should be accessible (flexible, location, and responsive to needs of parents).	#4 (C1, C2)	#10 (P2, P3, P4)	
4. Services should be long term and of adequate intensity.		#11 (P1, P2, P4)	#9 (R2, R3, R4, R5)
5. Provide home visitation services.		#2 (P1, P2, P4)	#3 (R1, R2, R3, R4, R5)
6. Provide community-based services that are available on a continuum.		#9 (P2, P3, P4)	#8 (R2, R3, R4, R5)

Potency: Quality of Sources

The author attempted to quantify the quality of the sources. Peer-reviewed journals and quality of study rating criteria are based on generally agreed-upon standards amongst researchers. However, quality standards are not as apparent for the consumer and professional sources. To assess quality, consumer and professional sources were reviewed in five areas. For consumer sources the areas were: systematic data collection, reach (size of sample), relevance to inquiry question, significance to the field, and the program's relationship to theory. Two points were possible for each category with a potential total of eight points for each source. Two points were awarded if the quality trait was fully present, one if partially addressed, and no points if not mentioned. One consumer source C4 did not provide enough information to be assessed. However, it was included in this inquiry because it reports study results from Circle of Parents (2004), a parent support group with a mission to prevent child maltreatment. The total number of points received by the four sources was 34 points out of 40. Converting the score to a proportion, the level of quality was .85.

Professional sources were assessed in a similar manner. The quality categories differed slightly and included the strength of the research base, programmatic influence, relevance to the inquiry question, significance to the field, and the program's relationship to theory. The same consumer scoring method was applied to the professional sources. The overall score of the professional perspective was 37 points out of 40 or .92.

Quality standards for the research perspective were more objective and have widespread acceptance in the social science community. Table 3.6 shows the quality standards used to rate the sources. Scores of the five research sources ranged from 78 to 91 points out of 100 or an average of .85.

Research criteria were more stringent than the criteria for consumer and professional perspectives. While research scores may be lower than scores for the consumer and professional perspectives, the significance and overall quality may be higher. For this reason, research scores were assigned a weighted value of .60. Consumer and professional perspectives were each weighted at .20.

The quality equation for sources included in this inquiry is:

$$\begin{array}{ccccc} \text{Consumer} & + & \text{Professional} & + & \text{Research} & = & \text{Quality of Inquiry} \\ .20(85) & + & .20(92) & + & .60(85) & = & .86 \end{array}$$

Standards (research) with the highest weighting may underestimate the level of quality, however, the author finds a quality rating of 86 out of 100 points to demonstrate a high level of quality overall. Criterion that were especially strong (over 90%) among the research perspective were method, theory of change, data collection/sample size, outcome measures, replication/fidelity, significance, and relevance to the best practices inquiry.

Potency: Level of Agreement

This section explores the level of endorsement of the six best practices within and across perspectives. Level of agreement is presented in order of most accepted best practices (BP) to lesser accepted. BP1 (provide a support system) received the most endorsement within and among the consumer, professional, and research sources. All of the consumer perspectives, three of the professional sources, and four of the research sources confirmed the practice. BP2 (parent education) was also confirmed by the three perspectives. While the practice registered the same level of support within the professional (three out of four) and research (four out of five) perspectives, the consumer perspective was not as affirming (two out of four).

The four remaining practices were supported by either the consumer and professional perspective or the professional and the research perspective. The professional perspective tended to be the hub of agreement, as the consumer and research perspectives did not intersect without the professional perspective. BP3 (accessibility of services) was endorsed by the consumer and professional perspectives. Among consumers, two of the four sources listed this practice along with three of the four professional sources. BP4 (services should be long term and of adequate intensity), BP5 (home visitation), and BP6 (community-based services) were common to professional and research sources. BP4, BP5, and BP6 were noted by three of the four professionals. BP4 and BP6 were mentioned by

Table 3.6 Quality Summary of Research Perspective

Area	Points Possible	R1*	R2*	R3*	R4	R5	TOTAL
Method	10	10	10	8	10	10	48
Theory of change	10	10	10	10	10	7	47
Data collection? Sample size?	10	10	10	10	10	10	50
Outcome measures are valid and reliable	10	10	10	10	8	8	46
Program effectiveness	20	18	15	15	17	15	80
Replication/Fidelity	10	10	10	10	9	8	47
Significance	10	10	10	10	9	10	49
Relevance to best practices inquiry/well-written	10	10	10	10	10	10	50
Cost-benefit relationship	10	0	0	0	8	0	8
	100	88	85	83	91	78	425

Notes

* Denotes a meta-analysis. If the authors used the quality area as a criterion for inclusion the source received full points. If the area was discussed in the article, points were awarded accordingly.

— R3 did not specifically mention sample size, however adequate size was assumed because sample sizes had to be sufficient to calculate effect size.

four out of the five research sources. BP5 (home visitation) received unanimous endorsement from the researcher perspectives.

It must be noted that a mere count of the number of sources endorsing a best practice can be misleading. Daro and Donnely (2002) (P4) reviewed accomplishments in child abuse prevention over the last 30 years. A specific count of the number of articles reviewed for the summary was not given. Nonetheless, the article represents more than one professional's opinion of best practices. Endorsement by one of the meta-analyses in the research perspective multiplies the level of support substantially. For example, R1 reviewed 23 studies, R2 included 56 program reviews, and R3 selected 43 studies. Therefore, those best practices from the research perspective (support system, home visiting, community-based services, and parent education) may be considered as widely accepted best practices within the research community.

Recommendations for Increasing Potency of Sources

Consumer and professional perspectives provide the how-to for the delivery services. The research perspective provides the justification and rationale for funding. The three perspectives are critical to provide families with quality and effective services. A policy/practice feedback loop is essential to connect these areas and is central to the best practices of this inquiry. Strengthening the policy/practice feedback loop as a value will also strengthen the potency of each perspective.

On the consumer level, social services need to help parents and families find their voice. Parent involvement and parent participation is often a requirement of funding. Participation often takes the form of parent representation on boards or state-level teams. These two or three individuals are expected to represent all parents, express their opinion in the presence of "experts," and commit time and energy to attend meetings. Another form of parent participation is parent leadership. Approaches such as Strengthening Families (CSSP, 2004) recognize the need to give parents an authentic voice. Rather than empowering parents, the approach partners with parents. Evaluations should be participatory and ensure that parents get the information they want and need.

Comprehensive and community-based programs address families holistically and use a myriad of practices (e.g., home visiting, parent education, parent–child interaction). Networks or umbrella agencies oversee a range of services to support families. National and state organizations disseminate research results and best practices. However, inadequate funding makes full implementation of research-based programs financially and practically unfeasible. Increased accountability requirements of the federal government and funding sources require increased accountability. Professional organizations have an opportunity to take a lead role in communicating research to the field and vice versa. Individual programs often do not have the capacity to conduct solid evaluations. Consequently, their experiences and collective wisdom are not communicated to the research community. The lack of agreed-upon measures of maltreatment impacts the ability of local and state programs to develop a rationale for continued funding. A more fluid boundary between the professional and research perspectives would serve both well.

On the research level, more emphasis needs to be placed on conducting rigorous evaluations in the communities in which these services occur. Experimental designs are often not feasible for prevention services. Many programs offer a range of services with varying levels of intensity and duration. Modeling techniques and other designs could be employed to explore the cumulative effect such combinations of services have on strengthening families and decreasing risk factors.

Value Critique and Recommendations

Best practices were explored on several value criteria used by professionals working in child maltreatment. Values were not discussed at length in the sources, therefore the author's assessment and recommendations are based on the provided descriptions with the intention to strengthen best practices.

Values strongly represented by the best practices include social work values of self-determination, dignity of the individual, and importance of human relations (NASW, 1999). Self-determination is manifested as the ability to choose services and voluntarily participate. The continuum of services allows clients to select from an array of services.

Most best practices were strongly rooted in theory, were client centered, and approached the reduction of maltreatment from a strengths perspective. The flexibility of services and location offer participants choices and can reduce the stigma of mandatory treatments. Client-centered best practices include home visitation, the provision of a support system, and accessibility.

The client–worker relationship, cultural competence, and a continuum of services for families were key components of the consumer and professional perspectives, while accountability/outcomes were the focus of the research perspective. Perhaps a consistent emphasis on these values across the perspectives can be explained by article length limitations and the intended audience. The client–worker relationship was heralded as an essential practice by all of the consumer sources. Programs could further facilitate a trusting relationship by minimizing staff turnover, providing consistent workers, and maintaining high standards for staff behavior and conduct. Staff should be warm, friendly, helpful, knowledgeable, and punctual. Workers should not be too intrusive or critical (Taban and Lutzker, 2001). Programs could train staff in family-centered attitudes and practices that are advocated by many consumers (Allen & Petr, 1996; Dunst, 1995)

Cultural competence could be infused into the home visiting (BP5), parent education (BP2), and other services (BP6). Home visiting programs could match the culture and language of participants to home visitors. Parent education materials should be provided in the language of parents. Program planners should provide culturally competent services that match clients' stated needs and interests. Practitioners can also use a cultural inquiry method to understand their own cultural bias, family and cultural values of clients, and strategies to balance the two (Williams-Gray, 2001).

According to the Child Abuse Prevention and Treatment Act (Department of Health and Human Services, 2002), community-based programs should develop "a continuum of family centered, holistic, preventive services for children and families" (p. 55). This continuum of care value could be integrated more fully into best practices through community collaborations that consist of planning efforts in which stakeholders (e.g., potential participants, local service providers, faith-based organizations, parent groups, funders) come together, determine the scope of the problem, and conduct an environmental scan of services. Next a service delivery system is designed to address the various needs of families. Various models of a continuum of services exist such as wrap-around services, multidisciplinary teams, and adjusting the level of services based on the needs of parents. A continuum of family and holistic prevention services can also be obtained through a community or state child abuse and neglect prevention plan in which the six best practices could be addressed through coordinated services and funding streams.

Two of the best practices, providing a support system (BP1) and parenting education (BP2), are conducive to promoting the value empowerment. Many programs are structured to empower parents by providing resources and strategies. However, empowerment as a value could be expanded by partnering with parents and engaging them to determine what are the best program practices. By including parent-run support groups or offering universal programs that strengthen parenting, parents can learn skills that will make them better parents and less likely to maltreat their children. Increased self-management and self-development promote a better understanding of the importance of taking care of themselves and managing stress and anger. Such skill development also increases confidence in parenting and promotes a feeling of being able to be in more control of the situation (Circle of Parents, 2004). Parents can also reach out to other parents and feel empowered by helping others. Training and support should be provided to nurture parent leadership. By offering a ladder of opportunities for parents within an organization, parents can stay involved, continue to grow as leaders, and support other parents. Promoting parent leadership and opportunities for input into program operations can help programs to better understand the parent perspective and alter program-matic elements to be more responsive to families.

The best practices in the research perspective were identified through the value criteria of accountability/outcomes. While most programs must be based on a logic model or include outcomes in order to be funded, the field of maltreatment prevention itself has limited proof of effectiveness according to the gold-standard of evidence-based practice—experimental designs with randomized trials. Such designs may not be feasible for prevention programs due to cost, limited evaluation capacity, fear of finding negative results, challenges to control for variables that threaten standardized programs, ethical issues around having a control group, among others (Tomison, 2000). These challenges should not be used as an excuse to limit evaluations of program effectiveness. Rather, funders should provide adequate resources to develop evaluation capacity within organizations. Instead of accepting experimental designs as the gold standard, funders, program staff, and evaluators should promote an evaluation framework that addresses the myriad of evaluation challenges. (See Tomison (2000) for a description of the framework and alternative evaluation approaches.)

Many of the reviewed sources cite a lack of adequate public funding and commitment to prevention. With the exception of the Olds (2002) Nursing Family Partnership home visitation and Healthy Families America, prevention programs have not done a sufficient job of developing a policy feedback loop that justifies increased funding and demonstrates positive outcomes. On the policy level, several of the best practices (support system, strengthening parenting, and community-based services) could be infused into existing institutions such as education, health, juvenile justice, and in particular early care and education. The relationship between researchers and policymakers must be bi-directional (Portwood & Dodgen, 2005). Professionals and researchers must have the outcomes to prove program effectiveness in order to justify more funding, but also to inform policymakers of what types of programs are working and should be brought to scale.

A practice feedback loop builds on the evaluation framework described earlier. Formative evaluation and a quality improvement feedback loop are essential. The feedback loop should consist of staff and participant input to continuously assess if the program is achieving its stated mission, goals, and objectives. Program practices should be revised accordingly. The practice–policy feedback loop is a critical link to promote fidelity in implementation.

References

Allen, R., & Petr, C. (1996). Toward developing standards and measurements for family-centered practice in family support programs. In G. Singer, L. Powers, & A. Olson (Eds.), *Redefining family support: Innovations in public-private partnerships* (pp. 57–86). Baltimore, MD: Paul H. Brookes Publishing.

Center for Study of Social Policy. (2004). *Protecting children by strengthening families: A guidebook for early childhood programs.* Washington, DC.

Center for Substance Abuse Prevention. (2003). *Building a successful prevention program.* Retrieved October 8, 2006, from http://casat.unr.edu/bestpractices/view.php?program =66.

Circle of Parents. (2004). *Summary of circle of parents, parent group interviews.* Interviews conducted with Illinois, North Dakota, Tennessee, Washington and Wisconsin participants.

Colorado Children's Trust Fund. (1992). Child abuse and neglect. Retrieved September 25, 2006 from www.cdphe.state.co.us/ps/cctf/canmanual/PreventionCAN.pdf.

Daro, D., & Donnely, A.C. (2002). Child abuse prevention: Accomplishments and challenges. In J.E.B. Myers, L. Berliner, J.N. Briere, C.T. Hendrix, T.A. Reid, & C.A. Jenny (Eds.), *The APSAC Handbook on Child Maltreatment* (2nd ed.). Thousand Oaks, CA: Sage Publications.

Daro, D., & Harding, K. (1999). Health Families America: Using research to enhance practice. *The Future of Children—Home Visiting: Recent Program Evaluations, 9*(1), 152–176.

DeMay, D. (2003). The experience of being a client in an Alaska public health nursing home visitation program. *Public Health Nursing, 20*, 228–236.

Department of Health and Human Services (U.S.), Administration on Children, Youth, and Families. (2002). *The Child Abuse Prevention and Treatment Act, As Amended by The Keeping Children and Families Safe Act of 2003*. Retrieved February 25, 2007, from www.friendsnrc.org/download/capta_manual.pdf.

Department of Health and Human Services (U.S.), Administration on Children, Youth, and Families. (2005). Child maltreatment: Fact Sheet. Retrieved September 2, 2006, from www.cdc.gov/ncipc/factsheets/cmfacts.htm.

DuMont, K., Mitchell-Herzfeld, S., Greene, R., Lee, E., Lowenfels, A., & Rodriguez, M. (2006, July). Healthy Families New York randomized trial: Impacts on parenting after the first two years. Paper presented at the Prevent Institute, Chapel Hill, NC.

Dunst, C. (1995). *Key characteristics and features of community-based programs*. Chicago: Family Resource Coalition.

Family Support America & New Jersey Task Force on Child Abuse and Neglect. (2003). *Standards for prevention programs: Building Success through Family Support*. State of New Jersey, Department of Human Services.

Faver, C.A., Crawford, S.L., & Combs-Orme, T. (1999). Services for child maltreatment: Challenges for research and practice. *Children and Youth Services Review, 21*, 89–109.

Felitti, V., Anda, R., Nordenberg, D., Williamson, D., Spitz, A., & Edwards, V. (1998). Relationship of childhood abuse and household dysfunction to many of the leading causes of deaths in adults. *American Journal of Preventive Medicine, 14*, 245–258.

Fromm, S. (2001). Total estimated cost of child abuse and neglect in the United States. Presentation by Frank W. Putnam to the American Association for the Advancement of Science meeting February 2004, Cincinnati, OH.

Geeraert, L., Noortgate, W., Grietens, H., & Onghenta, P. (2004). The effects of early prevention programs for families with young children at risk for physical child abuse and neglect: A meta-analysis. *Child Maltreatment, 9*, 277–291.

Lipsey, B.W., & Wilson, D.B. (2000). *Practical meta-analysis*. London: Sage.

Lundahl, B., Nimer, J., & Parsons, B. (2006). Preventing child abuse: A meta-analysis of Parenting Training Programs. *Research on Social Work Practice, 16*, 251–262.

MacLeod, J., & Nelson, G. (2000). Programs for the promotion of family wellness and the prevention of child maltreatment: A meta-analytic review. *Child Abuse & Neglect, 24*, 1127–1149.

McGuigan, W., Katzev, A., & Pratt, C. (2003). Multi-level determinants of retention in a home-visiting child abuse prevention program, *Child Abuse & Neglect 2*, 363–380.

Minnesota Department of Children, Families and Learning and the Children's Trust Fund. (2000). *Parent involvement and leadership: Study findings and implications for the field*. Received via email from Cynthia Savage, National Director of Circle of Parents, September 8, 2006.

National Association of Social Workers. (1999). *Code of ethics of the National Association of Social Workers*. Retrieved February 27, 2006, from www.socialworkers.org/pubs/code/code.asp.

National Child Abuse and Neglect Data System. (2004). *Summary Child Maltreatment 2004*. Retrieved September 14, 2006, from www.acf.dhhs.gov/programs/cb/pubs/cm04/summary.htm.

National Research Council: Panel on Research on Child Abuse and Neglect. (1993). *Understanding child abuse and neglect*. Washington, DC: National Academy Press.

National Resource Center for Community Based Child Abuse Prevention. (n.d.). Retrieved February 27, 2007 from www.friendsnrc.org/.

North Carolina Institute of Medicine. (2005). *New Directions for North Carolina: A Report of the NC Institute of Medicine Task Force on Child Abuse Prevention*. September.

Olds, D. (2002). Prenatal and infancy home visiting by nurses: From randomized trials to community replication. *Prevention Science, 3*, 153–172.

Oynskiw, J.E., Harrison, M.J. Spady, D., & McConnan, L. (1999). Formative evaluation of a collaborative community-based child abuse prevention project. *Child Abuse & Neglect, 23*, 1069–1081.

Portwood, S., & Dodgen, D. (2005). Influencing policymaking for maltreated children and their families. *Journal of Clinical Child and Adolescent Psychology, 34*(4), 628–637.

Runyan, D., Wattam, C., Ikeda, D., Hassan, F., & Ramiro, L. (2002). Child abuse and neglect by parents and caregivers. In E. Krug, L. Dahlberg, J. Mercy, & A. Swi (Eds.), *World report on violence and health* (pp. 59–86). Geneva, Switzerland: World Health Organization.

Taban, N., & Lutzker, J. (2001). Consumer evaluation of an ecobehavioral program for prevention and intervention of child maltreatment. *Journal of Family Violence, 16*, 323–330.

Tomison, A. (2000). Evaluating child abuse prevention programs. *The National Child Protection Clearinghouse, 12*, 1–18.

Williams-Gray, B. (2001). A framework for culturally responsive practice. In N.B. Webb (Ed.), *Culturally diverse parent-child and family relationships* (pp. 55–83). New York: Columbia University Press.

4 Best Practices for Preventing Teen Pregnancy

Emily McCave

By examining the perspectives of consumers (teenagers), practitioners, and researchers, five best practices on preventing teen pregnancy emerged. These best practices include sex education, access to contraceptives, and involvement of parents, as well as peer mentoring /youth development, and building community alliances. Consistent with multidimensional evidence-based practice (MEBP), these findings were then analyzed using potency and value criteria, including examining the best practices for strengths and weaknesses in the areas of community centeredness, empowerment, and respect for diversity. Four recommendations emerge for improving best practices for preventing teen pregnancy.

Overview of the Population and Problem of Concern

Each year, an estimated 800,000 to 900,000 young women under the age of 20 experience an unintended pregnancy in the United States (Center for Disease Control and Prevention, 2000). Additionally, more than 500,000 children are born annually to adolescent mothers; this is one of the highest rates of all developed nations (Knopf & Paluzzi, 2005). While increases in contraceptive use have brought down the rate of teenage pregnancies in recent decades, the CDC considers the issue of teenage pregnancy to be of paramount concern, largely because "adolescent pregnancy and childbearing have been associated with adverse health and social consequences for young women and their children" (2000, p. 605).

The literature points to distinct subgroups of teenagers that are at high-risk for experiencing teenage pregnancy in the United States. Teens who come from economically disadvantaged backgrounds, who have less education, and who are either Latina or African American, are particularly at risk for becoming pregnant (Mayden, Castro, & Annitto, 1999). Latina youth have recently surpassed African Americans in the birth rates for teens aged 15–19 because of the higher number of abortions used by African Americans.

The literature has consistently highlighted the negative outcomes associated with teenage motherhood for the teenage parent, the child, and for society. Teenage mothers are often impacted negatively in regards to economic outcomes. The ability to graduate from high school and obtain higher education is severely impeded by having a child as a teenager, which often is associated with higher rates of welfare use and experiences of poverty (Yampolskaya, Brown, & Greenbaum, 2002). Moreover, teen mothers accumulate less human capital than teens who do not become parents, in that they are less likely to receive job training and early job skills, which results in less earned income (Klepinger, Lundberg, & Plotnick, 1999).

The impact on teenage mothers is highly linked to the outcomes of their children. Teenage parents tend to experience heightened stress and lower self-esteem, which has broad impacts on their children, such as being raised in lower quality environments that provide less stimulation than what is provided typically by adult parents (Andreozzi, Flanagan, Seifer, Brunner, & Lester, 2002; Moore, Morrison, & Greene, 1997). Additionally, research consistently shows that children of teenage mothers are more likely to be born premature and have higher infant mortality rates than children born to adult women (King, 2003). Such children are more likely to experience cognitive delays, as well as emotional and behavioral difficulties (Hillis et al., 2004). Moreover, teenage parents are more likely to experience negative feelings and unrealistic expectations for their child, which can lead to abuse or neglect, particularly if the child is frequently ill or was born premature (Zalenko et al., 2001). The issue of intergenerational abuse is often present, given that teenage mothers are more likely to have an abuse history than teens who are not parents (Elders & Albert, 1998). Weinman, Smith, Geva, and Buzi (1998) comment on these negative outcomes, stating that teenage mothers "have few psychological and social resources, are cognitively immature, and tend to adopt more punitive ways to discipline their children" (p. 288).

In responding to the consequences of teenage pregnancy, society ends up paying a high cost. In 1994, the Office of Population Options reported that $34 billion in public funds were distributed to pay for the needs of teen mothers and their children, namely for health care, food stamps, welfare, and Medicaid (Solomon & Liefeld, 1998).

In response to the problem, national efforts to establish primary prevention programs to prevent teens from becoming pregnant have been initiated. Ideally, the primary outcome of any successful program would be fewer pregnancies, as evidenced by reduced birth rates and fewer abortions by adolescents. However, such statistics are difficult to capture, mainly because they come from self-reports by teens, which may not be accurate (Kirby et al., 1994). Mediators of teen pregnancy are more frequently measured and typically include delayed sexual initiation, increased contraceptive use, increased knowledge and skills regarding sexual decision-making, and increased communication between parents and adolescents about sex.

In this chapter, the author will utilize the multidimensional evidence-based practice (MEBP) method to address the following question: what are best practices to prevent teen pregnancy in the United States?

Best Practices Inquiry Search Process

Given the extensive amount of resources devoted to teen pregnancy prevention, often with little documented success, it is not surprising that there has been a push for "evidence-based practices." Large national organizations, such as the National Campaign to Prevent Teen Pregnancy and Healthy Teen Network, have started reviewing national prevention programs, presenting the most salient features of successful teen pregnancy prevention programs.

The overall search process for this inquiry included viewing abstracts and documents, published after 1995, in the following Databases: Google Scholar, Proquest Dissertation and Theses; Social Work Abstracts, Psych Info, PubMed, and Social Services Abstracts. Additionally, the University of Kansas library catalog and the table of contents in relevant electronic journals, such as *Journal of Public Health* and *Adolescence*, were examined for possible sources. Finally, a social work resources link from the University of Wisconsin's School of Social Work was utilized to locate national teenage pregnancy prevention organizations. For the research perspective, some studies were excluded after reading the abstracts and determining that the scope was too broad or narrow (e.g., academic success programs or HIV prevention programs, respectively) or that the studies had considerable methodological limitations (e.g., a convenience sample with a very small "N").

Results of Best Practices from the Three Perspectives

All of the sources for the three perspectives were given a code (e.g., C1, P1, R1, etc.). The codes are utilized in this section as well as in Tables 4.1, 4.2, and 4.3, which highlight the best practices from the three different perspectives. Each perspective has a brief summary of the source as well as a brief description of the criteria it met to be included in this analysis. A brief description of the best practices identified by each perspective is also provided.

Consumer Perspective: Sources

For the consumer perspective, sources were judged on the following qualities: 1) Authenticity—representation of consumer's voice; 2) Credibility—reputability of the source; 3) Influence—impact on the topic of teenage pregnancy prevention; 4) Specificity—clarity in describing the "best practices" and whether it distinguishes if consumers actually received the interventions or are speaking about what they need; 5) Systematic—level of rigor in gathering and disseminating the "best practices"; and finally 6) Appropriate Match—specific focus on teenage pregnancy prevention.

Summary C1: The National Campaign to Prevent Teen Pregnancy (2006) has a comprehensive website that includes a "Teens Tell All" section, in which teen responses from a number of topics about teen pregnancy were gathered and posted from an online survey.

Criteria C1: This source was chosen primarily because it was authentic, specific, and credible—the site leads to specific quotes from teens across the country. Additionally, this organization is highly influential; it is one of the most commonly cited national organizations that is solely devoted to preventing teenage pregnancy. This particular perspective is not highly systematic; it lacks detail about the methodology and design, which is why it is not included under the research perspective. Moreover, it does not distinguish whether adolescents who commented had participated in teen pregnancy programs that worked or whether they were speaking about the practices they needed.

Summary C2: Corcoran, Franklin, and Bell (1997) gave teens the chance to be the "experts" on what can be done to prevent teen pregnancy. Focus groups were conducted with 105 teens who were attending 18 different state-wide teen pregnancy prevention programs.

Criteria C2: This source was selected because of its attention to consumer voice and the exact fit with the topic. Because it was a qualitative study, it was rated using the qualitative rating scale (discussed in research perspective section). This study's strength included recruiting a diverse sample from multiple teen pregnancy preventions programs, using systematic data collection, including quotes to enhance authenticity. It was influential as a peer-reviewed article and contributes knowledge to the field. The main weakness was that it did not specify best practice interventions at the individual program level.

Summary C3: Hacker, Yared, Strunk, and Horst, (2000) conducted a quantitative study using a written survey that explored how teens view the problem of teen pregnancy and how to prevent it. For a research article, it was highly consumer driven, with teens serving as members on the community committee responsible for developing the surveys.

Criteria C3: This source was authentic and credible; it systematically created the survey using committee input that included teens, parents, school officials, public health workers, and pregnancy prevention workers and had a sample of 1,000 students from six high schools in Boston. As a publication in a peer-reviewed journal, it was influential. Additionally, youth surveyed were exposed to a variety of health education curricula, suggesting that youth had a wide exposure to a variety of practices aimed at preventing teen pregnancy.

Consumer Perspective: Results

To be considered a "best practice" by consumers, a practice had to be discussed by at least two of the three consumer sources. Thus, the first seven best practices from Table 4.1 fit these criteria.:

Best practice #1, sex education, entailed school-based curricula for mixed gender classrooms. Aspects of sex education included focusing on pregnancy and proper contraceptive use. Closely tied to this was best practice #2, access to

Table 4.1 Consumer Perspective on Best Practices

Best Practices	C1	C2	C3
1. School-based sex education	X	X	X
2. Access to contraceptives	X	X	X
3. Encouraging abstinence	X	X	X (or sexual initiation delay)
4. Peer support/Mentorship and community-based youth development	X	X	X
5. Communication with parents and partners	X	X	X
6. Improving attitudes and morals	X	X	
7. Having online resources and hotlines	X	X	
8. Involving the media	X		
9. Planning for sexual encounters	X		
10. "In Your Face" programs	X		
11. Counseling, support groups, shelters		X	
12. Involving young males		X	
13. Self-defense classes		X	

contraceptives, which emphasized that youth have access to *free* and *anonymous* contraceptives, and that condoms in particular should be distributed in schools. It also included access through community clinics. A differing approach that was commonly identified was best practice #3, which focused on promoting abstinence and delaying sexual initiation. This particular intervention was often tied into best practice #6, increasing healthy attitudes and morals, which often encompassed healthy self-image and self-esteem, along with utilizing religion to support abstinence.

Best practice #4, peer mentorship and youth development, entailed having youth participate in extracurricular activities and having teen parents provide sex education to peers. Best practice #5 consisted of promoting communication between youth and parents and with their partners, which asserted that if youth talk with their parents and partners about the realities of sex, they are less likely to get pregnant. Finally, for best practice #7, youth indicated that having information on how to access online resources, such as Planned Parenthood, or telephone hotlines, particularly for youth on the streets after running away or who are experiencing sexual abuse, was important for teen pregnancy prevention.

Professional Perspective: Sources

For the professional perspective, the selection criteria were the same as for the consumer perspective, with the exception of a seventh criterion (Theory Driven). This considers whether the source operates from a particular theoretical framework.

Summary P1: Vincent et al. (2000) replicated a multicomponent community-wide teen pregnancy prevention program in Kansas that had demonstrated a 54% reduction of estimated pregnancy rates in South Carolina during the early 1980s. Achieving some, but not all, of the same results, the authors presented the "realities and challenges" of replication.

Criteria P1: This source was a suitable match with the topic, along with being credible, systematic, influential, and authentic, as the originator of the model worked with the replication team. Additionally, the model asserts that the more breadth and depth of knowledge and services are provided to educators and youth, the more effective the programs will be in its goals.

Summary P2: The Child Welfare League of America brought together practitioners, advocates, Latina youth, and researchers to create a dialogue about what works in teen pregnancy prevention programs, particularly those that are involved with Latina youth (Mayden et al., 1999). Out of the symposium came specific guidelines for the best practices in preventing teen pregnancy, particularly for Latina youth.

Criteria P2: This source had credibility, authenticity, and a sufficient match to the problem area. It appeared to be empowerment focused and operated from a multicultural/ethnic perspective. Given that Latinas are a growing group who are at high risk for teen pregnancy, it was important to include this professional perspective in this best practices inquiry.

Summary P3: Franklin, Corcoran, and Ayers-Lopez (1997) are practitioners who have worked with teenage parents in the field. Based on their experiences, they presented guidelines for preventing teen pregnancy.

Criteria P3: This source was considered credible and authentic, given that these professionals are sharing their practice wisdom in this topic area. This source was part of a larger book operating from an ecological perspective and it systematically provided specific interventions for reducing teen pregnancy.

Summary P4: The National Association of Social Workers (NASW) presented its official position on adolescent pregnancy in its series, Social Work Speaks (2003). In this most recent edition, NASW put forth a set of recommendations that social workers should consider when working to prevent teen pregnancy.

Criteria P4: As social work's professional association, NASW is credible and lends authenticity and influence to this source. It is well-matched to the problem, and described the interventions needed to prevent teen pregnancies. It appeared empowerment and systems oriented.

Professional Perspective: Summary of Best Practices

The first six best practices listed in Table 4.2 were presented by at least three out of the four professional sources.

Table 4.2 Professional Perspective on Best Practices

	Best Practices	P1	P2	P3	P4
1.	School-based sex education	X	X	X (But community-based as well)	X (Community as well)
2.	Access to contraceptives	X	X	X	X
3.	Community alliances	X	X	X	X
4.	Peer support/Mentorship and community-based youth development	X	X	X	
5.	Cultural and developmental sensitivity		X	X	X
6.	Involve parents		X	X (and also extended family)	X (and also extended family)
7.	Involving the media	X		X	
8.	Involve young men		X		X
9.	Involve faith organizations	X		X	
10.	Collaboration with school administrators	X			

The #1 best practice, sex education, focused on curricula both in schools and in the community that were comprehensive in nature (e.g., K-12 sex education, graduate classes for teachers, alliances with public health and medical professionals, cultural values and sexual decision-making) and that were accessible for youth of all learning styles and abilities. The #2 best practice, access to contraceptives, emphasized utilizing nurses in schools as well as having adequate referral processes to public health clinics and private physicians, particularly for identified high-risk youth. Having affordable and accessible contraceptive services for youth was also stressed. The #3 best practice, forming community alliances, focused on building alliances between local government officials, schools, health and helping professionals, and faith groups. Interventions including having community residents serve on community advisory boards and social support programs run together by schools, churches, and community groups.

The #4 best practice, youth mentoring and development, focused on peer health educators, community service projects, tutoring, and job placement for youth. The #5 best practice, developmentally and culturally appropriate interventions, emphasized community cultural values, age-appropriate activities, and specific interventions for high-risk groups, such as Latinas, migrants, emotionally disabled youth, and homeless youth. The #6 best practice, involving parents, focused on having parents involved with either planning or participating in the intervention, such as working with churches and the media, receiving sex education, serving as sex educators, and passing down child-rearing stories to youth. It also included targeting families to prevent sexual abuse of teens (to ward off early sexual involvement).

Research Perspective: Sources

A more rigorous inclusion process was established for the research perspective. Two quality-of study rating scales were developed to accomplish this process, one for quantitative sources and another scale for qualitative sources. Both rating scales included ten criteria each with its own weight attached. While most of the criteria categories were the same for both scales, the descriptions and points awarded for these criteria differed for the two scales. The total possible score for both scales was 100 points. Six sources were rated (including the one qualitative study from the consumer perspective mentioned in the prior section), five of which were included in the research perspective. Additional sources could have been rated; however, the research sources often identified numerous best practices, so it was important to keep the amount of information gathered manageable for the inquiry process. Moreover, as there were five sources with solid rating scores, it is seemed less imperative to include sources with much less rigorous methods, as they would most likely not be viewed as credible in the best practices potency critique (discussed in a later section on critique of best practice sources).

Table 4.3 highlights a summary table for the research quality ratings of each article. This table highlights the overall strengths and weaknesses of the research sources in the last column.

Table 4.3 Summary Table for Quality Ratings of Research Perspective Sources

Quantitative	R1	R2	R3	R4	Total
Contributes relevant knowledge (10 pts.)	7	8	8	10	33 (40) 83%
Theoretical/Conceptual development (10 pts.)	6	7	8	6	27 (40) 68%
Research design (15 pts.)	11	13	10	11	45 (60) 75%
Data collection (10 pts.)	8	8	7	8	31 (40) 78%
Sample (10 pts.)	9	7	6	8	30 (40) 75%
Data analysis (10 pts.)	6	8	6	6	26 (40) 65%
Specificity (10 pts.)	6	6	7	7	26 (40) 65%
Acknowledgment of researcher bias (5 pts.)	0	0	0	0	0 (40)
Significance of results (15 pts.)	9	10	12	14	45 (60) 75%
Clearly organized and well written (5 pts.)	3	4	3	4	14 (20) 70%
Total (100 pts)	65	71	67	74	277 69%

Summary R1: Basen-Engquist et al. (2001) conducted a quasi-experimental study of the Safer Choices curriculum, which is a cognitive–behavioral, multifaceted program targeting ninth through twelfth graders. It includes school-wide activities, class-based curriculum, peer educators, parent activities, and linking youth to community resources. This study's main strengths included having three different data collection periods: baseline, 19 months, and 31 months. Additionally, it used cohort data as well as cross-sectional data and had a large sample (between 7,000 and 10,000 for each data collection point). It showed significant improvements in condom use at 19 and 31 months post-baseline, with no significant differences in the frequency of sexual intercourse. The study's main weakness was that it was a quasi-experimental design rather than true experimental design and that it did not track actual pregnancy outcomes.

Summary R2: Allen, Philliber, Herrling and Kuperminc (1997) carried out an experimental study that evaluated The Teen Outreach Program in 22 different nationwide sites, with 695 students. Instead of focusing on sexuality, this program takes an indirect developmental approach to promote healthy socialization of youth through volunteer experiences and using a life options classroom-based curriculum. This study's main strengths included a true experimental design and a large sample (N = 695). Most importantly, it demonstrated significant reductions in reported pregnancies at nine months and results confirmed past studies of the program. Its main weakness was that it lacked specificity regarding the inter-ventions and compensated by referring to a prior article for more in-depth review.

Summary R3: Lonczak, Abbott, Hawkins, Kosterman, and Catalano (2002) conducted a longitudinal quantitative study to evaluate the long-term impacts of the Seattle Social Development Project on sexual behavior, including the numbers of pregnancies experienced. Participants received the intervention at various points from first through sixth grade. Follow-up interviews were conducted with 93% of those youth at age 21. The intervention draws from social development theory and includes parenting classes, in-service trainings for teachers, and social competency training for the students. This study was strong in that it included a longitudinal cohort sample (N = 349) and the control group received no intervention. The authors clearly delineated the interventions. The study demonstrated significant reductions in reported pregnancies for intervention group compared to controls (38 and 56% respectively). It highlighted the importance of early intervention without a sex education component. The main weakness of the study was that it was nonrandomized.

Summary R4: Philliber, Kaye, and Herrling (2001) presented the three-year evaluation of the Children's Aid Society Carrera-Model Program spanning 12 different sites in six different states, with over 900 middle and high school students. This program is multifaceted and includes a job club, educational support, family life and sex education, as well as arts and sports. This program is unique in viewing youth "at promise" rather than "at risk." The main strength of this study included that the data was collected over a three-year period and that it obtained a large sample (N = 941 at third year data collection point). It demonstrated significant reductions in reported pregnancies (49% less pregnancies than comparisons). This model has contributed extensively to the knowledge base in this area and has won national awards. The study's main weakness was that it was a quasi-experimental design rather than true experimental design.

Summary R5: Kirby, Laris, and Rolleri (2006) carried out a qualitative content analysis using a meta-analysis approach to determine which sex and HIV education programs around the world are effective. Out of 83 total studies examined, there were 13 studies that measured pregnancy rates, three of which achieved significant positive effects. The study then reported the important characteristics of those programs that were effective.

Criteria R5: This study used its own inclusion criteria: 1) curriculum and group-based programs; 2) focused on ages 9 to 24; 3) either experimental or quasi-experimental designs with both pre-test and post-test data; 4) a sample of at least 100 participants; 5) examined specific behavioral outcomes; 6) measured these outcomes for at least three to six months; and 7) the study was completed or published after 1990. Limitations of the analysis were offered as were specific programmatic characteristics of successful intervention programs. Consequently, this study was included automatically into this analysis because of the rigor employed in the inclusion process.

Research Perspective: Results

Table 4.4 reveals the best practices according to researchers, with the first seven practices that have at least four sources that identified them as "best practices."

Best practice #1 entailed using interventions that are theory based, such as developmental theory, social learning theory, and social control models. Emphasis was on enhancing positive social identity and promoting autonomy, while also promoting the development of supportive adult relationships. Additionally, a strengths-based approach was used in all of the studies, though not always explicitly, which recognized the unique needs of individuals and provided an environment where youth could reach their full potential. Best practice #2, speaks to having a multifaceted, broad-based program utilizing multiple interventions, such as focusing on teachers and parents, along with youth. Best practice #3, group-based sex education/life options curriculum, included topics such as vulner-abilities and consequences of sexual activity and proper use of contraceptives. A life options curriculum instead focused on decision-making, recognizing and handling emotions, managing relationships, and dealing with transitions from adolescence to adulthood; this curriculum was used in only one program reviewed.

Best practice #4, youth development, included activities to enhance the social and emotional development of the youth and increase positive attitudes,

Table 4.4 Research Perspective on Best Practices

Best Practices	R1	R2	R3	R4	R5
1. Theory based	X	X	X	X	XX*
2. Multifaceted, broad-based program	X	X	X	X	XX
3. Group-based sex education/life options curriculum	X	X (emphasis on life options, not sex education)		X	XX
4. Youth development		X	X	X	XX
5. School-community linkages	X	X		X	XX
6. Teacher/Instructor training	X	X	X		XX
7. Sequential sessions over multiple years	X		X	X	XX
8. Access to reproductive health services	X			X	XX
9. Developmentally and culturally appropriate activities			X	X	XX
10. Parent education	X		X	X	
11. Careful curriculum development					XX
12. Peer leadership	X				
13. School-wide organization of activities	X				

Note: *R5 was given two X marks for each best practice because it reviewed multiple studies

knowledge, and skills for managing relationships. Interventions included community service, developing problem-solving skills, and refusal skills. Youth participated in arts, sports, job placement, tutoring, and college preparation. Best practice #5, linking schools and the community, entailed providing activities to inform youth about health-related community services, such as bringing in speakers and a community resource guide. It also involved professionals from the community acting as key players in the program curriculum development. Best practice #6, training teachers, included preparing instructors to communicate effectively with youth and increasing their knowledge and skill base in the area of sexuality/life options. Teachers received training on classroom management and on interactive and cooperative teaching methods. Finally, best practice #7, sequential interventions over multiple years, entailed multiple sessions or aspects of the intervention in a sequential, logical manner, such as increasing in complexity as youth age.

Summary Conclusions of Current Best Practices

There were five best practices that were common across the perspectives (see Table 4.5). Two of those best practices were consistently identified throughout all three perspectives: 1) sex education and 2) youth leadership and development.

Table 4.5 Chart of Best Practices across Perspectives

Best Practices	Consumer	Professional	Research
1. Sex education	X #1 (1, 2, 3)	X #1 (1, 2, 3, 4)	X #3 (1, 2, 4, 5)
2. Peer mentoring and youth development	X #4 (1, 2, 3)	X #4 (1, 2, 3)	X #4 (1, 2, 3, 4, 5)
3. Involve parents	X #6 (1, 2, 3)	X #6 (2, 3, 4)	
4. Community alliances		X #3 (1, 2, 3, 4)	X #5 (1, 2, 4, 5)
5. Access to contraceptives	X #2 (1, 2, 3)	X #2 (1, 2, 3, 4)	
6. Developmentally and culturally sensitive		X #5 (2, 3, 4)	
7. Focusing on abstinence	X #3 (1, 2, 3)		
8. Promote healthy morals	X #5 (1, 2)		
9. Access to online resources and telephone hotlines	X #7 (1, 2)		
10. Teacher/Instructor training			X #6 (1, 2, 3, 5)
11. Theory based			X #1 (1, 2, 3, 4, 5)
12. Multifaceted, broad-based program			X #2 (1, 2, 3, 4, 5)
13. Sequential lessons/experiences over multiple years			X #7 (1, 3, 4, 5)

The remaining three best practices were identified by two of the perspectives: involving parents and access to contraceptives was identified by the consumer and professional perspectives, whereas the best practices of forming and maintaining community alliances was identified by both the professional and the research perspectives, but not the consumer perspective.

This chapter has examined the question: what are the best practices for preventing teen pregnancies in the U.S.?

The first best practice is group-based sex education/life options curriculum. While there are a variety of types of sex education, the curricula that were identified as being most important for preventing teen pregnancy included curricula that were provided in schools as well as the community, and that sex education should include mixed genders. Successful programs were comprehensive in nature (e.g., providing K-12 sex education and graduate classes for teachers, forming alliances with public health and medical professionals, and considering cultural values and sexual decision-making). Curricula included topics such as vulnerabilities and consequences of sexual activity as well as information about proper use of contraceptives. Curricula should be accommodating to youth of all learning styles and abilities. Programs that focus entirely on a life options component can be an appropriate alternative for those communities who have a significant contingent of community members and groups who are uncomfortable with direct sex education. Namely, this involves talking about decision-making, recognizing and handling emotions, managing relationships, and dealing with transitions from adolescence to adulthood. Both forms of education have been found to be beneficial to students. Administrators may want to consider both the maturity level of the students and the professional readiness of the instructors to deal with direct sexual education as well as the community support. If sufficient program funds exist, it may be beneficial to offer both forms of education, requiring students to opt in to one form or the other, and then conducting longitudinal program evaluation to determine significant differences in behavioral outcomes, particularly pregnancy rates. Additionally, it may be beneficial to utilize the life options curriculum for pre-adolescent and early adolescent youth and then move into a direct sex education curriculum in the high school years.

The second best practice identified is providing teens with access to reproductive health care. Youth should have access to *anonymous* and *affordable (free when possible)* contraceptives, with condoms in particular available in the communities and within schools. It involves utilizing nurses in schools and having adequate referral processes to public health clinics and private physicians, as well as developing internal mechanisms for ensuring accessibility for identified high-risk youth. It is imperative that students learn about the reproductive health resources available in their communities and that, if possible, youth are linked directly to reproductive health services in the community.

The third best practice, youth development, is one that often does not focus on sexuality, but rather provides activities that enhance the social and emotional development of youth. Such activities include providing younger youth with older peer mentors and having youth participate in activities outside of school. Activities that foster peer leadership, such as having teen parents to serve as peer health educators, are important to consider. A variety of projects, such as community service, tutoring, school clubs, arts, sports, job placement, and college preparation are part of youth development. With such programs it is important to have classroom-based discussion to process the youth's experiences with the program. Activities can focus on developing refusal and problem-solving skills, particularly regarding interpersonal relationships. Effective programs include activities aimed at promoting healthy psychosocial factors, such as positive attitudes, knowledge and skills for managing relationships.

The fourth best practice is involving parents in teen pregnancy prevention programs. Notably, this was a best practice that was identified by consumers and professionals, but not as an evidenced-based practice identified by researchers. However, three of the four research sources did identify the use of parent education as a critical component to teen pregnancy prevention. Given that only those practices that received support by four out of the five sources were selected for the final best practices, it is apparent that more research would most likely support the beliefs of consumers and professionals who indicate this is an essential aspect of teen pregnancy prevention. Such parent involvement can entail promoting communication between youth and parents, particularly talking with their parents about the realities of sex. Parents can also be involved with working with churches and the media to promote dissemination of program information. Parents should be involved as much as possible as sex educators and in receiving education from programs, in an effort to strengthen the family. Encouraging parents to pass down child-rearing stories and practices is also important. Finally, efforts targeting the family to prevent sexual abuse of teens (to ward off early sexual involvement) are key.

The fifth best practice is building school and community alliances. This entails forming alliances between local government officials, schools, health and helping professionals, and faith groups. It means bringing in community residents to serve on community advisory boards and developing social support programs run together by schools, churches, and community organizations. It is important to have well-coordinated multidisciplinary teams of professionals working together to implement early prevention programs and sex education curricula. It can include providing activities to inform the youth about health-related community services, such as bringing in speakers and providing a community resource guide. It can also included supervised volunteer experiences at local community agencies. For programs that are held in the community, program planners can use schools as a way to recruit and retain youth.

Critique of Current Best Practices

Potency of the Best Practices Sources

In order to determine the level of support for the common best practices found in this inquiry, the strength or quality of the best practices was assessed by examining the following for each of the six best practices: 1) quality of sources for each perspective; 2) level of agreement within perspectives; and 3) level of agreement across perspectives. The quality of consumer and professional perspectives were not overly rigorous, which excluded them from the research perspective. Yet these two perspectives are critical to the discussion on teen pregnancy prevention. As such, research that is more rigorous needs to focus on including professionals and consumers in the research samples as well as in the development of the research study, so that their experiences are incorporated into the best practices literature. Regarding the quality of research sources for each perspective, Table 4.3 compares the total scores of each research source, as well as compares the subtotals of the quality criteria across research sources, thereby highlighting the strengths and weaknesses of the research sources overall (last column). In general, it can be said that the research sources were strong on the knowledge that was contributed, the data collection procedures, the research design (that included several longitudinal studies), the sample sizes, and finally the significance of results. The sources were seriously lacking, however, in the acknowledgment of bias by the researchers, and slightly lacking in theoretical development, data analysis, and specificity.

With regard to level of agreement within and across perspectives, there was strong support for best practice #1, given that all three perspectives identified sex education as a best practice. Consumers consistently identified school-based sex education, and professionals agreed and added community-based sex education to the mix. The research perspective added a life options intervention either in conjunction with or as a substitute for group-based sex education.

The second best practice, access to contraceptives, can be considered well-established given that all three perspectives agreed it was important to include in prevention programs. Within the research perspective, there were two programs that did not focus on contraceptive use at all, indicating that interventions need to consider that some communities might not approve of youth accessing contraceptives.

The third best practice, peer mentoring and youth development, has a great deal of support across perspectives, although the specific characteristics differed somewhat. Consumers emphasized peer mentorship, particularly from teen parents; professionals emphasized providing social, educational and job training opportunities for youth; and research employed various extracurricular activities.

Involving parents, the fourth best practice, also received strong support across consumer and professional perspectives, but not the research perspective. Within the professional perspectives, there was some variation in the specificity and type of parent involvement, ranging from having parents as sex educators to serving on planning committees. Within the consumer perspective, there was strong agreement that interventions should focus on enhancing communication between parents and youth.

The last best practice, building community alliances, cannot be considered as strong as the other best practices, given that the consumer perspective did not identify this as a best practice. Perhaps this could be related to the fact that the consumers are teens, and, given their age and experiences, such issues as community alliances might not be paramount to their immediate needs.

Overall, the conclusion is that the strength, or potency, of "best" practices for preventing teen pregnancy is quite high. There have been many methodologically rigorous studies yielding strong empirical support, as well as number highly credible sources in the consumer and professional perspective.

Value Criteria

An additional way of assessing the strength of the best practices is to examine their fit with specific values criteria. While there are a number of values that the best practices could be weighed against, for this chapter the following values are seen as critical in evaluating the best practice for preventing teen pregnancy: empowerment, community centeredness, and respect for diversity. The reasons for choosing these particular values are twofold. First, these values have been discussed in the teen pregnancy prevention literature as important considerations (Mayden et al., 1999; Philliber et al., 2001; Vincent et al., 2000). Second, these values are particularly salient in social work practice; therefore social work practitioners involved in teen pregnancy prevention programs will readily be able to evaluate the programs they are involved with by these criteria.

Overall, the best practices can be viewed as offering strong opportunities for *empowerment* to youth and other stakeholders invested in interventions. Sex education and life options curriculum provide an opportunity for empowerment for youth who are seeking information and may interact with their peers and parents in a more confident manner. Involving parents is an excellent form of empowerment, and not only for parents who want to communicate with their youth; a majority of youth indicate that they would prefer to talk with their parents about their sexual health needs (Hacker et al., 2000). Similarly, most youth report wanting access to reproductive health care services, either in school or in the community (National Campaign to Prevent Teen Pregnancy, 2006). Providing an opportunity to get connected with such information and services, may afford youth a sense of control over their well-being. Moreover, youth development activities can offer opportunities for personal growth and a positive outlet, which may foster empowerment for youth receiving such interventions. Finally, creating partnerships between schools and communities to develop the interventions already mentioned can certainly be a method for empowerment, as it allows communities to combine resources and tackle the problem of teen pregnancy with a united purpose.

Overall, the level of *community centeredness* across the identified best practices is not as readily apparent as with the value of empowerment. Regarding sex education, many programs have an "opt-out" policy; this aspect of best practice can be considered community centered because it reflects community values, though that opt-out option may only be available for parents, not youth (Santelli, Ott, Lyon, Rogers, & Summers, 2006). However, sex education also may not be viewed as community centered, as many parents and religious leaders argue that it is inappropriate to offer sex education to youth. Sex education as community centered is difficult because it involves being respectful of parents as stakeholders within the community, along with other community stakeholders such as educators and health providers. Managing conflicting values is difficult and in the end it may be that sex education creates community conflict. Providing access to reproductive health services is community centered if it provides for the entire youth community, however, it is more likely that program planners may be faced with certain populations who are not automatically included in the program's catchment area, such as youth with severe disabilities and youth who are in group homes. Youth development and fostering school and community alliances are the only two best practices that are clearly community centered, as it often involves the direct link between communities and schools. Overall, the majority of best practices include elements of community centeredness, but current obstacles prevent full realization of this goal.

Depending on the curriculum, sex education programs vary regarding *respect for diversity*. Youth who are receiving abstinence-only education (AOE) may not receive information that is sensitive to the diverse needs of youth. One challenge regarding the involvement of parents is the conflict between the rights of the parents with the rights of youth, who may feel pressured by their parents to conform to family values, particularly if the program involves AOE. This issue is closely related to access to reproductive health care, as AOE programs also do not allow for discussion of contraceptives, except for the failure rates. Collaboration via school and community alliances may enhance sensitivity regarding diversity if different stakeholders come together, such as health practitioners and religious leaders. Youth development activities incorporate a respect for diversity, in that youth are able to take part in activities that are of particular interest to them and their needs.

Overall, the sources across perspectives were lacking in specific interventions targeting race, sexual orientation, and cultural factors. The two sources that did incorporate cultural factors, namely the professional source on Latina teens (Mayden et al., 1999) and the research source on the Children's Aid Society Carrera-Model Program (Philliber et al., 2001) emphasized the importance of recognizing unique cultural factors of teens. Given that Latina and African American young women have the highest teen pregnancy rates, it is critical to develop best practices that reflect the unique cultural factors that influence these racial groups. This is a weakness in most programs, in that a "one size fits all" approach is used; none of the sources across perspectives considered gay, lesbian, bisexual, and transgendered (GLBT) youth and their particular needs. Given that this particular group is at risk for participating in high-risk sexual activity, it is certainly possible that GLBT youth will experience unintended pregnancies, particularly if they are trying to "pass" successfully (Morrow & Messinger, 2006); as such, GLBT youth should be included as a target population within teen pregnancy prevention programs.

Recommendations

From the potency and value critique come important considerations for current best practices and how they can be improved upon. The following is a list of recommendations with a brief example of how each recommendation might be implemented.

1. *Explore further the validity of the best practices identified by the consumer and research perspective that did not make the final cut.* While all of the best practices identified by professional perspective were included in the final best practices summary, this was not the case for either the research and consumer perspective. This leaves a question as to why these remaining best practices were not synthesized with each other and with the professional perspective. It would seem that both of these perspectives have important best practices to offer; a way

to bring together such practices would be to carry out more consumer-driven research that seeks to explore the validity and generalizability of the practices consumers have indicated as important to them in preventing teen pregnancy, such as offering online resources and telephone hotlines to youth in teen pregnancy programs. Notably, youth identified both abstinence and fostering healthy morals as best practices; however, research has yet to identify these as best practices, which may be reflective of the ingrained social norms of teens. Additionally, more programs could incorporate those remaining practices identified by researchers as critical to teen pregnancy prevention and thus have more frequent professional and consumer critiques of these practices, such as incorporating teaching training, and using long-term multifaceted programs that are theory based. Additionally, it is important to carry out research to determine what type of parent involvement is particularly beneficial in preventing teen pregnancy, as it was identified by both the consumer and the professional perspectives, but not the research perspective. In a similar vein, consumers should be given the opportunity to voice their levels of satisfaction and dissatisfaction with the level of cultural and developmental sensitivity presented in the programs they participate in at various points and to develop opportunities to develop community alliances with peers from other schools to focus on building connections and positive peer influences.

2. *Expand the scope of the research perspective to include marginalized sub-populations of youth.* The professional perspective consistently pointed out the need to provide teen pregnancy programs to marginalized youth—such as youth with disabilities, youth in residential care, immigrant youth, and youth of color. However, from reviewing the research perspective, it is apparent that most research is focused on mainstream youth in the school system. This often does include youth of color; however, it is important for researchers to make considerable efforts to study what programs specifically work for nonmainstream youth, such as youth are who are homeless, youth who attend alternative schools, youth who have had multiple pregnancies, youth who are in special education classrooms, and GLBT youth. While we do have a sense for what works with most youth, it is imperative that we do not generalize for the vastly diverse population of youth in the U.S. With the current foundation in place, it would behoove the field to focus now on what works (or does not) for subpopulations.

3. *Promote respect for diversity within community alliances.* This is particularly important when certain best practices, such as access to contraceptives and involving parents, may be in conflict and which might make forming community alliances difficult. Holding a symposium or an ongoing open dialogue group to discuss differences in values might be useful in promoting community-wide respect for diversity. Moreover, incorporating abstinence education into teen pregnancy prevention programs in a respectful manner, focusing particularly on pre-adolescents and older youth who choose to remain abstinent may enhance community alliances.

4. *Finally, it is important to note that abstinence-only sex education programs were not found to be a best practice to prevent teen pregnancy.* One of the most widely used forms of sex education across the nation is abstinence-only education

programs, largely because states and local organizations can receive significant federal financial support. This specific form of sex education was *not* found to be a best practice for preventing teen pregnancy, which is consistent with the literature on the efficacy of abstinence-only education (for a review, see McCave, 2007). Program planners, funders, and policymakers should consider this when developing and implementing sex education curricula and teen pregnancy prevention programs.

Conclusion

This best practices inquiry attempted to answer what are "best practices" for preventing teen pregnancy. By reviewing several quality sources from consumers, professionals, and researchers, five best practices emerged: sex education, access to contraceptives, parent involvement, peer mentoring and youth development, and community alliances. After conducting a potency and values critique, it is apparent that while most of the best practices come from high-quality sources and fit a social work values criteria, there are still areas for improvement in both areas. In an effort to facilitate such improvement, recommendations were offered as a starting point. With the vast knowledge collected from consumers, professionals, and researchers, it is likely that future programs can capitalize on this information and make significant gains in preventing teen pregnancy.

References

Allen, J.P., Philliber, S., Herrling, S., & Kuperminc, G.P. (1997). Preventing teen pregnancy and academic failure: Experimental evaluation of a developmentally based approach. *Child Development, 68*(4), 729–742.

Andreozzi, L., Flanagan, P., Seifer, R., Brunner, S., & Lester, B. (2002). Attachment classifications among 18-month-old children of adolescent mothers. *Archives of Pediatrics & Adolescent Medicine, 156*, 20–26.

Basen-Engquist, K., Coyle, K.K., Parcel, G.S., Kirby, D., Banspach, S.W., Carvajal, S.C., & Baumler, E. (2001). Schoolwide effects of a multicomponent HIV, STD, and pregnancy prevention program for high school students. *Health Education & Behavior, 28*(2), 166–185.

Center for Disease Control and Prevention. (2000, July). National and state specific pregnancy rates among adolescents: United States, 1995–1997. *MMWR: Morbidity and Mortality Weekly Report, 49*(27), 605–631.

Corcoran, J., Franklin, C., & Bell, H. (1997). Pregnancy prevention from the teen perspective. *Child and Adolescent Social Work Journal, 14*(5), 365–382.

Elders, M.J., & Albert, A.E. (1998). Adolescent pregnancy and sexual abuse. *JAMA, 280*(7), 648, 649.

Franklin, C., Corcoran, J., & Ayers-Lopez, S. (1997). Adolescent pregnancy: Multisystemic risk and protective factors. In M. Frazer (Ed.), *Risk and resilience in childhood: An ecological perspective* (pp. 195–219). Washington, DC: NASW Press.

Hacker, K.A., Yared, A., Strunk, N., & Horst, L. (2000). Listening to youth: Teen perspectives on pregnancy prevention. *Journal of Adolescent Health, 26*(4), 279–288.

Hillis, S.D., Anda, R.F., Dube, S.R., Felitti, V.J., Marchbanks, P.A., & Marks, J.S. (2004).

The association between adverse childhood experiences and adolescent pregnancy, long-term psychosocial consequences, and fetal death. *Pediatrics, 113*(2), 320–327.

King, J.C. (2003). The risks of maternal nutritional depletion and poor outcomes: Increases in early or closely spaced pregnancies. *American Society for Nutritional Sciences.* 1732S–1736S.

Kirby, D., Laris, B.A., & Rolleri, L. (2006). Sex and HIV education programs for youth: Their impact and important characteristics. Scotts Valley, CA: ETR Associates.

Kirby, D., Short, L., Collins, J., Rugg, D., Kolbe, L. Howard, M., Miller, B., Sonenstein, F., & Zabin, L.S. (1994). School-based programs to reduce sexual risk behaviors: A review of effectiveness. *Public Health Reports, 109*(3), 339–360.

Klepinger, D., Lundberg, S., & Plotnick, R. (1999). How does adolescent fertility affect the human capital and wages of young women? *The Journal of Human Resources, 34*(3), 421–448.

Knopf, M., & Paluzzi, P. (2005). Replicating success one program at a time: Lessons from replicating community-based programs that effectively address the complex issues associated with teen parents and teen pregnancy prevention in the United States (pp. 1–20). Washington, DC: Healthy Teen Network.

Lonczak, H.S., Abbott, R.D., Hawkins, D., Kosterman, R., & Catalano, R.F. (2002). Effects of the Seattle Social Development Project on sexual behavior, pregnancy, birth, and sexually transmitted disease outcomes by age 21 years. *Archives of Pediatric and Adolescent Medicine, 256,* 438–447.

Mayden, B., Castro, W., & Annitto, M. (1999). *First talk: A teen pregnancy prevention dialogue among Latinos.* Washington, DC: CWLA Press.

McCave, E.L. (2007). Comprehensive sexuality education vs. abstinence-only sexuality education: The need for evidenced based research and practice. *School Social Work Journal, 31*(2), 14–27.

Moore, K.A., Morrison, D.R., & Greene, A.D. (1997). Effects on the children born to adolescent mothers. In R.A. Maynard (Ed.), *Kids having kids: Economic costs and social consequences of teen pregnancy* (pp. 145–180). Washington DC: Urban Institute Press.

Morrow, D.F., & Messinger, L. (2006). *Sexual orientation and gender expression in social work practice: Working with gay, lesbian, bisexual, and transgender people.* New York: Columbia University Press.

National Association of Social Workers. (2003). *Social work speaks: National Association of Social Workers Policy Statements, 2003–2006* (6th ed.). Washington, DC: NASW Press.

National Campaign to Prevent Teen Pregnancy. (2006). *Teens tell all.* Retrieved September 10, 2006 from www.teenpregnancy.org/resources/teens/voices/default.asp.

Philliber, S., Kaye, J., & Herrling, S. (2001). The national evaluation of the Children's Aid Society Carrera-Model Program to prevent teen pregnancy. Accord, NY: Philliber Research Associates.

Santelli, J., Ott, M.A., Lyon, M., Rogers, J., & Summers, D. (2006). Abstinence-only education policies and programs: A position paper of the Society for Adolescent Medicine. *Journal of Adolescent Health, 38,* 83–87.

Solomon, R., & Liefeld, C.P. (1998). Effectiveness of a family support center approach to adolescent mothers: Repeat pregnancy and school drop-out rates. *Family Relations, 47,* 139–144.

Vincent, M.L., Paine-Andrews, A., Fisher, J., Devereaux, R.S., Dolan, H.G., Harris, K.J., & Reininger, B. (2000). Replication of a community-based multicomponent teen pregnancy prevention model: Realities and challenges. *Family & Community Health, 23*(3), 28–45.

Weinman, M.L., Smith, P.B., Geva, J., & Buzi, R.S. (1998). Pregnant and postpartum adolescents' perceptions of the consequences of child abuse. *Child and Adolescent Social Work Journal, 15*(4), 287–301.

Yampolskaya, S., Brown, E.C., & Greenbaum, P.E. (2002). Early pregnancy among adolescent females with serious emotional disturbances: Risk factors and outcomes. *Journal of Emotional and Behavioral Disorders, 10*(2), 108–115.

Zelenko, M.A., Huffman, L.C., Brown, B.W., Daniels, K., Lock, J., Kennedy, Q., & Steiner, H. (2001). The child abuse potential inventory and pregnancy outcome in expectant adolescent mother. *Child Abuse & Neglect, 25*, 1481–1495.

5 Best Practices for Facilitating Access to Health Care for Children of the Poor

Karen Flint Stipp

Despite escalating medical expenditures in the United States there remain millions of children without access to health care. This inquiry identified that best practices for facilitating access to health care are administrative appointment-keeping supports; nonmedical supports including referrals, parent education and outreach; provider–parent relationships built upon effective communication; and usual sources of care maintained by continuity of care and a primary provider. Conversely, the use of emergency departments for preventable conditions was a costly indicator that families experienced health-care barriers. It behooves communities to consider the high cost of foregone care and work collaboratively to pre-empt suffering, to preclude loss of children's potential and to prevent costly emergency department utilization.

Overview of the Problem and Population

Eliminating health disparities and increasing quality and years of healthy life are among the U.S. Department of Health and Human Services (HHS) goals for 2010 (2000). Access to health care, alongside policies and environmental factors that affect health, is essential for reaching HHS goals for healthy people in healthy communities (Figure 5.1).

Access to health care is defined by the Institute of Medicine (IOM) as "the timely use of personal health services to achieve the best possible health outcomes" (Millman, 1993, p. 4). Timely interventions are nowhere more salient than for children. Preventive health care and sick child health care delivered at the right time can avert ill effects on lifelong health for young people and on the communities in which they live and grow.

Both HHS and IOM recognize the multicausational nature of access to health care. IOM states that "having insurance or nearby health care providers is no guarantee that people who need services will get them. Conversely, many who lack coverage or live in areas that appear to have shortages of health care resources do, indeed, receive services" (Millman, 1993, p. 4). HHS similarly identifies three predictors of access to health care: (1) having health insurance; (2) being of a higher socioeconomic status (SES); and (3) having a usual source of health care (2000). Neither health-care insurance, nor affluence, nor a usual source of care, is

Determinants of health

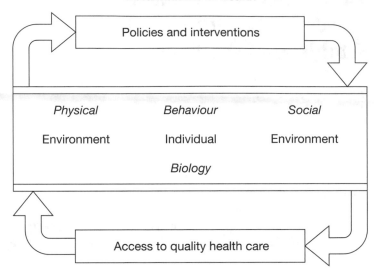

Figure 5.1 Determinants of Health Chart

Source: HHS (2000). *Healthy People 2010: Understanding and Improving Health*, p. 6.

sufficient to guarantee access to health care, yet health-care systems must consider each of these in their developing practices. Of these predictors, usual source of care may be the one most influenced by health care system practices, and as such will be a particular focus of this chapter.

Predictors of Access to Health Care: Insurance

Most uninsured children live in a family with one or more working parent (Byck, 2000). From 1989 to 1996, increased cost precipitated decreased employer-based health-care insurance coverage for children. Nearly three-quarters of the nation's children were privately insured in 1989; only two-thirds of the nation's children remained privately insured by 1996 (Slifkin, Freeman, and Silberman, 2002). There was a similar decline in the likelihood of a child having health-care insurance from any carrier, public or private (DeNavas-Walt, Proctor, & Lee, 2006).

State Children's Health Insurance Program (SCHIP) provisions of the 1997 Balanced Budget Act were developed in response to mushrooming numbers of uninsured children. SCHIP precipitated a brief reversal in the rate of uninsured children. Declining health-care insurance coverage for children recommenced in 2000 and persisted into 2007 (O'Brien & Mann, 2003). More than nine million U.S. girls and boys currently lack health-care insurance (Children's Defense Fund, 2007).

Insurance holds sway over the continuum between barriers to care and access to care. Uninsured children "are less likely to be treated for injuries (including serious injuries such as broken bones) and are less likely to get care for common childhood illnesses" (Slifkin et al., 2002, p. 1223). Declines in health-care insurance coverage have been borne out among children in poverty more than among children who live in median-income and affluent families. In 2005, 11.2% of all children and 19% of children in poverty were without health-care insurance. Declines in health-care insurance coverage were further borne out among nonWhite children more than among White children. In 2005, 19.6% of Black children were uninsured and 32.7% of Hispanic children were uninsured (DeNavas-Walt et al., 2006; U.S. Senate Finance Subcommittee, 2006). An estimated one in six children without health insurance is Black; one in four uninsured children is Hispanic (Raphel, 1999). This inquiry includes practices that facilitate both health care and insurance enrollment for children who are uninsured and underinsured.

Predictors of Access to Health Care: Socioeconomic Status

Ill health perpetuates poverty, and poverty perpetuates lack of access to health care. "Children in the lower socioeconomic hierarchy suffer disproportionately from almost every disease and show higher rates of mortality [sickness] compared with those in families that are better off" (Hughes & Ng, 2003, p. 154). Any consumer might face barriers to health care, but disproportionate barriers exist for children in economically poor families, that is, for children living in families with incomes below 200% of the federal poverty level (FPL).

The financial burden of health care for economically poor families is disproportionate to financial burdens of the middle class and the affluent. Consumers of every SES pay for health care through co-pays, fees for service, taxes and insurance premiums (Lee, 2000). However, a 2005 study by Galbraith, Wong, Kim, and Newacheck indicated that the poor pay proportionally more. Low-income families spent a mean of $120 on child health care from every $1000 earned, such that more than one in four economically poor families' out-of-pocket expenses exceeded 10% of their incomes. Families with annual earnings below the FPL spent a significantly higher proportion of their incomes on health care than did median-income and affluent families.

NonWhite and nonEnglish-speaking children face particular risk (Becker, 2004; Williams, 1999). They are represented disproportionately in the lower socioeconomic hierarchy, so that as a group, they are apt to have fewer physician contacts and more unmet health needs (Hughes & Ng, 2003). This inquiry will include practices that reduce extant ethnic and socioeconomic disparities in access to health care.

Predictors of Access to Health Care: Usual Source of Care

Best practices can support development of usual sources of care, particularly where economic disparity persists, that is, where there are children living in economically poor families. It is incumbent upon health-care professionals to apply best practices to helping children connect with a usual source of health care so that they might grow up as healthy people in healthy communities. Micro- and meso-level practices that connect children of the poor with a usual source of care will be a focus of this inquiry. Because uninsured children and children in families with few financial resources have poorer health outcomes than do insured children and children living in median-income and affluent families, the call of distributive justice is to social workers and other health-care professionals to facilitate access to health care for all children. Professionals can facilitate access to usual sources of care even as lawmakers persist in their efforts to develop policy that supports child health.

Research Methodology

The keywords *access, barrier, health care, best practices, child, working poor,* and *poverty* guided searches for consumer, professional and research perspectives on best practices. Interdisciplinary databases such as Wilson OmniFile, Google Scholar and Expanded Academic ASAP allowed searches of social work and other health-related fields including community health, nursing, pediatrics, and family medicine. To find consumer perspectives on best practices, additional material outside peer-reviewed journals was considered. Sources available through the Lexis-Nexis Academic database were useful, as was the website for *Exceptional Parents Magazine* (www.eparent.com).

For practice and research perspectives on best practices, the Web of Science database proved valuable for excavating reference citations. Searches led to several useful websites including Georgetown University's National Center for Education in Maternal and Child Health (www.ncemch.org); *Journal of the American Academy of Pediatrics* (pediatrics.org); the pediatric site for the *Journal of the American Medical Association* (archpediatrics.com); and *The Future of Children* (futureofchildren.org).

Articles considered and selected for this best practices inquiry focused on or asked research questions relevant to access to health care for children of the poor. Relevant populations included economically poor families with children, ethnic minority families, and families of children with special health-care needs (CSHCN). The latter group was included because of the economic burden faced by families with CSHCN.

The consumer perspective was represented by five articles, the professional perspective by four articles, and the research perspective by seven articles, each selected in part on the basis of agreement with other articles in the perspective. There is agreement between each source and at least two other sources within each perspective.

The literature search commenced with consumer perspectives, which hermeneutically informed later reading of the professional and research perspectives. Qualitative studies provided narratives of consumer perceptions and quantitative studies gave voice to a multitude of parents. Articles written by, with, and for parents and adult consumers informed the consumer perspective of this inquiry.

Table 5.1 Quantitative Rating Scale

Quality of Quantitative Sources	Possible Points
Theoretical & historical context	15
Research question	10
Research design	10
Sample & data collection	10
Analysis of data	10
Limitations & researcher bias	10
Results: effect size & cost/benefit	15
Clearly written	10
Relevance to the current study	10
Total	100

For professional sources, an additional criterion was inclusion of innovations that facilitate access to health care for children. For research sources, an additional criterion was the research design, adjudged according to a quantitative rating scale developed by the author to provide points of comparison between quantitative research studies (Table 5.1). Sources representing each perspective were selected on the basis of their potent expressions of consumer voice, their strong linkages to prior and ongoing research, and their publication in venues that reach and influence parents, professionals, researchers, and policymakers.

Results of Best Practices from Consumer, Professional and Research Perspectives

This section provides brief descriptions of sources representing each perspective. Following source descriptions for each perspective are results sections organized according to four practice foci: administrative practices, nonmedical supports, provider–patient relationships, and usual sources of care. Results sections for each perspective include a table summary of best practices for that perspective.

Consumer Perspective: Sources

The consumer perspective was informed by adult perceptions of access to health care. C1 reported discourse analyses of focus group transcripts by Sobo, Seid, and Gelhard (2006). C2 presented a qualitative analysis of barriers to health care from focus group transcripts and an analysis of descriptive statistics from survey data of households by Thomas, Kohli, and King (2004). C3 was a report about the Parents as Partners Medical Home Project (Burstein & Bryan, 2000). Medical Home, which is discussed in several of the articles that were selected to inform this inquiry, is a model designed to help pediatricians deliver continuous, comprehensive, family-centered, coordinated, culturally effective care for CSHCN (R1). C4 was a quantitative study reporting multivariate analyses of HMO administrative data by Newacheck et al. (2001). C5 was a review of practice recommendations from adult patients by Ngo-Metzger et al. (2006).

C1 reported barriers to health care experienced by English-speaking and Spanish-speaking parents whose children were students in San Diego public schools and had chronic health conditions (*N=20*). The study likened the health system to other cultural systems, and recommended health-system practices that would improve access. C1 was included because of its consumer narratives, relevance to low income and nonEnglish speaking families, and placement within prior and subsequent research.

C2 reported barriers to health care experienced by families with children aged birth to three (*N=207*). The study was included because it suggested practices to ameliorate barriers and support the HHS goal of eliminating health disparities for minority and low-income families.

C3 was a report of parent-recommended best practices that became the *Family-Centered Medical Bill of Rights and Measures*. C3 was included because its author was a CSHCN parent who supports other CSHCN parents in ongoing research, because of the study's link to prior and subsequent Medical Home research, and because of the study's potential influence via the widely distributed *Exceptional Parents Magazine*.

C4 reported access to health care for two groups of children enrolled in the same health maintenance organization (HMO). One group was commercially insured (*N=512*) and the other group was Medicaid insured (*N=510*). There was no statistical difference in access based upon insurance purchaser. This study was selected because it gave voice to parents who were either economically poor or had CSHCN, and because of its implications beyond insurance type for supporting access to health care.

C5's authors compiled recommendations for providers from a literature review of adult patient perspectives on culturally competent care as quality health care. C5 was selected because it reflected first-hand experiences of health disparities along ethnic lines, and it was widely disseminated by the Commonwealth Fund.

Consumer Perspective: Results

Consumers perceived both barriers and access to care that were resultant of health-care system practices. Table 5.2 is a summary of practices suggested by at least three of the five Consumer Perspective sources. C1, C2 and C5 recommended practices based upon consumers' health-care experiences and ongoing need. An asterisk in Table 5.2 denotes recommendations based upon need rather than on current practices. C3–C4 based recommendations on practice outcomes.

Consumer Perspectives on Administrative Practices. C1–C4 indicated that offices and clinics can create administrative barriers to health care, and they can likewise facilitate access to health care. C1 and C4 found phone prompts confusing and wait times excessive. Parents in C2 found it difficult to make appointments and reach providers for advice. C1, C2, and C4 recommended making it easier to access their health-care systems by phone, and C3 provided 24-hour phone support.

Table 5.2 Consumer Perspectives

	C1	C2	C3	C4	C5
Administrative Practices					
Appointment-keeping supports	X*	X*	X	X	
Nonmedical Supports					
Referrals & collaboration	X*	X*	X		X*
Parent education	X*	X*	X		X*
Outreach	X*	X*	X	X	
Provider–Patient Relationships					
Effective communication	X*	X*	X		X*
Respect for patients/parents	X*	X*	X		X*
Partnering with pts/community	X*	X*	X		X*
Usual Source of Care					
Primary provider	X*	X*		X	
COC	X*	X*	X	X	

Notes:
X denotes effectiveness indicated by the research study.
X* denotes consumer suggestions based on need.

C1–C4 suggested early and late office hours. They recommended appointment times that accommodate bus schedules, and wait times that allow parents to quickly return home with their sick child.

Consumer Perspectives on Nonmedical Supports. Parents requested referrals to community supports and collaboration between their child's primary providers and their mental health and education services (C1–C3, & C5). It should be noted that the use of "primary provider" in this inquiry connotes not a managed care gatekeeper but a health-care clinician from whom a child receives preventive care. Parents requested education about child health and the medical milieu (C1–C3, & C5). Outreach activities in C1–C4 included insurance enrollment and paperwork assistance (C1 & C3); on-time immunization supports (C2); and keeping "Medicaid" out of front office records (C4).

Consumer Perspectives on Provider–Patient Relationships. Positive relationships with providers support children's access to health care (C1–C3, & C5). Effective communication and perceived respect were integral to positive relationships. Conversely, comments reflecting prejudice and disrespect evidenced cultural incompetence that erected relational barriers to health care (C1, C2, & C5). Partnership perspectives on health care view parents as active problem solvers and care team members. Partnering with families, and with families' community supports such as educators and mental health professionals, supported provider–patient relationships (C1–C3, & C5).

Consumer Perspectives on Usual Source of Care. C1–C4 identified continuity of care (COC) as supportive of usual sources of care. COC coordinates treatment for preventive well-child care (WCC) with chronic and acute conditions. Immunization is a cornerstone of WCC, and not being on schedule for immunizations was an indicator of failed COC (C2), as were chart mix-ups, referrals to a closed lab, and a doctor who discarded medication prescribed by a different provider and purchased by the parent (C1–C2). C3 recommended a written care plan and 24-hour support for parents. A primary provider was the usual source of care for C1–C2, and C4.

Professional Perspective: Sources

Sources presented practices of health-care professionals who serve children in a variety of settings. P1 was a review of outreach programs across the U.S. by Carpenter and Kavanagh (1998). P2 was a report of nursing practices in a rural setting by Henly, Tyree, Lindsey, Lambeth, and Burd (1998). P3 was a cost analysis of pediatric care coordination (Antonelli & Antonelli, 2004). P4 presented a model of scheduling for access to health care by Randolph, Murray, Swanson, and Margolis (2004).

P1 reviewed programs across the United States that incorporated outreach as a means of facilitating access to health care. Programs were initiated by insurers, providers and philanthropists. This article was selected because it provided an overview of innovative practices throughout the U. S. and because the innovations were widely disseminated by the National Institute of Health Care Management.

P2 reported use of the primary health-care paradigm as conceptualized by the World Health Organization (WHO). The paradigm was applied to work with rural families, by the University of North Dakota's College of Nursing. This article was selected because it was built upon WHO recommendations, it was relevant for children "who are place bound in rural areas or disenfranchised by reason of minority status" (p. 25), and it presented an innovative approach.

P3 compared cost of coordinating care to actual outcomes and to the projected cost of worse outcomes that would have likely occurred without COC (*N=444*). Cost did not prohibit the coordination of services in this pediatric practice. Inclusion of this article was based upon its relevance for CSHCN, its connection to Medical Home research, and its usefulness for informing fiscal decision-making.

P4 reported activities by health systems that facilitated access to care through timely scheduling. This report was included because of its relevance for uninsured children and its relationship to the IOM concept that access to health care must be timely.

Professional Perspective: Results

Many of the suggested practices did not require large financial investment, but each required change within medical community culture to better accommodate patients and their families. Table 5.3 is a summary of best practices identified by at least three of the five Professional Perspective sources.

Table 5.3 Professional Perspectives

	P1	P2	P3	P4
Administrative Practices				
Appointment-keeping supports	X	X	X	X
Ongoing program evaluations	X	X	X	X
Nonmedical Supports				
Referrals & collaboration	X	X	X	
Parent education	X	X	X	
Outreach	X	X	X	X
Provider–Patient Relationships				
Effective communication	X	X	X	X
Partnering with pts/community	X	X	X	X
Usual Source of Care				
Primary provider	X	X	X	X
COC	X	X	X	X

Note:
X denotes effectiveness indicated by the research study.

Professional Perspectives on Administrative Practices. Appointment-keeping supports were a component of best practices for each professional source. P1 recommended paying attention to the way staff treat patients waiting to see their provider. P2 delivered in-home scheduled health care for rural families with special health-care needs. P3 identified telephoning as a way to increase access without the inconvenience of office visits, though that is not "economically sustainable because few third party payers reimburse for telephone management efforts" (p. 1527). P4 reported that appointment delays, long office waits, and inadequate visit lengths were barriers to health care that could be offset by Open Access (OA) scheduling for same-day WCC and treatment. Each professional source viewed emergency department (ED) use as an administrative failure, and suggested improving scheduling to decrease ED visits. The professional sources also commended administrators to ongoing program assessments and evaluations.

Professional Perspectives on Nonmedical Supports. Nonmedical supports for access to health care included referrals (P1–P3), parent education (P1–P3) and outreach (P1–P4). Referrals included both connecting families with, and provider collaboration with, community supports such as mental health and special education. Parent education provided tips about navigating the medical milieu (P1 & P3), health information (P1 & P3), and community-wide health literacy efforts (P2). Outreach efforts helped parents access Medicaid and managed care (P1 & P3–P4) and provided home visits in rural settings (P2). P1 provided examples of innovative outreach practices, including Boston's Franciscan Children's Hospital's Kids Care-Van that treated children in their neighborhoods and made referrals to primary providers.

Professional Perspectives on Provider-Patient Relationships. Effective commu-nication supported positive relationships. Same-language provision of services was included only in P1 and P3, whereas relational components of communication were part of P1–P4. Positive relationships included provider respect for patient preferences and cultural competence education for "staff and health care providers who work directly with children and families" (P1, p. 9). Partnering with families and community supports was a component of provider–parent relationships in P1–P4.

Professional Perspectives on Usual Source of Care. COC was facilitated by care coordinators and case managers (P1–P2), nurse/physician teams (P3) and Medical Homes (P3–P4). ED use indicated failed COC. A primary provider, rather than a place or a health-care system, was the identified usual source of care (P1–P4).

Research Perspective: Sources

Seven quantitative studies informed the research perspective. Sources were selected on the basis of the quantitative rating scale (see Table 5.1). R1 was a comparison of descriptive statistics after a Medical Home demonstration (Farmer, Clark, Sherman, Marien, & Selva, 2005). R2 was a cross-sectional study with multiple regression analyses of data from parent surveys about perceptions of pediatric care by Seid, Stevens, and Varni (2003). R3 was a cross-sectional study with multiple regression analyses of California Health Interview data about access to health care and usual sources of care by Stevens, Seid, Mistry, and Halfon (2006). R4 reported logistic regression analyses of scheduling methods by O'Connor, Matthews and Gao (2006). R5 was a one-year longitudinal study with factorial analyses of timely medical feedback to providers by Kattan et al. (2006). R6 was a retrospective cohort study with a survival analysis of HMO data about effects of usual sources of care by Christakis, Mell, Koepsell, Zimmerman, and Connell (2001). R7 was a retrospective cohort study with multivariate regression analyses of parent surveys about school-based health center (SBHC) by Kaplan, Brindis, Phibbs, Melinkovich, Naylor, and Ahlstrand (1999).

R1 examined effects of a Medical Home on health care in the rural Midwest (*N=51*). Usual sources of care were enhanced by a Medical Home, resulting in declines in the health needs of CSHCN, of family needs, and of missed days of work/school for parents/children. The quality and importance of R1 for this inquiry was 89/100.

R2 examined effects of usual sources of care on children from 18 San Diego elementary schools (*N=3000*). Researchers controlled for SES, chronic health conditions, gender, and age. English proficiency exerted a strong independent effect on access to health care and reduced the effect of race and ethnic group for Asians, African Americans, and Latinos. The quality and importance of R2 for this inquiry was 80/100.

R3 examined effects of 1) visits to a provider, 2) usual sources of care, and 3) comprehensiveness of care, on risk factors of elementary school children served by public health programs (*N=19,485*). Higher risk profiles were associated with fewer visits and lack of usual sources of care. Once entering the health-care system, however, children with more risk factors received more comprehensive care than did children with fewer risk factors. The quality and importance of R3 for this inquiry was 86/100.

R4 found that next day and same day WCC scheduling and same language providers decreased missed appointments, increased contact with the usual source of care and increased on-time immunizations for babies (*N=878*) in a community pediatric clinic with ten providers. The quality and importance of R4 for this inquiry was 90/100.

R5 collected health data in bi-monthly phone calls to families of 5 to 11-year-old inner-city children with asthma, and sent bi-monthly reports of those calls to the children's providers (*N=937*). The letters included patient symptoms, medications, health service use and recommendations for improving care. The letters were shown to increase scheduled visits with the usual source of care and to reduce ED visits. The quality and importance of R5 for this inquiry was 90/100.

R6 identified strong associations between children who have a usual source of care, and decreased rates of hospitalization and ED use. The study sample had been enrolled in a Medicaid HMO for two years or since birth (*N=46,097*). The quality and importance of R6 for this inquiry was 89/100.

R7 identified more health-care provider visits by children in a Denver elementary school with SBHC than by children who attended a school without SBHC. The SBHC was shown to reduce ED use and increase the number of physician visits. The quality and importance of R7 was 82/100.

Research Perspective: Results

Table 5.4 is a summary of best practices from at least three of the seven Research Perspective sources. R2–R3 and R6 recommended interventions based upon the study's clarification of need. An asterisk in Table 5.4 denotes recommendations based upon a clarification of need rather than upon intervention outcomes. R1, R4, R5, and R7 recommended interventions based upon practice outcomes.

Research Perspectives on Administrative Practices. R4–R6 identified the importance of reminder systems for either patients or providers, which would trigger appointments for WCC or for chronic conditions such as asthma. R4 recommended OA for decreasing missed appointments and improving immunization rates. Feedback to providers for child asthma patients in R5 resulted in a 24% drop in ED visits. R6 recommended using databases to track low incidence of primary provider visits. R1 additionally suggested lengthier appointments for CSHCN and R7 found that SBHC referrals decreased time to appointments.

Research Perspectives on Nonmedical Supports. R1, R3, and R7 recommended making patient referrals to and collaborating with community resources. R1–R2 and R6 suggested educating parents for the medical milieu. R7 implemented community-based education. R3 suggested that providers should help "families feel empowered to obtain care" (p. 527) through health literacy education for

Table 5.4 Research Perspectives

	R1	R2	R3	R4	R5	R6	R7
Administrative Practices							
Appoint-keeping supports	X		X	X+	X*+	X	
Nonmedical Supports							
Referrals & collaboration	X		X*				X
Parent education	X	X*	X*			X*	X
Outreach	X		X*	X		X*	X
Provider–Patient Relationships							
Effective communication	X	X*	X*	X	X		X
Usual Source of Care							
Primary provider	X	X*	X	X*	X	X*	X
COC	X		X	X*	X	X*	X

Notes:
X denotes effectiveness indicated by the research study.
X* denotes researcher suggestions based on indicated need.
X+ denotes a reminder to providers rather than to patients.

parents and adolescents. Outreach in R3–R4 and R6–R7 included supporting public insurance enrollment. R1 outreach was in-home care in rural settings.

   Research Perspectives on Provider–Patient Relationships. Six researchers identified effective communication as a best practice. R2–R4 and R7 suggested that linguistically appropriate services support parent–provider communication and relationships. Linguistically appropriate services are those delivered at the patient's level of health literacy and in languages that families understand. Nurse practitioners and social workers were employed to facilitate communication (R1) as was a system that reminded providers about patients' asthma care needs (R5).

   Research Perspectives on Usual Source of Care. Six research studies (R1 & R3–R7) identified COC methods as useful for supporting a usual source of care. Specific COC methods varied widely among settings. For instance, R1 applied the medical home model to rural families; R3 and R5 increased the dose of care (number of visits) for treating children with chronic health conditions; and R7 employed a case manager to connect SBHC students with primary providers. Each of the research studies supported a primary provider as the usual source of care.

Best Practices Summary

Best practices across perspectives are presented in this section. Table 5.5 is a summary of practices suggested by at least three sources within each perspective. Sources and practices were excluded if there did not exist consensus across

Table 5.5 Summary of Best Practices across Perspectives

	Consumers					Professionals				Researchers						
	1	2	3	4	5	1	2	3	4	1	2	3	4	5	6	7
Administrative Practices																
Appts.	X	X	X	X		X	X	X	X	X			X	X	X	X
Nonmedical Supports																
Referrals	X	X	X		X	X	X	X		X		X				X
Parent ed	X	X	X		X	X	X	X		X	X	X			X	X
Outreach	X	X	X	X		X	X	X	X	X		X	X		X	X
Provider–Patient Relationships																
Eff Com	X	X	X		X	X	X	X	X	X	X	X	X	X		X
Usual Source of Care																
Primary	X	X		X		X	X	X	X	X	X	X	X	X	X	X
COC	X	X	X	X		X	X	X	X	X		X	X	X	X	X

perspectives. The summary includes identification of practices that support the three HHS predictor(s) of access to health care: insurance enrollment, extant ethnic and socioeconomic disparities, and having a usual source of care.

Administrative Practices: Similarities, Differences and Best Practices

A best practice across perspectives was support for appointments. "Some of the most promising contemporary interventions to improve children's access involve individual clinicians and primary care practices improving their scheduling systems" (P4, p. e231). C1, C2, C4, and each professional source, and researchers in R1 and R7, expressed that confusing phone prompts, inconvenient hours and egregious office wait times are barriers to families' appointment-making and appointment-keeping. C3, P2–P4 and R4–R6 recommended a variety of techniques for getting children to their primary providers, according to age-appropriate and condition-specific protocols. Each perspective called for health-care systems to consider administrative practices that impede or could better support making appointments, for reduction of ethnic and socioeconomic disparities, and to support usual sources of care.

Nonmedical Supports and Barriers: Similarities, Differences, and Best Practices

Consumers, providers and researchers reflected the outlook that patients "have the right to guidance and assistance with needs which are not problem- or illness-related, for the sake of primary prevention" (p. 26). Consumers recognized the need for guidance and assistance because there are health care system barriers (C1–C2 & C4). Researchers identified the need for guidance and assistance based upon patient characteristics (R1–R3). Practice models that provided guidance and assistance were those that incorporated nonmedical supports (C3, P1–P4, R1, R4, & R6–R7). The three nonmedical best practices across perspectives were referrals, education and outreach.

Referrals would coordinate medical care with interventions by educators, social service agencies and mental health (C1–C3, C5, P1–P3, R1, R3, & R7) as well as with alternative medicine (C5). C1–C2, P1and R1 specifically mentioned referrals that help families coordinate transportation to and from appointments. It was suggested across perspectives that referrals and coordination with community resources would reduce ethnic and socioeconomic health-care disparities.

Parent education for medical milieu-related and health-related knowledge facilitates access to health care. Consumers C1–C3 and C5, along with research source R1, suggested that education would help families maneuver through medical system barriers. Families wanted help with navigating the "arbitrary" and "capricious" medical system rules (C1), and with understanding medical "lingo" (C3). Families wanted to know how to get their questions answered about the risks and benefits of immunization (C2), and wanted providers to pass along the same amount of health-related information to families of lower SES as they do to families of higher SES (C5). The Medical Home empowered parents to advocate for their children through education (R1). Professional and research perspectives suggested that parent education would affect parent awareness of children's health needs (P1–P3, R1–R3, R6–R7) and with making informed health-care choices (P1 & P3). One-on-one education by providers at the time of care helped parents understand useful health promotion information in context (R2 & R3). Parent education for families of lower SES could reduce ethnic and socioeconomic health-care disparities.

Outreach facilitates care for children who do not currently receive care. C2, P2 and R7 suggested community-based education as a component of outreach. In-home care in rural settings (P2 & R1); phone or mail reminders of scheduled care (C2, P4, & R4); and offices and clinics near where families work, live and attend school (P1–P2, & R7) were approaches to outreach. Outreach would also secure care for children who were uninsured, underinsured, or publicly insured (C1, C2, P1, & R3) and provide Medicaid and SCHIP applications and assistance with insurance paperwork (C3, P1, P3, & R7). Outreach included equitable treatment of publicly and privately insured patients (C4, R3, & R6). Outreach would increase health-care insurance enrollment, reduce ethnic and socioeconomic health-care disparities and support usual sources of care.

Provider–Patient Relationships: Similarities, Differences, and Best Practices

From each perspective, effective communication was essential for developing provider–patient relationships that facilitate access to health care. Professionals and researchers identified same language providers and families as requisite to effective communication (P1, P3, R2–R4, & R7). C5 also mentioned same-language providers, but along with C1 and C3, expounded on other communication barriers including staff rudeness, discrimination, and provider ignorance of families' health beliefs. C5, P1, and P3 recommended ongoing staff education to address prejudices, to eliminate latent institutional discrimination, and to build awareness about peculiarities of the medical culture, including the power inherent in knowledge, and the goods and services to which staff are gatekeepers. Consumers and professionals identified cultural competence and partnering with families as aspects of effective communication (C1–C3, C5, & P1–P4), and consumers included acting respectful as a best practice for providers (C1–C3, C5), though these were not reiterated by researchers. The agreement across perspectives was that familiar providers who listen and respond to families can precipitate effective communication (C1–C3, C5, P1–P4, R1–R5, & R7). Communication that supports provider–patient relationships would reduce ethnic and socioeconomic health-care disparities.

Usual Source of Care: Similarities, Differences, and Best Practices

Usual source of care is itself a predictor of access to health care, but it differs from the other two predictors—insurance and socioeconomic status—in that it is also an approach to practice. Usual sources of care were supported across perspectives by primary providers and by COC. That no single provider can be available around the clock for her or his hundreds of patients was addressed by COC methods across perspectives.

COC methods support regular and timely visits for prevention and control of chronic conditions, and COC decreases the need for unscheduled sick-child visits. Each perspective recognized that COC supports usual sources of care (C1–C4, P1–P4, R1, & R3–R7). Three consumers identified failed COC. Offices and clinics changed providers without informing families (C1); different providers presented conflicting information (C2); and providers changed with insurance coverage changes (C4). C3, P1–P4, R1, and R3–R7 studied a variety of care coordination methods. C3 and P4 used Medical Home models of COC. P1 utilized case management and information technology to review encounter data and predict staffing needs. P2 provided a continuum of services by nursing students supervised by faculty familiar to families. P3 gave overall responsibility for case coordination to physicians, but initiated physician and nurse teams for families with complicated medical and psychosocial issues. Researchers called for COC for CSHCN who access care through multiple specialists (R1) and who require frequent follow-up care (R3 & R5). R6 used databases to coordinate care by usual sources to enhance patient trust and medical compliance. R7 provided case management to coordinate between an SBHC and children's primary providers.

While COC methods for coordinating care and facilitating usual sources of care varied across settings, there was agreement that it was a primary provider, rather than a particular setting or group of providers, who was effective as a usual source of care. An outcome in R1 indicated that staff who coordinated care precipitated improved outcomes on several variables, but declines in parent satisfaction with care, as COC activities in that setting decreased families' time with primary providers. In other settings, COC did support primary providers as usual sources of care. COC increased rates of health-care insurance enrollment and reduced ethnic and socioeconomic health-care disparities.

Critique of Best Practices

Potency: Strength and Quality of Sources

It is a strength of all articles in this inquiry that they reflect conditions as they exist under current policy. Policy changes instituted by the Personal Responsibility and Work Opportunity Reconciliation Act delinked Medicaid from cash welfare benefits (1996), precipitating a decline in public insurance enrollment for children (Mann, Rowland, & Garfield, 2003). SCHIP conversely precipitated an increase in the number of children enrolled in public insurance (O'Brien & Mann, 2003).

Consumer Sources. As a group, children of the poor neither organize their own websites nor write pithy slogans to call attention to their need for access health care. However, C1–C4 were useful proxies for children's voices as they captured views of economically poor and minority parents. C5 expressed the views of economically poor and minority adult patients. Each consumer source portrayed the need for access to health care, and captured parent and consumer voices for distribution among family health and pediatric professionals where individuals sometimes have difficulty being heard. C1 was written subsequent to studies of risk factors reported in R2 and R3, and focused on parent experiences with barriers perpetrated by the health-care system, rather than on individual patient character-istics. C2 and C4 were likewise peer-reviewed articles with ties to prior and subsequent research.

Professional Sources. Professional articles provided examples of innovative practices. P1 and P2 were program descriptions. P3 and P4 yielded statistical outcomes, but with results that were not generalizable beyond their local settings. The strength of the professional articles for this inquiry came from their look beyond the responsibilities of policy to responsibilities borne by providers and insurers for the health of the children in their communities. Though most outcomes were not generalizable to other settings, studies suggested innovations for further development.

Research Sources. Table 5.6 presents a summary of overall quality for the seven research sources. Each study was conducted by teams of medical researchers. Data analyses in these studies were meticulous (96% rating) though the studies did not always produce anticipated effects (74% rating). All but R4 were follow-up studies. R2 and R3 were cross-sectional studies of risk factors, with implications for facilitating access to care. R1 and R4–R7 provided statistical outcomes of specific practices.

Level of Agreement. Practices by the same name are operationalized differently in each unique setting, requiring careful comparison to capture similarities and distinctions. Best practices for facilitating access to health care are still emerging,

Table 5.6 Quality of Quantitative Research Sources

Quality of Quantitative Sources	R1	R2	R3	R4	R5	R6	R7	Assigned/Possible	Overall
Context	12	13	15	12	12	13	12	89/105	85%
Research question	10	8	10	8	7	9	8	58/70	83%
Research design	10	6	8	10	10	9	10	61/70	87%
Sample; Data collection	8	6	8	10	10	9	10	57/70	81%
Data analysis	10	10	10	10	9	10	8	67/70	96%
Limitations	8	8	8	10	9	10	8	59/70	84%
Results & cost/benefit	14	10	10	10	15	12	10	78/105	74%
Writing	9	10	10	10	9	9	8	63/70	90%
Relevance	8	9	7	10	9	8	8	57/70	81%
Total	89/100	80/100	86/100	90/100	90/100	89/100	82/100	689/700	84%

and need further development for generalizability across settings. There can be confidence that the best practices reviewed here are relevant for guiding future research and practice in health systems and communities that are invested in facilitating children's access to health care.

Of the four practice foci identified in this inquiry, the greatest degree of specificity exists in best practices by nonmedical supports. The quality of sources and agreement across perspectives engenders confidence in the need for implementing nonmedical supports including coordinated referrals, parent education, and outreach.

There is likewise confidence instilled by this inquiry that COC and primary providers support usual sources of care. Usual source of care has been a theme throughout this summary of best practices, mentioned by 15 of the 16 sources. Fourteen sources identified COC methods that supported a usual source, though there was not full consensus about specific COC models such as Medical Home or OA. There is a need for further development of COC models. Fourteen sources identified a primary provider, rather than a clinic or a provider group, as a usual source of care. COC methods supported the practicalities of a primary provider being consistently available for prevention and treatment for each of her or his own patients.

There was less agreement and specificity among sources about administrative supports and provider–parent relationships. The administrative best practice that emerged across perspectives was support for making and keeping appointments. There was not a consensus about exactly what an appointment support model should look like. The only provider–parent relationship support across perspectives was effective communication. Researchers measured language issues, but did not capture the essence of relationships presented through consumer experiences. It will be helpful for future research to study the effects of partnering, respect, and cultural competence.

Gaps in current knowledge/practice. The fragmented U.S. health-care system can be as unwieldy to those who would improve it as it is for parents of a child in need of care. Its parts, though related, have varying degrees of disconnectedness with each other and with the communities they serve. There is not a single point of intervention that will facilitate access for every child, and the points that would be malleable to intervention vary between communities and health-care systems. R3 called for a multifactorial approach to access, though there is not a model of exactly what that would look like. It befalls provider systems, insurers, hospital systems, departments of health, and consumer organizations to advocate for and apply recommended best practices locally.

The bane of a fragmented health-care system is the lack of an overall design conducive to a single point of correction. The blessing is that local settings can implement practices on a small scale, which, if effective, might likewise be useful on a broader scope. Best practices identified in the previous section will improve child and community health where they are implemented. Further research within communities known to provide exceptional access to health care would yield additional indicators about effective practices. Of particular interest are community-wide practices in areas where there are high rates of on-time immunizations and low rates of preventable ED use.

The model developed from this inquiry is a compilation of recommendations developed out of needs assessments and outcome studies of local health-care system practices. The administrative, nonmedical, relational, and usual source supports presented here form an idealized model that may not exist *in toto* in any one setting. The inquiry provides a model, or an ideal, against which health-care systems can judge their own practices and further development of best practice guidelines across the country.

Judging Best Practices by Value Criteria

The identified best practices are consistent with many of the values that guide human services professions. Social justice is a social work ethical principle, which along with the principles of fiscally responsible provision of health-care goods and services that guide health-care economics creates a call for distributive justice in health-care services. Other social work ethical principles considered in this section include service to others; dignity and worth of the person; and human relationships. Cultural competence is a social work ethical standard included in this critique. Values criteria for the strengths perspective are presented here in tandem with primary prevention. Empowerment and the ecological perspective are also used to judge best practices. At this writing, the ongoing lack of access to health care experienced by children of the poor indicates that there remains work to be done in implementing best practices that satisfy these values.

Social justice is the social work ethical principle that pursues change on behalf of vulnerable populations (NASW, 1999). Health-care economic principles call for *fiscally responsible provision of health-care goods and services* (Lee, 2000). The marriage of social work and health-care economics produces a demand for *distributive justice*. The nation's most vulnerable must experience some benefit from the 14% of gross domestic product that consists of health-care goods and services (Kopelman, 2002). A child's need for health care is scarcely comparable to other goods and services, as "diseases and disabilities inhibit children's capacities to use and develop their talents, thereby curtailing their opportunities" (Kopelman, 2002, p. 263). Yet, U.S. dollars are spent without concomitant procurement of adequate health care for every child.

About half of U.S. pediatricians either do not accept children on Medicaid, or restrict the number of their Medicaid patients (Berman, Dolins, Tang, & Yudkowsky, 2002). Medicaid-insured children without primary providers are often treated in a stopgap fashion through costly ED visits, after preventable or treatable conditions have escalated into acute or urgent conditions. Other publicly insured, underinsured, and uninsured children face similar dilemmas. ED is the component of the American health-care system that is prohibited "from denying emergency medical treatment as a way of cutting costs" (Schaffner, 2005) by the Federal Emergency Medical Treatment and Active Labor Act (2000). However, an ED provides suboptimal care for meeting the ongoing health needs of a child, and it is quite costly because of equipment and staffing requirements. ED cost is substantial in terms of child health outcomes, and in terms of financial burden to families, insurers, hospital systems, and government entities. A quantitative consumer study (C4), professionals (P1–P4) and researchers (R1 & R5–R7) recognized ED utilization as a measure of failed health-care practices.

To answer the call of distributive justice, health-care systems must adopt practices that coordinate WCC and treatment. Coordinating care includes assistance with public insurance outreach efforts. It includes HMOs that involve themselves in reducing financial barriers to health care (C4). R5 studied a telephone system that showed cost savings and an increased number of provider visits. Professional sources (P1–P4) suggested reimbursement for care coordination and telephone strategies that increase low-cost contact between patients and providers. When widely implemented, *appointment supports* (C1–C4, P1–P4, R1, & R4–R7), *nonmedical supports* (C1–C5, P1–P4, R1–R4, & R6–R7) and *usual sources of care* (C1–C4, P1–P4, & R1–R7) can answer the call of social justice, health-care economics and distributive justice.

Other social work ethical principles include *service to others*; *dignity and worth of the person*; *and human relationships*. These are addressed by practices that bring knowledge and resources out of safekeeping in the medical milieu to be shared with parents (C1–C3, C5, P1–P3, & R1–R3); that do not leave sick children waiting for hours (C1–C4, P1, P3–P4, & R7); and that promote provider–patient relationships (C1–C3, C5, P1–P5, R1–R5, & R7), respectively. However, consumers and researchers indicated that in many settings these practices are ideal rather than realized (C1–C2, C5, R2–R3, & R6).

Cultural competence is a social work ethical standard that views service delivery within a cultural context. Ethnocentrism, including deference to the medical milieu, impedes care and is debilitating in its disregard for the wisdom families bring from their own cultures. Consumers (C1–C2 & C5) and researchers (R2–R3) identified lapses of cultural competence; P1 presented innovative remedies for medical-centric milieu, that were implemented in various U.S. settings. This inquiry suggests that *non-medical supports* (C1–C5, P1–P4, R1–R4, & R6–R7) and positive *provider–patient relationships* (C1–C3, C5, P1–P4, R1–R5, & R7) can support culturally competent care.

Empowerment is a "personal sense of control that one has over his/her realm of influence" (Williams & Wright, 1992, pp. 24–25). This inquiry calls for training parents to understand the health-care system (C1 & R1) and for health-care professionals to listen to parents and answer their questions (C2–C3 & C5). Empowerment would reach out to families unable to access care for their children (P2). Intentionality in empowering families is warranted because children with the most complex needs have the greatest difficulty obtaining care (R3). Empowerment views a child in need of treatment and his or her family as the nexus of care, the reason why everybody else is there, and drives practices that instill a confidence in parents befitting their pivotal role in the care system. Current practices, however, have not alleviated ongoing need (C1–C3, C5, P2, & R1). When widely implemented, the *nonmedical supports* (C1–C5, P1–P4, R1–R4, & R6–R7) and *provider–patient relationship supports* (C1–C3, C5, P1–P4, R1–R5, & R7) suggested herein will empower families and support child health.

The strengths perspective recognizes that most children are healthy children who need only minimal care to prevent illness, coordinated with treatments that address illness when it does strike. This is "problem reversal coupled with helping people move forward to realize their dreams and potential" (McMillan, Morris, & Sherraden, 2004, p. 324). *Primary prevention* similarly calls for the use of finite resources for "people who do not yet show any signs of disturbance" (Lurie & Monahan, 2001, p. 69). Primary prevention is relatively inexpensive yet indispensable, as children "develop rapidly, underscoring the importance of longitudinal, comprehensive primary care" (R2, p. 1010). Best practices for the strengths perspective and primary prevention connect children with providers for WCC, to circumvent problems that are more serious in their consequences for the child and more costly to health-care systems (R1).

During the first two years of life, however, only 18% of U.S. children receive recommended immunizations on time (Luman, McCauley, Stokley, Chu, & Pickering, 2002). Poor and minority children's immunization rates are lower yet (P4). Though most children are in excellent health, health has been shown to decline with SES (P1). Low immunization rates (C2 & R4), high ED utilization (C4, P1–P4, R1, & R5–R7) and that poor children experience poorer health than is enjoyed by wealthier peers, are indicators of health-care systems not yet facilitating primary prevention for every child. The strengths perspective and primary prevention call for implementation of widespread *nonmedical supports* (C1–C5, P1–P4, R1–R4, & R6–R7), *provider–patient relationship supports* (C1–C3, C5, P1–P4, R1–R5, & R7) and *usual source of care supports* (C1–C4, P1–P4, & R1–R7), to prevent illness and debility.

The ecological perspective is "based on the work of Urie Bronfenbrenner that calls for family-centered, community-based services to improve the health of individuals in the context of their own life situation" (P2, p. 29). This is consistent with the HHS goals for healthy people in healthy communities. The ecological perspective views children, providers, families and community constituents as members of the same environment, and urges health-care professionals to partner with each of these entities to support the health of all in community-wide systems of care rather than in patchworks. The current fragmentation of services does not recognize that child health is a by-product of community health. Consumers (C1–C3 & C5), professionals (P1–P4), and researchers (R1 & R4–R5) identified the need for practices that are family centered and community centered, and for changing the medical milieu so that health-care systems cooperate and are part of community systems. *Appointment supports, nonmedical supports, provider–patient relationships* and *usual sources of care* will include more children in community systems of health care.

Recommendations

The best practices presented here have emerged from what is working within individual health-care systems. **Distributive justice** will be advanced through community-wide strategies that connect all children—and particularly children who are underinsured, are of minority status or are living in poor families—with a usual source of care. Strategies will include referral systems that decrease communities' ED utilization and cost by increasing provision of primary care. A Texas hospital system responded to the economics and care issues of ED by initiating a pilot program that provided preventive care to uninsured patients. The patients were people who made frequent ED visits because they lacked health-care insurance for maintenance of chronic conditions. Hospital officials stated that the preventive care program saved the hospital money (Eckholm, 2006, Health-1). Similar cost analyses and pilot programs, expanded to community-wide responses, will help planners reinforce the economics of securing a place within community-care systems for all children, and garner support for community-wide referral systems. A systematic, community-wide approach to health care will result in decreased suffering and debility, improved community health, and fiscally responsible allocation of finite health-care resources.

Community strategies for connecting children with primary providers will include referrals for children who present at an ED with conditions preventable by primary care. Referrals will certainly not exclude children from emergency care after urgent situations arise, but will link children to primary providers for follow-up care and for prevention of further morbidity. Referrals to a primary provider are consistent with *primary prevention's* emphasis on averting morbidity; with the *strengths perspective's* emphasis on keeping children healthy; and with *empowerment's* emphasis on supporting children's physical and mental capabilities.

Emergency departments are not the only settings from which strategic community planners would establish referral protocols. Community-wide strategies will require collaboration among health-care professionals to accommodate referrals from public health departments, clinics, schools, and services to recent immigrants. Referrals to providers accepting new patients will include assistance with making and keeping the initial appointment and information about the provider's office hours, location, and nearby public transportation. Referrals will include a form, available in each of a community's languages, for application to Medicaid, SCHIP, and other financial resources, and assistance with completing that form as needed. The social work principle of *service to others* is consistent with community-wide information dissemination and coordination of preventive and sick-child care, even for children who do not have means to pay.

For referrals to be of value, however, planners must attend to whether there are enough pediatric and family-care providers, including medical doctors, doctors of osteopath, nurse practitioners, and physician assistants, to accept each of the community's children as patients. If forced to choose, community health-care planners will place more emphasis on attracting generalist rather than specialty care providers, to develop appointment availability of a frequency and length sufficient to forestall preventable suffering. Connecting children to usual sources of care is consistent with social work principles including *the worth and dignity of children* and the importance of *human relationships*.

A community-wide approach will require change from medical milieu-centered practices to client- and community-centered practices. Collaborative community-wide solutions are consistent with the *ecological perspective* that views child health in the context of community health preparedness; looking outside the medical milieu is consistent with social work's ethical standard of *cultural competence*.

Expanding best practice approaches into community-wide strategies is consistent with the values and principles that guide social work and other human service professions. Strategies that connect children with usual sources of care will facilitate access to health care for entire communities of children.

References

Antonelli, R.C., & Antonelli, D.M. (2004). Providing a Medical Home: The cost of care coordination services in a community-based, general pediatric practice. *Pediatrics, 113*(5), 1522–1528. Retrieved October 18, 2006, from www.pediatrics.org.

Balanced Budget Act of 1997, H.R. 2015,105th Cong., 2nd Sess.

Becker, G. (2004). Deadly inequality in the health care "safety net": Uninsured ethnic minorities' struggle to live with life-threatening illnesses. *Medical Anthropology Quarterly, 18*(2), 258–275.

Berman, S., Dolins, J., Tang, S., & Yudkowsky, B. (2002). Factors that influence the willingness of private primary care pediatricians to accept more Medicaid patients. *Pediatrics, 110*, 239–248.

Burstein, K., & Bryan, T. (2000). Parents as partners in the Medical Home. *The Exceptional Parent, 30*(8), 29–31.

Byck, G. (2000). A comparison of the socioeconomic and health status characteristics of the uninsured. *Pediatrics, 106*(1), 14–21.

Carpenter, M., & Kavanagh, L. (1998). Outreach to children: Moving from enrollment to ensuring access. *National Institute for Health Care Management*. Retrieved October 18, 2006 from www.nihcm.org.

Children's Defense Fund. (2007, January 11). *Children's Defense Fund announces plan to cover 9 million uninsured children*. Retrieved May 24, 2007 from www.childrens defense.org.

Christakis, D., Mell, L., Koepsell, T., Zimmerman, F., & Connell, F. (2001). Association of lower continuity of care with greater risk of emergency department use and hospitalization in children. *Pediatrics, 103*(3), 524–529. Retrieved October 4, 2006, from www.pediatrics.org.

DeNavas-Walt, C., Proctor, B., & Lee, C., United States Census Bureau, Current Population Reports, P60–229. (2006). *Income, poverty and health insurance coverage in the United States: 2005*. Washington, DC: U.S. Government Printing Office. Retrieved May 24, 2007, from www.census.gov/prod/2006pubs/p60-231.pdf.

Eckholm, E. (2006, October 25). Hospitals try free basic care for uninsured. *The New York Times*, Health, 1. Retrieved October 26, 2006 from www.nytimes.com.

Emergency Medical Treatment and Active Labor Act of 2000, P.L. 106–554, 114 Stat. 2763.

Farmer, J., Clark, M., Sherman, A., Marien, W., & Selva, T. (2005). Comprehensive primary care for children with special health care needs in rural areas. *Pediatrics* *116*(3), 649–656. Retrieved October 18, 2006, from www.pediatrics.org.

Galbraith, A., Wong, S., Kim, S., & Newacheck, P. (2005). Out-of pocket financial burden for low-income families with children: Socioeconomic disparities and effects of insurance. *Health Research and Educational Trust, (40)*6, 1722–1736.

Henly, S., Tyree, E., Lindsey, D., Lambeth, S., & Burd, C. (1998). Innovative perspectives on health services for vulnerable rural populations. *Family and Community Health, (21)*1, 22–31.

Hughes, D., & Ng, S. (2003). Reducing health disparities among children. *The Future of Children, 13*(1), 153–167. Retrieved September 21, 2006, from www.futureofchildren. org.

Kaplan, D., Brindis, C., Phibbs, S., Melinkovich, P., Naylor, K., & Ahlstrand, K. (1999). A comparison study of an elementary school-based health center: Effects on health care access and use. *Archives of Pediatric and Adolescent Medicine 153*, 889–893. Retrieved October 6, 2006, from www.archpediatrics.com

Kattan, M., Crain, E., Steinbach, S., Visness, C., Walter, M., Stout, J., et al. (2006). A randomized clinical trial of clinician feedback to improve quality of care for inner-city children with asthma. *Pediatrics, 117*(6), e1095–e1103. Retrieved October 18, 2006, from www.pediatrics.org.

Kopelman, L. (2002). Children's right to health care: A modest proposal. In R. Rhodes, M. Battin & A. Silvers (Eds.), *Medicine and social justice* (pp. 259–269). New York: Oxford University Press.

Lee, R. (2000). *Economics for healthcare managers*. Chicago: Health Administration Press.

Luman, E., McCauley, M., Stokley, S., Chu, S., & Pickering, L. (2002). Timeliness of childhood immunizations. *Pediatrics, 110*, 935–939.

Lurie, A., & Monahan, K. (2001). Prevention principles for practitioners: A solution or an illusion? *Social Work in Health Care, 33*(1), 69–86.

Mann, C., Rowland, D., & Garfield, R. (2003). Historical overview of children's health care coverage. *The Future of Children 13*(1). Retrieved March 13, 2007 from www. futureofchildren.org.

McMillan, J.C., Morris, L., & Sherraden, M. (2004). Ending social works grudge match: Problems versus strengths. *Families in Society: The Journal of Contemporary Social Services, 85*(3), 317–325.

Millman, M. (Ed.) (1993). *Access to health care in America: Committee on monitoring access to personal health care services, Institute of Medicine*. Washington, D.C.: National Academy Press.

National Association of Social Workers. (1999). *Code of ethics of the National Association of Social Workers*. Washington, DC: NASW.

Newacheck, P., Lieu, T., Kalkbrenner, A., Chi, F., Ray, G., Cohen, J. et al. (2001). A comparison of health care experiences for Medicaid and commercially enrolled children in a large, nonprofit health and maintenance organization. *Ambulatory Pediatrics, 1*, 28–35.

Ngo-Metzger, Q., Telfair, J., Sorkin, D., Weidmer, B., Weech-Maldonado, R., Hurtado, M. et al. (2006). Cultural competency and quality of care: Obtaining the patient's perspective. *The Commonwealth Fund*. Retrieved October 19, 2006, from www. commonwealthfund.org.

O'Brien, E., & Mann, C. (2003). Maintaining the gains: The importance of preserving coverage in Medicaid and SCHIP. *Covering Kids & Families: The Robert Wood Johnson Foundation*. Retrieved February 5, 2007, from http://coveringkidsandfamilies. org.

O'Connor, M., Matthews, B., & Gao, D. (2006). Effect of open access scheduling on missed appointments, immunizations, and continuity of care for infant well-child care visits. *Archives of Pediatric and Adolescent Medicine. 160*, 889–893. Retrieved October 6, 2006, from www.archpediatrics.com.

Personal Responsibility and Work Opportunity Reconciliation Act of 1996, P.L. 104–193, 110 Stat. 2105.

Randolph, G., Murray, M., Swanson, J., & Margolis, P. (2004). Behind schedule: Improving access to care for children one practice at a time. *Pediatrics, 113*(3), e230–e237. Retrieved October 4, 2006, from www.pediatrics.org.

Raphel, S. (1999). Eye on Washington: Access to health care for America's children. *Journal of Child and Adolescent Psychiatric Nursing, (12)*2, 87–90. Retrieved September 9, 2006, from Expanded Academic.

Schaffner, D.E. (2005). EMTALA: All bark and no bite. *University of Illinois Law Review* (1021). Retrieved August 31, 2006 from web.lexis-nexis.com.

Seid, M., Stevens, G., & Varni, J. (2003). Parents' perceptions of pediatric primary care quality: Effects of race/ethnicity, language, and access. *Health Services Research and Educational Trust, (38)*4, 1009–1032.

Slifkin, R., Freeman, V., & Silberman, P. (2002). Effect of the North Carolina state children's health insurance program on beneficiary access to care. *Archives of Pediatric and Adolescent Medicine, 156*, 1223–1229. Retrieved October 6, 2006, from www.archpediatrics.com.

Sobo, E., Seid, M., & Gelhard, L. (2006). Parent-identified barriers to pediatric health care: A process-oriented model. *Health Services Research and Educational Trust, (41)*1, 148–172.

Stevens, G., Seid, M., Mistry, R., & Halfon, N. (2006). Disparities in primary care for vulnerable children: The influence of multiple risk factors. *Health Services Research and Educational Trust, 41*(2), 507–531.

Thomas, M., Kohli, V., & King, D. (2004). Barriers to childhood immunization: Findings from a needs assessment. *Home Health Care Services Quarterly, 23*(2), 19–39.

U.S. Department of Health and Human Services. (2000). *Healthy people 2010: Understanding and improving health*. Washington, DC: Government Printing Office.

U.S. Senate Finance Committee Subcommittee on Health Care. (2006). *CHIP at 10: A decade of covering children: Hearings before Cong*. (Testimony of Voices of America). Washington, DC. Retrieved October 3, 2006 from www.voices.org.

Williams, D. (1999). Race, socioeconomic status, and health: The added effects of racism and discrimination. *Annals of the New York Academy of Science, 896*, 173–188.

Williams, S., & Wright, D. (1992). Empowerment: The strengths of Black families revisited. *Journal of Multicultural Social Work, 2*(4), 23–36.

6 Best Practices for Engaging Parents of Children Receiving Mental Health Services

Tara McLendon

This chapter examines consumer, professional, and research perspectives regarding ways to engage parents in the provision of children's mental health services. An overview of the population and issue of concern is discussed, each of the three perspectives is considered, practices identified by each perspective are compared and contrasted with the other two perspectives, and current best practices are identified. Finally, these best practices are considered within the context of particular societal and professional values, and recommendations for improvements are made.

Overview of Population and Problem of Concern

Population of Concern

Beginning in 1969, the Joint Commission on Mental Health examined the quality of mental health services for children, and found them to be sorely inadequate (Duchnowski, Kutash, & Friedman, 2002). In an effort to address the numerous gaps in care, the National Institute of Mental Health (Duchnowski, Hall, Kutash, & Friedman, 1998) created the Child and Adolescent Service System Program. The over-arching goal of this initiative was to create a "system of care" for children with mental health difficulties and their families. This "system of care" included, among other things, facilitating inter-agency planning and service delivery, and involving families in the planning process (Lourie, Stroul, & Friedman, 1998). In 1993, at the request of the United States Congress, the Center for Mental Health Services developed a standardized definition of Serious Emotional Disturbance (SED), a term used to more clearly identify the population of concern. This definition included the child having a psychiatric diagnosis and some type of impairment impacting family life, school functioning, and/or participation in the community (Duchnowski et al., 2002).

This inquiry focuses on better understanding how to engage parents in the provision of children's mental health services. As a point of clarification, the term "parents" is infrequently utilized in the literature. Instead, "family" involvement is commonly the way in which participation in a child's treatment is conceptualized. For the purpose of this inquiry, the term "parents" will be utilized, with the understanding that it is consistent with the terms "family," "caretaker," or terms implying any person(s) functioning in the parent role. Furthermore, while the role and needs of the entire family are important considerations, the specific focus of the conclusions and recommendations of this inquiry will focus on parental involvement.

Population Strengths and Needs

Parents of children with SED have many strengths, as well as clearly identified needs. Strengths of this population can include well-developed advocacy skills, perseverance, knowledge of mental health and social services, willingness to provide support to other parents of SED children, and wisdom about the needs of their children and themselves (Ditrano & Silverstein, 2006; Spencer & Powell, 2000). Needs of these people can include the desire for a family-centered approach, cohesive and coordinated care that involves structured communication between service providers, being treated with respect by service providers, geographically accessible services, and culturally competent care (Ditrano & Silverstein, 2006; Kruzich, Jivanjee, Robinson, & Friesen, 2003; Spencer & Powell, 2000; Williams Adams, 2006).

Prevalence of SED

Despite the fact there has been no large-scale nationwide study of psychiatric disorders among children (ages 4 to 18 years), it is estimated that 17% to 22% of this population experiences some type of emotional, behavioral, or developmental problem (Kazdin, 2000). Moreover, it is thought that 3% to 8% of this total population meet the criteria for SED (Kuperminc & Cohen, 1995; Quinn & Epstein, 1998). In 2004, almost 900,000 SED children throughout the United States received services from the State Mental Health Authority, with 60% of this population being Caucasian, 25% African American, 5% Hispanic American, and the remainder is comprised of Native Americans, Pacific Islanders, people of Asian decent, "other" or "not available" (SAMHSA, 2005). Broadly speaking, children with SED are a diverse group with complex service needs. In addition to mental health services, these children are often involved in other systems including education, child welfare, and juvenile justice, a dynamic which makes meeting their needs all the more complex (Pires & Stroul, 1996).

Monetary and Human Costs

The monetary cost of SED to society is significant. Nationally, during 2004, roughly $4 billion was spent on outpatient care for this population, while about $2.5 billion was spent on state hospital and inpatient care (SAMHSA, 2005). In reference to human costs, Davis and Vander Stoep (1997) found that children with SED have a school dropout rate ranging from 43% to 56%; 3 to 5 years after leaving school, are employed at a rate of only 47%; show high rates of criminal involvement; have high numbers of unplanned pregnancies; and are at increased risk for substance abuse and suicide. Furthermore, SED children are at increased risk for out-of-home placement (Petr & Barney, 1993).

Desired Outcomes

There are several desired outcomes that increased parental engagement in the provision of children's mental health services could produce. Primary effects potentially include increased parental investment in the helping process, improved information exchange between the parent(s) and service provider(s), greater potential for reinforcement of treatment goals in the home, and enhanced parent/service provider alliance. Secondary outcomes of these primary effects could prospectively include more children avoiding out-of-home placement, as well as addressing concerns outlined above by Davis and Vander Stoep (1997).

It has been documented that parents who are engaged in the treatment of their child(ren) are a crucial component to positive outcomes and lasting change (Coatsworth, Santisteban, McBride, & Szapocznik, 2001; Cunningham & Henggeler, 1999; Liddle, 1995; Szapocznik et al., 1988). Hogue, Liddle, Dauber, and Samuolis (2004) point out that,

> Rigorous empirical studies have shown that family-based therapy can produce engagement and retention of drug users and their families in treatment (Henggeler et al., 1991); reduction or elimination of drug use (Liddle et al., 2001; Waldron, Slesnick, Brody, Turner, & Peterson, 2001); decreased involvement in delinquent activities (Henggeler, Melton, Smith, Schoenwald, & Hanley, 1993); improvement in multiple domains of psychosocial func-tioning such as school grades, school attendance, and family functioning (Liddle et al., 2001); and increased quality of parenting behavior (Mann, Bourdin, Henggeler, & Blaske, 1990; Schmidt, Liddle, & Dakof, 1996).
>
> (p. 84)

Focus of Best Practice Inquiry

This multidimensional evidence-based practice (MEBP) inquiry incorporates consumer, professional, and research perspectives regarding the best practices to engage parents in the provision of children's mental health services. Each perspective is considered separately and best practices are summarized from each perspective. Finally, using a value framework, gaps in service delivery are identified and recommendations for improvement are made.

Best Practices: Consumer, Professional, and Research Perspectives

A search of the literature regarding parental engagement in the provision of children's mental health services was conducted to identify consumer, professional, and research perspectives. Databases searched included: Expanded Academic ASAP, PsychINFO, Social Work Abstracts, and Lexis/Nexis Academic. Key terms included: children's mental health, Seriously Emotionally Disturbed (SED), family-centered practice, family-centered care, family involvement, family empowerment, family engagement, parent management training, parent(al) involvement, parent support, parent(al) engagement, barriers to mental health service provision, and system(s) of care. Finally, websites for Keys for Networking (www.keys.org), The Research and Training Center on Family Support and Children's Mental Health at Portland State University (www.rtc.pdx.edu), The Federation of Families for Children's Mental Health (www.ffcmh.org), Family Voices (www.family voices.org), and the University of Wisconsin Library (www.library.wisc.edu) were searched for relevant information.

Consumer Perspective: Sources

In an effort to include a consumer perspective regarding best practices to engage parents in the provision of children's mental health services, studies and articles incorporating this viewpoint were examined. The sources included were selected because they incorporate consumer thoughts and opinions, and this "voice" is clearly evident. The two empirically based studies have an unambiguous research design and systematic data collection. The third article is an interview of a mother of a SED child, and speaks to parental involvement in short-term and long-term placement. Finally, the newspaper article expresses the voice of parents of SED children as articulated via a summit sponsored by the National Alliance for the Mentally Ill (NAMI). These consumer perspectives are summarized in Table 6.1.

Ditrano and Silverstein (2006) (C1) utilized a participatory action research (PAR) design to identify ways schools and parents can work together to more effectively meet the needs of children with emotional disturbances. Although this study took place in an educational setting, because of the population studied and the goal of increasing parent engagement and involvement, it is reasonable to assume the findings are applicable to mental health service provision. A group of nine parents met seven times and a theoretical narrative was created by the researchers. This narrative described the parents' stories, their action projects, and conclusions reached regarding their need to become more effectively involved in their child's educational experience.

In Spencer and Powell (2000) (C2), the author (John Powell) interviewed Sandra Spencer, who is a parent of a child with SED and Executive Director of the Federation of Families for Children's Mental Health, a national advocacy organization. Her son was placed in a residential treatment setting for one-and-a-half years, and later in an inpatient psychiatric unit for 30 days. Throughout the interview, Ms. Spencer spoke of staff behaviors or institutional policies she saw as barriers to her involvement in her son's care, as well as behaviors and policies she perceived to engender parental engagement and ongoing involvement in care.

A survey of 102 family caregivers in 31 states examined perceptions of barriers to and supports of their participation in their children's out-of-home treatment (Kruzich et al., 2003) (C3). The data were gathered via a questionnaire mailed to parents of children who had received at least three months of in-home treatment or at least 30 continuous days of out-of-home treatment for emotional, behavioral, or mental disorders from September 1, 1996 to August 31, 1998. Finally, a NAMI-sponsored summit held in January 2006, the Children's Mental Health Voice of Florida Summit , produced recommendations to fill service gaps and better involve parents in service delivery to SED children (C4).

Consumer Perspective: Results

In summary, parents identified several practices they found helpful to engage and involve them in the provision of mental health services to their children (see Table 6.1). Some of these services and practices are ones which parents currently have access to, while others are recommended based on positive past experience or theories about what might be helpful. These recommendations are indicated by "[R]" following the perspective citation. Practices or recommendations are included if cited by two or more sources. One of the most commonly cited current or recommended best practices to engage parents in the provision of mental health services to their children is the demonstration of a respectful attitude by service providers (C1[R], C2, and C3). Consumer suggestions to facilitate this include: workers validating positive actions being taken by parents (Spencer & Powell, 2000); welcoming parents to the agency or school (Ditrano & Silverstein, 2006); and helping parents to feel that their participation is important (Kruzich et al., 2003).

The provision of culturally competent care is also cited three times (C2, C3, and C4[R]). Suggestions to assist in implementing this component of service provision include: training workers in cultural differences (Williams Adams, 2006); increased responsiveness to a family's cultural values (Kruzich et al., 2003); and asking about religious preferences (Spencer & Powell, 2000).

Better inter-agency collaboration was noted three times (C2[R], C3, and C4[R]). Specifically, consumers state that increased assistance with transition from residential settings to the family home and outpatient care is needed (Spencer & Powell, 2000; Kruzich et al., 2003).

Increased knowledge of resources/treatment options/educational system is cited twice (C1 and C2). Consumers note that bringing a support person with them to meetings helped them to be more confident and ask questions of providers and educators (Ditrano & Silverstein, 2006). Spencer and Powell (2000) point out it is important for service providers to share information with parents about techniques and language they use when working with a child. Support from other families is also cited twice (C1 and C2[R]). Families point out that sharing of experience and knowledge helps to normalize their experience and increase their familiarity with the system, both of which facilitate family participation in service delivery to their child (Ditrano & Silverstein, 2006; Spencer & Powell, 2000).

A positive service provider attitude and "provision of hope" to parents (C1 and C2) is also identified. Ditrano and Silverstein (2006) illustrate the way in which families who have a sense "their children would be successful in the future . . . (and) could achieve happiness" were able to advocate for them and take steps

Table 6.1 Best Practices Consumer Perspective

Best Practice	*Consumer #1 (C1)*	*Consumer #2 (C2)*	*Consumer #3 (C3)*	*Consumer #4 (C4)*
Inter-agency/interdisciplinary collaboration/more effective transition from placement to placement		R	X	R
Support from other consumers	X (after PAR Project)	R		
Instilling hope/optimism	X (after PAR Project)	X (at hospital)		
Increasing consumer knowledge of resources, and treatment options (including educational system)	X (after PAR Project)	X (at hospital)		
Culturally competent services		X (at hospital)	X	R
Developing consumer advocacy skills	X (after PAR Project)	X		
Respectful service provider attitude/no blaming of parents/ willing to engage parents/parent participation valued	R	X (at hospital)	X	
Giving families voice in treatment/program design		X (at hospital)		R
Access to primary care physicians competent in child and family assessment				R
Communication between parents & service providers/provision of contact person		X (at hospital)	X	
Flexibility in scheduling of meetings			X	
Inclusion of all family members			X	
Geographically accessible services		X (at RTC)		

Notes:
X=Current Best Practice
R=Recommended Best Practice (based on theory of what might work or positive past experience)

toward institutional change (p. 370). Spencer and Powell (2000) state, "Service providers need to listen to parents, follow their approach, and share their hopes and dreams" (p. 42). The importance of constructive communication between service providers and parents (C2 and C3) was also cited twice. These two consumer sources discuss the need for communication between residential treatment staff and parents; however, it is reasonable that parents whose children are receiving services in the community would see this as a way to become engaged and more involved in the service provision process, as well.

Giving families greater voice in treatment/program design is a recommendation by the NAMI sponsored Children's Mental Health Voice of Florida (Williams Adams, 2006) (C4[R]) and Spencer and Powell (2000) illustrate how a mother's awareness of her son's needs in the transition from a residential setting to home and school shaped the treatment plan (C2). Finally, the development of parent advocacy skills was cited by two sources (C1 and C2). The Participatory Action Research Project facilitated by Ditrano and Silverstein (2006) demonstrates the effect of increased advocacy skills on parents' ability to engage and change the educational system for their children with emotional disorders. Spencer and Powell (2000) illustrate the positive impact a parent with well-developed advocacy skills can have on the treatment system.

Professional Perspective: Sources

In addition to consumer perspectives, professional perspectives of best practices to involve parents in the provision of children's mental health services were examined. Criteria for selection included rigorous research design and/or significant study and implementation of the particular model or paradigm. One of the articles represents the perceived needs of service providers to more effectively involve families in service delivery (P1). Articles two, three, and four are conceptual papers based on well-developed and thoroughly studied models of service delivery, all of which include a framework for engaging/involving parents. Refer to Table 6.2 for summary of findings.

Craft-Rosenberg, Kelley, and Schnoll (2006) (P1) conducted four focus group interviews with the purpose of describing service provider views of family-centered practice. Seventy-six service providers from social work, nursing, and other helping professions participated. Pre- and post-meeting questionnaires were utilized.

Liddle (1995) (P2) describes engagement strategies specific to Multidimensional Family Therapy (MDFT). The author conceptualizes engagement not as an event which takes place at the beginning of therapy, but as an ongoing therapeutic process. Strategies and methods to engage parents in their child's treatment include providing hope, looking for parent strengths, and attending to transportation and childcare barriers, among others.

Santisteban and Szapocznik (1994) (P3) provide strategies to engage families of substance abusing and emotionally/behaviorally troubled youth. This framework is the result of 30 years of service provision and study at the Spanish Family

Guidance Center at the University of Miami. This approach to family involvement is based on Brief Strategic Family Therapy and specifically aims to address family interactional patterns that prevent families from engaging in services.

Through the development of Multisystemic Therapy, Cunningham and Henggler (1999), identify ways in which multiproblem families can be engaged in the therapy process (P4). Multisystemic Therapy is a home-based services approach that provides integrative, family-centered treatment. It was specifically designed to respond to the needs of adolescents who exhibit serious anti-social behavior and conduct disorder. The authors discuss universal engagement strategies, as well as those specific to MST.

Professional Perspective: Results

As in the consumer perspective, the professional best practices were categorized according to whether they are currently in use, or are recommended, based on past experience or theory regarding practices which might be helpful (see Table 6.2). Practices or recommendations are included if there were cited by two or more sources. One practice is cited four times, which was the provision of culturally competent care (P1[R], P2, P3, and P4). A survey indicated that service providers sometimes worked with families displaying "more ethnic diversity than partici-pants felt prepared to handle" (Craft-Rosenberg et al., 2006, p. 23). A conclusion of this survey was that service providers could benefit from a greater understanding of how to work with culturally diverse families. Within the context of engagement, Liddle (1995) stresses the importance of understanding social context and circumstances particular to that family. Cultural competence and the understanding of a family, their values, and beliefs is a cornerstone of Brief Strategic Family Therapy and the corresponding engagement process (Santisteban & Szapocznik, 1994). Cunningham and Henggeler (1999) cite lack of understanding for cultural and value-based differences on the therapist's part as a significant barrier to engagement.

The provision of a framework to engage/involve families is discussed in three articles in this section (P2, P3, and P4). Various techniques to engage the adoles-cent subsystem, the parental subsystem, and facilitate engagement between these two subsystems are an essential component of Multidimensional Family Therapy (Liddle, 1995). Santisteban and Szapocznik (1994) provide a specific engagement framework, as well as commenting, "In the absence of specialized engagement procedures, families are often left to their own devices in terms of bringing all of their members to therapy" (p. 11). Cunningham and Henggeler (1999) outline universal engagement techniques service providers can use, including showing empathy and normalizing parental guilt and anxiety.

The demonstration of service provider respect/concern for parents/attempting to understand the family is also discussed (P2, P3, and P4). Liddle (1995) stresses the importance of understanding the family's history and past experiences with therapy. The author operationalizes this tenet by stating, "One should assume that parents have tried their best to deal with the difficult challenges presented by their

Table 6.2 Best Practices Professional Perspective

Best Practice	Professional #1 (P1)	Professional #2 (P2)	Professional #3 (P3)	Professional #4 (P4)
Inter-agency/interdisciplinary collaboration	R	X		
Time/administrative support of working with families	R	X		X
Skills to work with multi-need families/"hands on experience"	R			
Culturally competent services/skills to work with ethnically diverse families	R	X	X	X
Showing concern/respect to family/attempting to understand family (including their perception of the service provider)		X	X	X
Framework to engage families—could include strategies to engage "identified patient", disengaged parent, family fear of therapy		X	X	X
Addressing parents' problems (substance abuse, mental illness)				X
Establishing therapist credibility				X
Providing families with "hope"		X		X
Normalizing child's behavior/situation		X		X
Attending to transportation, child care barriers		X		
Allowing parents to "vent" and tell their story		X		
Looking for/acknowledging parental strengths	R	X		X

Notes:
X=Current Best Practice
R=Recommended Best Practice (based on theory of what might work or past experience)

children" (p. 49). Santisteban and Szapocznik (1994) emphasize the therapist being attuned to and trying to understand familial structure and communication patterns that hinder engagement. Cunningham and Henggeler (1999) discuss understanding the parent's point of view as a way for the therapist to enhance the engagement process.

The need for adequate time to engage families and administrative support to do so is also noted. Focus group participants conclude "complex families require more time" and the lack of time to engage and work with these families is a barrier to service delivery (Craft-Rosenburg et al., 2006, p. 25). Administrative support, including adequate training and supervision, and low caseloads are also cited as dynamics vital to the engagement of parents (Cunningham & Henggeler, 1999; Liddle, 1995).

Finally, looking for/acknowledging parental strengths is also cited three times (P1[R], P2, and P4). Focus group participants note the use of a strengths-based practice as a desired area for change in their practice (Craft-Rosenburg et al., 2006). Liddle (1995) stresses looking for parental strengths and supporting positive behaviors, and Cunningham and Henngeler (1999) point out the identification of family strengths is a technique basic to the therapeutic process.

The importance of interdisciplinary/inter-agency collaboration was cited twice (P1[R] and P2). The lack of interdisciplinary teamwork was one of the most commonly cited weaknesses in the provision of family-centered care, as reported by the focus group facilitated by Craft-Rosenberg et al. (2006). Liddle (1995) stresses involving "extra therapy resources" (e.g., school and probation personnel) in the helping process (p. 57).

Providing parents with hope that the problematic situation can improve, and they do have an important role in this process, is cited as a technique instrumental to engagement (Cunningham & Henggeler, 1999; Liddle, 1995). Finally, both Cunningham and Henggeler (1999), and Liddle (1995) point out that normalizing the family's situation can be helpful to the engagement process. By helping a parent to understand the complexity of their circumstances and that frustration and anger are to be expected, the presenting problems can be normalized to some extent.

Research Perspective: Sources

A research perspective of parental involvement in children's mental health service delivery was also considered. Each selection criteria was worth ten points, with a possible total of 100 points. Selection criteria included: design type (Lyness, Walsh, & Sprenkle, 2005); length of study; sample size (Lyness et al., 2005); quality of instruments (e.g., reliability, validity) (Lyness et al., 2005); intervention fidelity (Schoenwald, Sheidow, & Letourneau, 2004); thoroughness of data analysis/reporting; consistency with inquiry; strength of conceptual/theoretical base; transportability of practices/findings (Schoenwald & Hoagwood, 2001); and acknowledgement of inquiry limitations/researcher bias. A thorough literature review revealed 11 quantitative studies that specifically examined *means by which* to engage parents in children's mental health service provision. The five which scored the highest on the selection criteria were included, with scores ranging from 72 to 89. Table 6.3 summarizes the research perspective's best practices.

McKay, McCadam, and Gonzalez (1996) (R1) report the effects of a engagement intervention delivered during the initial parent telephone contact that was designed to increase attendance at intake assessment. One hundred and eight inner-city families requesting child mental health services were randomly assigned to one of two conditions. The first condition (n=55) involved a 30 minute intensive telephone engagement intervention. It was designed to clearly identify the child's needs, help the caretaker to take steps to address the situation prior to the initial appointment, and examine and address barriers to service (e.g., negative experience with previous helping experiences, problems with transportation and/or childcare). This service was provided by two master level social workers. The second condition (n=53 families) consisted of a routine telephone screening, lasting approximately 30 minutes. This screening, provided by a master level social worker, specifically related to the child's functioning and the need for service. Forty of the 55 intervention families (72.7%) attended the first appointment or called at least one day in advance to reschedule. Conversely, only 45.3% of comparison families attended the first appointment or called to reschedule.

Santisteban et al. (1996) (R2) utilized Strategic Structural Systems Engagement (SSSE) with 193 Latino families that were randomly assigned to experimental or control conditions. The experimental condition consisted of SSSE, which is based on concepts of Brief Strategic Family Therapy and purports that a family's resistance to therapy will manifest itself during the intake process, and as such, can be more effectively addressed within that context. Control families received usual intake services. The study found that 81% of the experimental group was successfully engaged (attending at least two sessions), while only 60% of the control families attended at least two sessions.

McKay, Nudelman, McCadam, and Gonzalez (1996) (R3) report the effects of an engagement model designed to be delivered during the initial session. One hundred and seven inner-city families requesting child mental health services were randomly assigned to one of two conditions. The first condition (n=33) involved an interview protocol designed to involve families in mental health care. This condition had the purpose of engaging the child and family in the helping process, focusing on immediate and practical concerns, and identifying and addressing barriers to engaging in the helping process, among others.

In this study, 107 new families were randomly assigned to first interviewers trained in the above method, or a comparison group of therapists who did not receive this specific training. Of the 33 families assigned to the intervention provided by trained interviewers, 29 families (88%) attended their first session, and 28 (97%) returned for a second session. In comparison, of the 74 families assigned to the routine first interview condition, 47 (64%) attended the first session, and 39 (83%) returned for a second session. Over the 18 week study period, the intervention group attended an average of 7.1 sessions, while the second group attended an average of 5.4 sessions.

McKay, Stowe, McCadam, and Gonzalez (1998) (R4) studied the effects of two different engagement interventions and their impact on attendance at the initial appointment, as well as retention in ongoing services. One hundred and nine families participated in the inquiry, being randomly assigned to one of three conditions: combined intake procedure (n=35); telephone intervention alone (n=35); and usual intake procedure (n=39). Briefly, the telephone intervention alone consisted of a 30 minute intervention which was designed to assist the primary caretakers to invest in the helping process, explore barriers to seeking help, as well as encourage participants to take concrete steps to improve the situation before the first session. The combined intervention consisted of the telephone intervention, as well as assignment to a therapist specifically trained to focus on engagement during the first session. Finally, the comparison procedure consisted of usual techniques (e.g., assessing the child's need for service, obtaining demographic information).

In summary, the combined intervention and telephone-only intervention were associated with increased attendance at the initial appointment, as compared to usual techniques. This difference, however, was not statistically significant. Families in the combined condition attended an average of 7.3 sessions during the 18 week study, while those receiving only the telephone intervention attended an average of 5 sessions during this time. Finally, the usual intake group attended an average of 5.9 sessions within the course of the study.

The Family Associate Intervention was examined by Elliot, Koroloff, Doren, and Friesen (1998) (R5). This approach utilizes trained paraprofessionals, who have a child that has utilized community mental health services, as "Family Associates" (FA). In this study, 239 families were assigned to either a group that received usual community mental health services and the Family Associate Intervention (n=96) or a group only receiving usual services (n=143). At the time of referral and before a family's first appointment, the FA contacted the parents to provide information about services, emotional support, and link families to community resources, and remained in contact with the parents for three months or until the child/family had completed three sessions. Follow-up information was collected four months after the three month/three session criteria were met. Each family also had access to $250 to assist with barriers to service (e.g., child care, transportation, and respite). It is important to note it appears the $250 was only made available to the families who received the FA Intervention. Moreover, the authors never speculate as to the influence of the money on the study outcomes (e.g., the influence of the money on families who had access to it, versus comparison families who did not have access to the funds), nor do they discuss limitations in general.

Results indicate that FA involvement increased parent/caretaker initiation of services (attending the first session) to a statistically significant degree. At the four month follow-up, however, the two groups were relatively similar in continuation of services. Specifically, approximately 25% of each group had dropped out of services and approximately 30% of each group had missed at least one appointment.

Research Perspective: Results

In summary, the research perspective reflects a variety of ways in which to engage parents in the delivery of mental health services to their children (see Table 6.3).

There is one practice cited by all five sources, assistance with/addressing child care/transportation (immediate barriers to seeking help). In the framework utilized by McKay, McCadam, and Gonzales (1996a) (R1), McKay et al. (1996b) (R3), and McKay et al. (1998) (R4), one of the tasks during the initial phone call and first session was to address barriers to utilizing ongoing services, such as lack of transportation or child care. Santisteban et al. (1996) address barriers including resistant "identified patients" or disengaged parents. The Family Associate intervention is specifically designed to address the many barriers which face families seeking mental health services for their children, including cost of services, lack of child care and transportation, lack of information about the mental health care system, and problems accessing community resources (Elliot et al., 1998) (R5).

Three practices were cited by four sources. The first of these three practices is the use of telephone calls to engage parents/caregivers (R1, R2, R4, and R5). McKay et al. (1996a) (R1), and McKay et al. (1998) (R4) utilized the initial help-seeking phone call to clearly identify presenting difficulties, convey that parental actions can positively impact the situation, and discuss specific steps which can be taken to improve the situation prior to the first appointment. Santisteban et al. (1996) (R2) employed Strategic Structural Systems Engagement (SSSE) during the initial phone call to address resistance to therapy. In the study examining the Family Associate intervention, Elliot et al. (1998) (R5), the Family Associate telephoned the parent(s) soon after the referral to mental health services was made, in order to facilitate parental involvement.

An emphasis on culturally competent care is also evident in the work of McKay et al. (R1, R3, and R4), in that the framework for responding the initial help-seeking phone call, as well as the ongoing engagement process, is based on an understanding of barriers which have traditionally kept people of low-income and minority groups from seeking mental health services. Culturally competent care is one of the core concepts of Santisteban et al. (1996) (R2), specifically as it pertains to working with people of Hispanic origin.

A framework of engagement/involvement for the first session and ongoing sessions is also cited four times (R1, R2, R3, and R4). McKay et al. (1996a) (R1) used a specific protocol to facilitate engagement, outlined above in the discussion of the use of the telephone to facilitate engagement. Strategic Structural Systems Engagement is a very specific framework utilized by Santisteban et al. (1996) (R2). This model includes expressing concern for the family, inquiring about the severity of the adolescent's problem, inquiring about the values and interests of different family members, asking if all family member are willing to attend the intake appointment, problem-solving around attendance at the intake appointment, and telephoning significant others for the purpose of gathering information. McKay et al. (1996b; 1998) (R3, R4) utilized a framework during the first interview which included the worker clearly introducing him or herself, the agency, and the intake process; allowing parents to "tell their story"; focusing on parents' concrete concerns; and assisting parents to effectively interact with other systems (e.g., beginning to discuss how to help the parent get the child's academic needs met).

Table 6.3 Best Practices Research Perspective—Summary of Research Scores

Best Practice Study Criteria	Research #1 (R1)	Research #2 (R2)	Research #3 (R3)	Research #4 (R4)	Research #5 (R5)	Total
Design type	10	10	10	10	8	48/50 (96%)
Length of study/follow-up	4	7	8	8	9	36/50 (72%)
Sample size	10	10	10	10	10	50/50 (100%)
Data collection/validity, reliability of instruments	5	8	5	5	10	33/50 (66%)
Interventions clearly designed, fidelity/ integrity checks	6	10	6	10	10	42/50 (84%)
Data analysis	7	10	7	5	10	39/50 (78%)
Consistency with BP inquiry/contribution to field/importance of findings	7	9	9	9	9	43/50 (86%)
Strength of conceptual and theoretical base	8	10	8	8	10	44/50 (88%)
Transferability of findings/practices to other settings	5	5	5	10	5	30/50 (60%)
Acknowledgment of limitations/researcher bias	10	10	10	10	0	40/50 (80%)
Total points	72	89	78	85	81	405/500 (81%)

Summary Conclusions of Current Best Practices

Similarities and Differences

There is little agreement across all three perspectives regarding what would be considered best practices to involve parents in the provision of children's mental health services. This is likely due to the limited research base specific to this issue (Hoagwood, 2005). There are, however, six distinct practices identified by at least two of the three perspectives examined. Table 6.4 summarizes similarities and differences across the three perspectives.

Within the context of the consumer and professional perspectives, current best practices are identified. In addition, "recommended" practices are identified as well. These recommended practices are based on practices which consumers and professionals think might facilitate parental engagement in the provision of mental health services to children, or are interventions based on positive past experience(s) which involved parents in service provision. The purpose of this inclusion of "recommended" practices is to interface practices to which consumers and professionals would like to have access/utilize, with best practices identified by the research community.

The two most commonly cited practices across all three perspectives are the provision of culturally competent services (C2, C3, C4[R], P1[R], P3, P4, R1, R2, R3, and R4) and showing respect and concern to families (C1[R], C2, C3, P2, P3, P4, R1, R2, R3, and R4). The next most frequently cited practice is the provision of a general framework for the initial phone call/first session/ongoing sessions (P2, P3, P4, R1, R2, R3, and R4). Increasing consumer knowledge of resources and treatment options (including increasing knowledge of the educational system) follows (C1, C2, R3, R4, and R5). The facilitation of inter-agency collaboration (C2[R], C3, C4[R], P1[R], and P2) is cited four times. Finally, providing hope to parents that their family's situation can improve is also noted four times (C1, C2, P2, and P4).

There are several practices referred to in one of the perspectives, but not in the other two. Specifically, consumers articulate the need for support from other parents/consumers to help them navigate and be more effectively involved in the system (C1 and C2[R]), as well as having the opportunity to contribute to the design of the treatment utilized with their children (C2 and C4[R]). Consumer perspectives two and three also make reference to the importance of communication with service providers as a practice to more effectively involve them in the care of their children.

Practices cited only within the professional perspective include the need for administrative support and allowance of adequate time to involve parents in the treatment process (P1[R], P2, and P4), as well as the importance of identifying parent and family strengths (P1[R], P2, and P4). Finally, there are practices cited by one source, including building skills to work with multi-need families (P1[R]), addressing parental problems which may interfere with engagement (e.g., substance abuse, mental illness) (P4), and establishing therapist credibility as ways

Table 6.4 Summary of Best Practices across Consumer, Professional, and Research Perspectives

Best Practice	Consumer	Professional	Research
Inter-agency collaboration	2R,3,4R	1R,2	
Culturally competent services	2,3,4R	1R,3,4	1,2,3,4
Showing respect to/concern for families	1R,2,3	2,3,4	1,2,3,4
Increasing consumer knowledge of resources/treatment options (including educational system)	1,2		3,4,5
General framework of engagement/framework for 1st session/ongoing sessions		2,3,4	1,2,3,4
Developing consumer advocacy skills/increasing family self-efficacy/empowerment	1,2R		5
Providing/instilling "hope" for families	1,2	2,4	

Notes:
X=Current Best Practice
R=Recommended Best Practice (based on theory of what might work or positive past experience)

to effectively engage parents in the provision of mental health services to their children (P4).

Practices noted only in the research perspective, include the use of the initial phone call for services as a way to facilitate increased parent investment and involvement in their child's care (R1, R2, R4, and R5). In addition, immediately addressing concrete parental concerns is cited three times (R1, R3, and R4).

Summary of Best Practices

Through the inquiry outlined above, six practices were identified in response to the question, "What are the best practices to engage parents of children receiving mental health services?" These practices include: providing culturally competent services; showing respect and concern to parents; increasing consumer knowledge of resources and treatment options (including increasing knowledge of the educational system); utilizing a framework for the initial phone call/first session/ongoing sessions; facilitating inter-agency collaboration; and providing hope to parents that the problematic situation can improve.

Critique of Current Best Practices

"Potency Factor"—Quality of Sources, Agreement Across and Among Perspectives

In order to evaluate the credibility and validity of the identified best practices as objectively as possible, three criteria were utilized. These criteria included quality of sources for each perspective, level of agreement across perspectives, and level of agreement within perspectives. As discussed in the introductory paragraph of the Consumer Perspective and Professional Perspective sections of this chapter, all eight sources utilized are considered to be of high quality, as the "voice" of each source is clearly heard, a rigorous research design was utilized, and/or the particular model or paradigm has been the subject of significant practice utilization.

Table 6.3 outlines the relative quality of the five research articles. The scores rating the quality of the research articles range from 75 (R1) to 89 (R2). All five studies combined received a total score of 405 out of 500. Sample size received 50 out of 50 points and is the strongest criteria across studies, as all studies have a sample size greater than 100. Transferability of findings to other settings received 30 out of 50 points, the weakest of the criteria. The dynamic that restricts transferability is that much of the research base regarding parental engagement has been built with Latino and African American families living in urban areas with low socioeconomic status. Thus, the applicability of findings to rural families of other racial and ethnic backgrounds is yet to be understood. Perhaps another weakness of the research perspective that affects its potency is that three of the five research articles come from the same group (McKay et al.). This section may have been strengthened by a greater diversity of authors, however, McKay et al. present the most rigorously studied methods and most promising outcomes.

While the quality of sources included in the inquiry are relatively high and there is some well-established research (Cunningham & Henggeler, 1999; Liddle, 1995; Santisteban et al., 1996), the study of specific ways to engage parents in the provision of mental health services to their children is not particularly well developed, generally speaking (Hoagwood, 2005). Moreover, in reference to agreement across perspectives, the existing literature does not appear to have a consistent focus. It is important to note that there is not *disagreement*, per se, across perspectives, but the emphasis varies from author to author and group to group. For example, parents consistently voice that communication with service providers and support from other parents helps to engage them in service delivery. The research literature, on the other hand, emphasizes specific techniques and strategies to involve parents, which may or may not be consistent with these consumer wishes. Furthermore, despite the fact a particular research author does not explicitly state parents should be treated with respect while utilizing specific engagement techniques, it is reasonable to assume that the author would not *disagree* that this is an important practice that engenders parental engagement.

These inconsistencies impact the strength of the identified best practices in that there is only some consistency across, and even within, perspectives. Specifically, because of a lack of predictable focus within the consumer perspective, only one practice is identified by three sources (no practice was identified by all four), thus necessitating the consideration of practices cited by only two sources. For the purpose of consistency, all professional practices with only two citations were also considered. While all of these factors bring into question the overall quality of "best" practices identified in this inquiry, there is some agreement across and among perspectives (e.g., culturally competent care, showing respect and concern to families), and all these dynamics should be considered while bearing in mind the limited amount of research in this area (Hoagwood, 2005).

Value-Critical Analysis

The first value considered is that service provision occurs in a System of Care, a concept that stems from the Child and Adolescent Service System Program (CASSP) which is discussed in the introductory paragraph of this chapter. Briefly, service provision within a System of Care refers to service delivery occurring in the least restrictive environment, with a child-centered, family-focused priority. Furthermore, this model emphasizes coordination of services between agencies. Thus, the best practice of inter-agency collaboration is consistent with this value. It is also reasonable to assume that practices of treating consumers with respect and increasing their knowledge about treatment are consistent with the value of providing services within a System of Care (Stroul & Friedman, 2001).

The next value considered is Brofenbrenner's (1979) ecological understanding of functioning. Within this framework, Swick and Williams (2006) state that service providers should "consider the personal, cultural, and community-based elements of the families we are helping" (p. 376), consistent with the best practice of cultural competence. Furthermore, it can reasonably be assumed that the best practice of showing respect and concern to parents and families is demonstrated in avoiding categorizing and stereotyping families (Swick, 2004) and the best practice of increasing parent knowledge is demonstrated in Swick and Williams' (2006) example of educating parents about their children's school experience. Finally, while a generic framework to engage parents might not necessarily be ecological in nature, four frameworks (R1, R2, R3, and R4) utilized by the research perspective were specifically ecological.

In reference to family-centered care, Craft-Rosenberg et al. (2006) state, "There is little agreement in the literature as to when family-centered care began, in what field it developed, and even how to define it. There is consensus however, that it developed concurrently in several fields, from several legal mandates, and with consumer activism as a driving force" (p. 18). These authors cite mutual trust, shared decision making, reciprocal relationships, facilitation of family participation in service, strengths-based practice, interdisciplinary team work, and cultural competence as components of family-centered care. Therefore, the best practices of culturally competent care, showing respect and concern, increasing parent knowledge of resources and treatment options, and inter-agency collaboration would all be commensurate with the value of family-centered care.

A strengths-based approach to service provision assumes that all consumers have positive capabilities, the capacity for success, and that while illness and struggle may be injurious, they can also be a source of opportunity. This perspective includes a sensitivity to cultural factors, is based on treating consumers with respect, and provides them with information about community resources (Saleebey, 2002). Furthermore, a concept fundamental to the Strengths Perspective is empowerment. According to Saleebey (2002), empowerment "indicates the intent to, and the process of, assisting individuals, groups, families, and communities to discover and expend the resources and tools within and around them" (p. 9). As illustrated above, several best practices identified in this inquiry are consistent with the conceptualization of the Strengths Perspective (and the concept of empowerment). These include a respect for diversity (cultural competence), an emphasis on treating consumers with respect, and the provision of information about services and resources, as well as service providers engendering a sense of hope and optimism.

Three of four practice perspectives place emphasis on identification of parent and family strengths (P1[R], P2, and P4). Four of the five frameworks utilized by the research perspectives (R1, R2, R3, and R4) were ecological in nature, but not specifically strengths oriented, and one (R2) came from a strategic orientation. Therefore, one recommendation could be that research conducted in this area could place greater emphasis on understanding the role that identifying parent strengths plays in the engagement process.

Petr and Walter (2005) also cite the importance of the values service affordability and accessibility, as well as service provider accountability. In reference to the relationship between affordability for the agency and its impact on accessibility, three frameworks for service provision are quite expensive (P2, P3, and R2), while the cost of the model of McKay et al. (R1, R3, and R4) is unclear. Thus, a gap in knowledge and practice may be one of cost/benefit. How much does it cost to staff and train positions to facilitate a relatively simple engagement protocol similar to McKay et al.? Is it cost effective? What impact does the high price tag which agencies must pay to utilize the models of (P2) Liddle (1995), (P3) Cunningham and Henggeler (1999), and (R2) Santisteban et al. (1996) have on accessibility? For example, Leschied (2002) notes that groups wishing to utilize MST (Cunningham & Henggeler, 1999) must pay a yearly licensing fee of $6,000, complete the 5-day MST training at a cost of $750 per therapist plus travel and expenses for the trainer, pay $1,500 per month for an MST consultant to provide weekly supervision; and provide for the MST consultant's travel and expenses to facilitate the quarterly booster sessions, amounting to approximately $10,000 per year. The other four practices identified by this inquiry are conceptual in nature and cost does not to appear to be a barrier to utilization.

Speaking strictly about accessibility, the practices of culturally competent care, showing families respect and concern, and increasing parent knowledge of resources and treatment options can all potentially enhance consumer accessibility to services. Consumer and professional literature also purport that the practice of inter-agency collaboration facilitates service accessibility (C2[R], C3, C4[R], P1[R], and P2). Finally, a clear framework guiding service provision could potentially enhance accountability, as this would provide a standard to which service providers could be held.

All of the best practices identified in this inquiry are components of or consistent with the Social Work Code of Ethics. The provision of culturally competent care is a clear ethical standard (section 1.05), and showing consumers respect is third of six guiding ethical principles. Increasing consumer knowledge of resources and treatment options facilitates the operationalization of self-determination, a core social work ethical standard. The use of a framework to guide service provision could contribute to competent service provision, both an ethical principle and a standard (section 1.04). Finally, interdisciplinary collaboration is cited as an ethical responsibility that social workers are obligated to uphold (section 2.03) (NASW, 1999).

In summary, within a value-based context, the identified best practices to engage parents of children receiving mental health services are generally consistent with a System of Care and family-centered service provision model. The best practices also reflect an ecological understanding of families and are consistent with the NASW Code of Ethics. While the specific practices are commensurate with a strengths perspective, the research base contributing to the identification of best practices is lacking in this regard. Finally, in reference to affordability, the cost/benefit of these particular practices is unexplored at this point.

Recommendations

As discussed in the "Potency" section of this chapter, there is a lack of focus among perspectives (four consumer articles identified 13 practices, four professional articles identified 11 practices, and five research articles identified nine practices) and across perspectives (all three perspectives identified 24 practices, including duplication). There is, however, agreement that parents should be involved in services and suggested practices used to facilitate this process are not contra-indicated to one another. Within this context, as well as that of a relatively limited understanding of any of the three perspectives, the first recommendation is that further study be undertaken to better understand the needs of all three perspectives. A more significant level of agreement will be possible only when the research base is adequate enough to potentially produce a greater amount of consistency.

One weakness of the research base that was reflected in the articles' respective research scores is that most work has been done with Latino and African American families in inner-city areas. Ways in which to facilitate the engagement of parents from other racial and ethnic groups, as well as parents from rural areas, is not yet understood. Therefore, the potency of this area of inquiry could be strengthened considerably by better understanding the needs of consumers and parents that have not been the subject of inquiry, and incorporating these perspectives in program design and evaluation.

Bearing in mind the value-critical analysis, there are at least three recom-mendations that could enhance currently identified best practices. First, there is not a consistent emphasis on identifying parent and child strengths in the engagement process. It has been documented that this can be an essential part of the helping process when working with families (Early & Linnea, 2000; Werrbach, 1996). Simple steps could be taken in the engagement process to utilize specific strengths-based questions such as, "What is one thing that is going well in your family?" or "When things were going better in your family, what was different?" (Saleebey, 2002).

Within the context of family strengths, the best practice of providing hope to parents that the problematic situation with their child can be improved, could also be more clearly operationalized. Saleebey (2002) states, "Often forgotten, but truly important in promoting beneficial change are hope (and) positive expectations" (p. 81). The concept of hope seems to be a rather nebulous concept which could benefit from being more clearly elucidated, perhaps via strengths-based inquiries such as, "What are your hopes for your child and your family?" or "Tell me about a time when you were optimistic about your child's and family's future."

In reference to accessibility and agency affordability, three models (Cunningham & Henggeler, 1999; Liddle, 1995; Santisteban et al., 1996) appear to have more limited accessibility because of cost of agency utilization (Leschied, 2002; Szapocznik, 1999). The cost of McKay et al.'s models was not discussed; however, it appears as if a similar model using components consistent with those discussed could be implemented at most any Community Mental Health Center. Therefore, a way in which best practices could be improved is to more clearly articulate program cost and how that impacts family accessibility. Moreover, improvement could also be facilitated in this area by an increased emphasis on the development of effective no or low-cost models to facilitate parental engagement in children's mental health services.

Within the context of what is already known about the three perspectives, improvement could be made by incorporating all of the identified best practices together, as well as including the recommendations for enhancements. In doing so, this would provide a model based on current best practices which could then be evaluated and continually developed. For example, consistent with the work of McKay et al. (2004), a clear model for the initial phone call, as well as the intake session, could be designed. In this model, parents would be encouraged to share their experience of their child's mental health difficulties; problem-solving around barriers to service delivery would be facilitated; knowledge about the treatment process, options for care, and community resources would be shared in a clear, respectful, and culturally sensitive manner; and inter-agency collaboration would be facilitated. An emphasis on parent and child strengths, as well as an optimistic service provider attitude, would be included throughout the process. Finally, development of this model in a rural setting would be valuable, as this is one area of research that appears to be non-existent.

References

Brofenbrenner, U. (1979). *Ecology of human development.* Cambridge, MA: Harvard University Press.

Coatsworth, J.D., Santisteban, D.A., McBride, C.K., & Szapocznik, J. (2001). Brief strategic family therapy versus community control: Engagement, retention, and an exploration of the moderating role of adolescent symptom severity. *Family Process, 40*(3), 313–332.

Craft-Rosenberg, M., Kelley, P., & Schnoll, L. (2006). Family-centered care: Practice and preparation. *Families in Society, 87* (1), 17–28.

Cunningham, P.E., & Henggeler, S.W. (1999). Engaging multiproblem families in treatment: Lessons learned through the development of multisystemic therapy. *Family Process, 38*(3), 265–281.

Davis, A., & Vander Stoep, A. (1997). The transition to adulthood for youth who have serious emotional disturbance: Developmental transition and young adult outcomes. *Journal of Mental Health Administration, 24*(4), 400–427.

Ditrano, C.J., & Silverstein, L.B. (2006). Listening to parents' voices: Participatory action research in the schools. *Professional Psychology: Research and Practice, 37*(4), 359–366.

Duchnowski, A.J., Hall, K.S., Kutash, K., & Friedman, R.M. (1998). The alternatives to residential treatment study. In M.H. Epstein, K. Kutash, & A. Duchnowski (Eds.), *Outcomes for children and youth with behavioral and emotional disorders and their families: programs, evaluation, and best practices* (pp. 55–80). Austin, TX: Pro-Ed.

Duchnowski, A.J., Kutash, K., & Friedman, R.M. (2002). Community-based interventions in a system of care and outcomes framework. In B.J. Burns & K. Hoagwood (Eds.), *Community Treatment for Youth* (pp. 16–37). New York: Oxford University Press.

Early, T., & Linnea, G.F. (2000). Valuing families: Social work practice with families from a strengths perspective. *Social Work, 45*(2), 118–131.

Elliot, D.J., Koroloff, N.M., Doren, P.E., & Friesen, B.J. (1998). Improving access to children's health services: The family associate approach. In M.H. Epstein, K. Kutash, & A. Duchnowski (Eds.), *Outcomes for children and youth with behavioral and emotional disorders and their families* (pp. 581–610). Austin, TX: Pro-Ed.

Henggeler, S.W., Bourdin, C.M., Melton, G.B., Mann, B.J., Smith, L.A., et al. (1991). Effects of multisystemic therapy on drug use and abuse in serious juvenile offenders: A progress report from two outcome studies. *Family Dynamics of Addiction Quarterly, 1*(3), 40–51.

Henggeler, S.W., Melton, G.B., Smith, L.A., Schoenwald, S.K., & Hanley, J.H. (1993). Family preservation using multisystemic treatment: Long-term follow-up to a clinical trial with serious juvenile offenders. *Journal of Child and Family Studies, 2*, 283–293.

Hoagwood, K.E. (2005). Family-based services in children's mental health: A research review and synthesis. *Journal of Child Psychology and Psychiatry, 46*(7), 690–713.

Hogue, A., Liddle, H.A., Dauber, S., & Samuolis, J. (2004). Linking session focus to treatment outcome in evidence-based treatment for adolescent substance abuse. *Psychotherapy: Theory, Research, Practice, Training, 41*(2), 83–96.

Kazdin, A.E. (2000). *Psychotherapy for children and adolescents*. New York: Oxford University Press.

Kruzich, J.M., Jivanjee, P., Robinson, A., & Friesen, B.J. (2003). Family caregivers' perceptions of barriers to and supports of participation in their children's out of home placement. *Psychiatric Services, 54*(11), 1513–1518.

Kuperminc, G., & Cohen, R. (1995). Building a research base for community services for children and families: What we know and what we need to learn. *Journal of Child and Family Studies, 4*(2), 147–175.

Leschied, A. (2002). Randomized study of MST in Ontario, Canada. Retrieved February 14, 2007, from www.lfcc.on.ca/MST5_MSToversight.pdf.

Liddle, H.A. (1995). Conceptual and clinical dimensions of a multidimensional multi-systems engagement strategy in family-based adolescent treatment. *Psychotherapy, 32*, 39–58.

Liddle, H.A., Dakof, G.A., Parker, K., Diamond, G.S., Barrett, K., & Tejeda, M. (2001). Multidimensional family therapy for adolescent drug abuse: Results of a randomized clinical trial. *American Journal of Drug and Alcohol Abuse, 27*(4), 651–688.

Lourie, I.S., Stroul, B.A., & Friedman, R.M. (1998). Community-based systems of care: From advocacy to outcomes. In M.H. Epstein, K. Kutash, & A. Duchnowski (Eds.), *Outcomes for children and youth with behavioral and emotional disorders and their families* (pp. 81–114). Austin, TX: Pro-Ed.

Lyness, K.P., Walsh, S.R., & Sprenkle, D.H. (2005). Clinical trials in marriage and family therapy research. In D.H. Sprenkle & F.P. Piercy (Eds.), *Research methods in family therapy* (pp. 297–317). New York: The Guilford Press.

Mann, B.J., Bourdin, C.M., Henggeler, S.W., & Blaske, D.M. (1990). An investigation of systemic conceptualizations of parent-child coalitions and symptom change. *Journal of Consulting and Clinical Psychology, 58*, 336–344.

McKay, M.M., Hibbert, R., Hoagwood, K., Rodriguez, J., Murray, L., Legerski, J., & Fernandez, D. (2004). Integrating evidence-based engagement interventions into "real world" child mental health settings. *Brief Treatment and Crisis Intervention, 4*(2), 177–187.

McKay, M.M., McCadam, K., & Gonzalez, J. (1996a). Addressing the barriers to mental health services for inner city children and their caretakers. *Community Mental Health Journal, 32*, 353–361.

McKay, M.M., Nudelman, R., McCadam, K., & Gonzales, J. (1996b). Evaluating a social work engagement approach to involving inner-city children and their families in mental health care. *Research on Social Work Practice, 6*, 462–472.

McKay, M.M., Stowe, J., McCadam, K., & Gonzalez, J. (1998). Increasing access to child mental health services for urban children and their caregivers. *Health and Social Work, 23*(1), 6–16.

National Association of Social Workers. (1999). Code of Ethics. Retrieved October 24, 2006, from www.socialworkers.org/pubs/code/code.asp.

Petr, C.G., & Barney, D.D. (1993). Reasonable efforts for children with disabilities: The parents' perspective. *Social Work, 38*(3), 247–254.

Petr, C.G., & Walter, U.M. (2005). Best practices inquiry: A multidimensional, value-critical framework. *Journal of Social Work Education, 41*(2), 251–267.

Pires, S.A., & Stroul, B.A. (1996). Family issues in health care reform. In C.A. Heflinger and C.T. Nixon (Eds.), *Families and The Mental Health System for Children and Adolescents* (pp. 1–17). Thousand Oaks, CA: Sage.

Quinn, K.P., & Epstein, M.H. (1998). Characteristics of children, youth, and families served by local interagency systems of care. In M.H. Epstein, K. Kutash, & A. Duchnowski (Eds.), *Outcomes for children and youth with behavioral and emotional disorders and their families* (pp. 81–114). Austin, TX: Pro-Ed.

Saleebey, D. (2002). *The strengths perspective in social work practice.* Boston, MA: Allyn and Bacon.

Santisteban, D.A., & Szapocznik, J. (1994). Bridging theory, research, and practice to more successfully engage substance abusing youth and their families into therapy. *Journal of Child & Adolescent Substance Abuse, 3*(2), 9–23.

Santisteban, D.A., Szapocznik, J., Perez-Vidal, A., Kurtines, W.M., Murray, E.J., & Perriere, A. (1996). Efficacy of intervention for engaging youth and families into treatment and some variables that may contribute to differential effectiveness. *Journal of Family Psychology, 10*(1), 35–44.

Schmidt, S.E., Liddle, H.A., & Dakof, G.A. (1996). Changes in parenting practices and adolescent drug abuse during multidimensional family therapy. *Journal of Family Psychology, 10*, 12–27.

Schoenwald, S.K., & Hoagwood, K. (2001). Effectiveness, transportability, and dissemination of interventions: What matters when? *Psychiatric Services, 52*(9), 1190–1197.

Schoenwald, S.K., Sheidow, A.J., & Letourneau, E.J. (2004). Toward effective quality assurance in evidence-based practice: Links between expert consultation, therapist fidelity, and child outcomes. *Journal of Clinical and Adolescent Psychology, 33*(1), 94–104.

Spencer, S., & Powell, J.Y. (2000). Family-centered practice in residential treatment settings: A parent's perspective. *Residential Treatment for Children & Youth, 17*(3), 33–43.

Stroul, B.A., & Friedman, R.M. (2001). The system of care concept and philosophy. In B.A. Stroul (Ed.), *Children's mental health: Creating systems of care in a changing society*. Baltimore, MD: Paul H. Brookes.

Substance Abuse and Mental Health Services Administration (SAMHSA). (2005). Center for mental health services uniform reporting system output tables. Retrieved September 23, 2006, from www.mentalhealth.samhsa.gov/cmhs/MentalHealthStatistics/URS 2004.asp.

Swick, K.W. (2004). *Empowering parents, families, schools and communities during the early childhood years*. Champaign, IL: Stipes.

Swick, K.W., & Williams, R.D. (2006). An analysis of Brofenbrenner's bio-ecological perspective for early childhood educators: Implications for working with families experiencing stress. *Early Childhood Education Journal, 33*(5), 371–378.

Szapocznik, J. (1999). *Brief strategic family therapy*. Retrieved September 8, 2005, from www.strengtheningfamilies.org/html/programs_1999/09_BSFT.html.

Szapocznik, J., Perez-Vidal, A., Brickman, A.L., Foote, F.H., Santisteban, D., Hervis, O., & Kurtines, W.M. (1988). Engaging adolescent drug abusers and their families in treatment: A strategic structural systems approach. *Journal of Consulting and Clinical Psychology, 56*(4), 552–557.

Waldron, H.B., Slesnick, N., Brody, J.L., Turner, C.W, & Peterson, T.R. (2001). Treatment outcomes for adolescent substance abuse at 4 and 7-month assessments. *Journal of Consulting and Clinical Psychology, 69*(5), 802–813.

Werrbach, G.B. (1996). Family-strengths-based intensive child case management. *Families in Society, 77*(4), 216–226.

Williams Adams, R. (2006, January 15). Better youth mental health care sought: Summit hears that many parents across Florida are facing similar challenges. *The Ledger* (Lakeland, FL)., p. B1.

7 Best Practices for Improving Levels of Functioning and Subsequent Discharge to Less Restrictive Environments for Children and Youth in Therapeutic Foster Care

Uta M. Walter

This inquiry identified two sets of practices that research, professional, and consumer sources considered "best" in Therapeutic Foster Care (TFC). The first set revolves around connecting to, involving, and supporting biological families; the second set focuses on TFC provider families to communicate clearly with agency staff and families, and to receive systematic support and training. While TFC overall can be considered an effective practice, current knowledge is still limited because of a lack of strong and consistent agreement within and across perspectives. For instance, the emphasis consumers and professionals put on relational practices, such as positive relationships between parties, or good communication, still awaits attention from researchers. In light of a value-critical analysis, suggestions are offered to further improve TFC practices by making them more family centered.

Overview: Children and Youth in Therapeutic Foster Care

In the past decades, Therapeutic Foster Care (TFC), which is also referred to as "treatment foster care," "family-based treatment," or "specialized foster care" (Hudson, Nutter, & Galaway, 1994a, 1994b), has gained empirical and conceptual support as a family-based alternative to residential group treatment for children and youth with serious emotional and behavioral difficulties (James & Meezan, 2002). With historical roots in three discrete service fields, namely child welfare, juvenile justice, and mental health (Dore & Mullin, 2006), TFC programs vary highly in characteristics and structures and there are no nationally binding definitions for therapeutic foster care (James & Meezan, 2002).

Nonetheless, TFC programs typically share a number of characteristics that set them apart from regular foster care and residential treatment (Bates, English, & Kouidou-Giles, 1997; Dore & Mullin, 2006; Hudson et al., 1994b). These include: 1) care is provided within a family setting and in the home of the foster care provider; 2) the program targets children with specials needs such as having a "serious emotional disorder" (SED) who would otherwise be placed in more restrictive settings; 3) the program has a philosophy that emphasizes community linkages, coordinated services, and individualized plans for treatment and education; 4) providers are specifically selected and trained to care for children and youth with special needs; 5) providers care for a limited number of foster children at a time and receive higher levels of ongoing support, consultation, crisis intervention, and supervision from professionals; 6) caseworkers carry a limited caseload; 7) and provider families receive higher reimbursement rates than general foster families.

Approximately 11% of all children with SED in out-of-home care live in Therapeutic Foster Care (James & Meezan, 2002). While not all youth served in TFC are formally classified as having a "serious emotional disorder", TFC programs serve a variety of special needs populations with SED characteristics including juvenile offenders (Chamberlain & Moore, 1998; Chamberlain & Reid, 1994, 1998), children and youth in child welfare, especially those with externalizing behavior disorders (Meadowcroft, Thomlison, & Chamberlain, 1994; Reddy & Pfeiffer, 1997; Smith, Stormshak, Chamberlain, & Whaley, 2001), and youth leaving psychiatric hospitals (Chamberlain & Reid, 1991). Young people in TFC are predominantly male Caucasian adolescents in either parental or state custody, who primarily exhibit disruptive behavior problems and diagnoses such as ADHD and conduct disorders (Hudson et al., 1994a; James & Meezan, 2002). Many children, especially girls, arrive at TFC programs with a significant history of trauma such as neglect, physical and sexual abuse, and after a series of previous out-of-home placements which often exacerbated their symptoms (Hussey & Guo, 2005).

As they enter into adulthood, failure to successfully assist young people with SED comes at a high human and fiscal cost (Geller & Biebel, 2006; Wagner, 1995). Poor long-term outcomes for youth with SED are well documented in the literature and include high dropout and unemployment rates, high incidence of engagement in illegal or high-risk behaviors including substance abuse, a lack of ability to function independently as adults, increased risk for homelessness, and for early pregnancy (Armstrong, Dedrick, & Greenbaum, 2003; Davis, 2003; Davis, Banks, Fisher, & Grudzinskas, 2004; Malloy, Cheney, & Cormier, 1998; Yampolskaya, Brown, & Greenbaum, 2002). Key resiliency factors associated with better long-term outcomes for SED are positive parent–child relations, higher levels of current family support, contact with prosocial peers, higher reading levels, good problem-solving abilities, and good social skills (Armstrong et al., 2003; Vance, Bowen, Fernandez, & Thompson, 2002).

TFC programs are designed to provide safe, stable, and therapeutic family environments with the goal of improving youths' behavioral, social, and emotional functioning to the point where they can move to less restrictive placements in the community, preferably, to the child's biological family[1] (Redding, Fried, & Britner, 2000). On the continuum of care, TFC is considered the least restrictive form of out-of-home therapeutic placements for children with SED (Dore &

Mullin, 2006; U.S. Department of Health and Human Services, 1999) and functions both as a step-down placement for children and youth leaving more restrictive out-of-home settings such as juvenile justice centers or psychiatric hospitals, or as a step-up for those deemed too impaired to be served effectively in general foster care (Baker & Curtis, 2006; Reddy & Pfeiffer, 1997).

The most commonly measured outcomes in TFC revolve around improvement of children's behavioral functioning. The next frequent measures are indicators of program success, such as planned discharge status, placement stability, and restrictiveness of living arrangement following TFC (James & Meezan, 2002). The following review focuses on best practices for youth in TFC to improve their functioning and subsequently lead to a discharge to less restrictive environments, typically their families. The question is: What are the best practices for children and youth in Therapeutic Foster Care to improve levels of functioning and subsequent discharge to less restrictive environments?

Best Practices Inquiry Search Process

Using key words of "therapeutic foster care," "treatment foster care," "specialized foster care," and "foster family based treatment," national literature databases (PsycInfo, PubMed, Social Work Abstracts, and Social Services Abstracts) and the internet were searched for documents published since 1993. Additional articles were identified through a review of reference lists.

Generally, sources were included for review if they provided views and knowledge pertinent to the question, and were deemed credible, authentic, and trustworthy through publication in peer-reviewed journals or on websites of nationally recognized organizations. Preference was granted to sources that represent knowledge about practices as actually delivered, rather than aspired practices only.

The perspective of consumers was informed by empirical studies involving consumer families as well as by internet resources of organizations representing the views of youth with SED and their families, such as the Federation of Families for Children's Mental Health. The professional perspective was illuminated by systematic reviews and studies about views and experiences of TFC providers published in peer-reviewed journals, as well as by materials published by professional organizations, such as the Foster-Family Based Treatment Association (FFTA). Finally, the research perspective was informed by searching for empirical studies, including meta-analyses, on the effects of TFC programs on functioning, placement stability, and discharge to less restrictive environments. To identify best practices, a systematic analysis of contents identified those practices deemed important by a majority of sources first within and then across perspectives.

Results of Best Practices Inquiry: Three Perspectives

The Consumer Perspective: Sources

For this review, "consumers of TFC" were defined as youth served in TFC, as well as their primary caregivers, typically their biological families. Evidence suggests that TFC children resemble peers in residential care more than their counterparts in general foster care. While not identical to youth in residential care (Drais-Parillo, not dated), they share histories of complex and unstable multiple placements, and significant impairments in the education domain (James & Meezan, 2002; Hudson et al., 1994b). Thus the inclusion of insights from consumers of residential care seemed warranted to expand the otherwise limited number of consumer sources on TFC. Also included are publications furnished by nationally recognized advocacy groups, such as the Federation of Families for Children's Mental Health, a consumer-run national organization. Highest rated were those sources which 1) reflected the voice of consumers, 2) spoke to the questions at hand, 3) came from a reputable source that bears some influence on mental health programming, 4) indicated a systematic form of gathering and presenting relevant knowledge (in case of empirical studies appropriately documented methodology and limitations of a study), and 5) identified specific practices.

The highest rated source is a qualitative study by Jivanjee (1999a, C1) who asked ten biological families of children about their experience of being involved in the process of Multidimensional Treatment Foster Care (MTFC), a TFC model developed by the Oregon Social Learning Center. (A related study by the same author involved interviews with TFC families and staff and is reviewed later under Professional Perspective.) Participating families were invited by caseworkers and were at least somewhat involved in the TFC program. The sample thus does not reflect the opinions of parents who remained entirely uninvolved. Participants included a wide range of parents such as with and without custody of their child, as well as with and without reunification as an identified treatment goal.

A study by Kruzich, Jivanjee, Robinson and Friesen (2003, C2) surveyed 102 family caregivers from 31 states whose children were in a residential treatment center, psychiatric unit, or group home asking about their participation in treatment, barriers and supports to their participation, and their relative satisfaction. Though not specific to TFC, a number of these families may very well be involved with TFC as a step-down placement for their children at a later point in time. Thus their ideas about preferred professional practices can also be valuable for TFC practitioners. The vast majority of respondents to the questionnaire were biological mothers of Caucasian youth placed in residential treatment centers. The study is limited by a sampling procedure that involved only caregivers who were on the mailing lists of family organizations. Participants were ethnically more homogeneous than the general population under study, better educated, and likely to be more engaged in advocacy for their rights to be involved in treatment. Probably drawing on the same data, and thus importing the same limitations, is a later publication examining the experiences of 102 families about parent–child contact in relation to national accreditation standards in mental health, and child welfare systems (Robinson, Kruzich, Friesen, Jivanjee, & Pullmann, 2005, C3).

As part of a literature review, Redding et al. (2000, C4) examined existing studies for factors associated with higher placement stability and higher child and family satisfaction in TFC. The authors do not indicate inclusion/exclusion criteria for their review.

Finally, a fact sheet put forth by the Federation of Families for Children's Mental Health (FFCMH) (1992, C5) outlines general principles and supports to enhance family involvement in the out-of-home treatment so that children can eventually return home. These guidelines point to practices recommended but not necessarily implemented in practice.

Consumer Perspective: Results

A majority of consumer sources (endorsed by at least three of the five sources) suggests that families find the following practices particularly important: involvement in planning and decisions regarding their child's placement and treatment; frequent contacts with their child, including phone contacts and visits; flexible schedules for meetings with staff and for contacts/visits with the child; practices enhancing positive relationship with TFC providers/agency staff, for instance frequent, clear, and open communication and sharing of information, receiving support and advocacy, and positive staff attitudes toward families, and encouragement to participate; clear communication and coordination between staff/agencies; and assistance with transportation. (See also Table 7.1.)

The Professional Perspective: Sources

Sources for the perspectives of professionals include published empirical studies exploring the experiences of TFC provider families, and/or TFC program staff, as well as TFC standards put forth by the Foster-Family Based Treatment Association (FFTA), and studies specifically related to those standards. Highest rated were those sources which 1) reflected the voice of practitioners, 2) spoke directly to the questions at hand, and 3) in case of empirical work appropriately documented methodology and practices.

The Foster-Family Based Treatment Association (FFTA) (1995, P1) is the main guiding professional association in TFC consisting of more than 300 mostly private, nonprofit TFC provider agencies and programs. FFTA has issued program standards and guidelines for the provision and administration of TFC currently used in over 20 states in the U.S. and in several Canadian provinces (Hudson et al., 1994a). FFTA program standards encompass three main domains: the program, treatment parents, and children, youth and their families (Hudson et al., 1994a; Farmer, Burns, Dubs, & Thompson, 2002). For each domain, the standards specify certain criteria to be met.

A secondary analysis of data from 210 TFC programs in the U.S. and Canada (Galaway, Nutter, & Hudson, 1995, P2), who subscribe to FFTA standards, found

Table 7.1 Overview of Practices in TFC from a Consumer Perspective

Practices	C1	C2	C3	C4	C5
Involvement in decisions re. child's placement and treatment*	X	X	X	X	X
Frequent contacts with child*	X	X	X	X	
Flexibility in meeting/visit schedules*	X	X		X	X
Positive relationship with TFC provider/agency staff*	X	X		X	X
Frequent, clear, and open communication and sharing of information*	X	X		X	X
Receiving support and advocacy*	X	X			X
Positive staff attitudes toward families: encouragement to participate*	X	X			X
Assistance with transportation*	X	X			X
Communication and coordination between TFC providers, staff/agencies*	X	X			X
Time to get to know/build trust	X				
Opportunities for education, learning strategies etc.	X				X
Close geographic distance from provider		X			
Supports offered after treatment/attention to transitional needs	X				X
Cultural competency/sensitivity		X			X

Note:
*=Qualified for best practice from this perspective

no clear correlations between program characteristics and discharge outcomes that would clearly support the importance of FFTA standards. The study did not assess youths' level of functioning directly but measured only if discharges were planned or unplanned.

A study by Farmer et al. (2002, P3) found that actual conformity with FFTA standards varied widely. The study involved TFC programs in only one state and assessed conformity with a selected number of FFTA standards. Program standards seemed best met in programs where supervisors oversaw no more than five caseworkers, who in turn supervised no more than eight foster parents. Most agencies provided 24/7 support for parents, 87% of supervisors provided similar support for caseworkers, and in 55% of programs caseworkers made contacts with foster parents at least once a week.

Three qualitative studies examined the perspectives and experiences of TFC agency practitioners and foster families, respectively. Wells and D'Angelo (1994, P4) conducted focus groups with 40 foster parents who described their experiences with children entering into their family, issues arising during their placement, and challenges when children left the home. Findings highlight the complex and multifaceted nature of the work but are not particularly specific to the question posed for this review.

As part of a larger study, Wells, Farmer, Richards and Burns (2004, P5) conducted a qualitative inquiry into the experience of being a treatment foster mother using an inductive iterative method (five minutes of free speech) with 43 TFC mothers caring for an adolescent. Though the unstructured method and short interview time poses limits to insights, the sample was quite diverse. Because mothers expressed their experience and role in highly relational terms rather than in terms of methods and strategies, authors suggests that the concept of "therapeutic alliance" be afforded more attention to guide research and practice in TFC.

Finally, a study by Jivanjee (1999b, P6) is related to the Multidimensional Treatment Foster Care (MTFC) model, and specifically explored the involvement of biological families in TFC. To this end, the author conducted interviews with 12 TFC provider families and 12 professionals in an MTFC program for children referred from child welfare agencies. (A related study by the same author explored the views of biological families and is included in the earlier Consumer Perspective.) The study provides an in-depth exploration of practices in MTFC and found that providers and professionals shared values and attitudes that were generally supportive of family involvement. Actual concrete actions toward such involvement, however, were tempered by sympathies or antipathies toward given families, and thus varied highly from case to case.

Professional Perspective: Results

Overall, at least three of the six professional sources endorse the following practices: low caseloads, ongoing training for TFC parents; provision of detailed, clear, and complete information in preparation for placement and efforts to match children to foster families; reliable and regular flow of information between agency staff (e.g. caseworkers) and TFC families, and inclusion of TFC families as treatment team members; involvement of biological family in planning, decision-making, and facilitating contacts between child and biological parents by fostering positive relationships with biological families and addressing organizational barriers to such involvement. FFTA standards represent aspired practices but are not reliably implemented, making it difficult to discern if they bear direct relationship to better outcomes. (See also Table 7.2.)

The Research Perspective: Sources

Criteria for evaluating qualitative and quantitative studies included the extent to which a study contributed knowledge to answer the question posed for this review, the level of theoretical and conceptual grounding of the study as indicated in the literature review and/or the described interventions, the appropriateness of the research design and the quality of data collection procedures, the size and quality of the sample accessed for the study, the appropriateness of data analyses, the clarity and specificity with which interventions are described, and the significance or trustworthiness of the findings. (Table 7.3 summarizes the quality rating of each individual study.)

Table 7.2 Overview of Practices in TFC from a Professional Perspective

Practices	P1	P2	P3	P4	P5	P6
Low caseloads*	X	X	X			
Pre-placement: detailed, clear, and complete information in preparation for placement; matching children to foster families*	X		X	X		
During placement: being informed by staff, frequent contact between agency staff (caseworker) and TFC family; TFC being included as treatment team member*	X			X		X
Involvement of biological family*: in planning and decision-making, through facilitating contacts between child and parents and a positive relationship with biological families	X			X		X
Ongoing in-service training for TFC parents*	X		X			X
Staff training and supervision	X		X			
Recruiting of TFC parents (stability, values/attitudes)	X					X
Pre-service training	X					
Clear goals, transition, discharge and permanency planning, regular reviews of plans	X		X			
Emotional and practical supports, access to resources for TFC parents and caseworkers	X			X		
Positive stance, attitude, and relationship with youth				X	X	

Note:
*=Qualified for best practice from this perspective

Utilizing similar quality criteria as indicated earlier, Reddy and Pfeiffer (1997, R1) conducted a meta-analysis of 40 outcome studies on TFC. (Studies that were part of this meta-analysis were excluded from further review of individual studies below.) The authors concluded that, by and large, children completed TFC as planned and responded favorably. Since too few studies included necessary statistical data to calculate effect sizes, the authors used the Weighted Predictive Value (WPV) procedure to pool results across studies. To this end they applied the comparatively crude measure of "positive," "negative," or "indifferent" outcomes for the areas of placement permanency, behavior problems, restrictiveness of placement at discharge, social skills and psychological adjustment. Intervention, or best practices, components identified in the meta-analysis were limited to provision of individual therapy, family therapy for biological and/or TFC families, group therapy, and consultations with schools or home.

The largest positive effect of TFC was noted for placement permanency and social skills, and medium-size positive effects on the reduction of behavior problems, a decreased level of restrictiveness in placement, and increased psychological adjustment. However, these results are neither uniformly positive nor particularly strong. Authors found their analysis hampered by the lack of methodological rigor in studies (such as small nonrandomized samples, lack

Table 7.3 Summary of Individual Studies' Quality

Criteria (points possible)	R1[1]	R2	R3	R4	R5	R6	R7	R8	Total
Contributes relevant knowledge for the topic and question *(15)*		15	15	10	8	9	12	12	*81 (77%)*
Theoretical/conceptual grounding (10)		10	8	10	8	8	8	4	*56 (80%)*
Research design *(15)*		15	15	15	9	5	0	8	*67 (64%)*
Data collection *(10)*		6	6	6	8	3	0	6	*35 (50%)*
Sample *(10)*		6	6	8	7	3	0	9	*39 (56%)*
Data analysis *(10)*		9	9	10	7	5	0	5	*45 (64%)*
Specificity of intervention description *(15)*		15	10	15	15	8	12	0	*75 (71%)*
Significance of results (15)		13	13	13	10	10	9	8	*76 (72%)*
Total Points (100)		*89*	*82*	*87*	*72*	*51*	*41*	*52*	

Note:
[1] R1 was a meta-analysis and is thus not included in this table.

of control or comparison groups), a lack of longitudinal follow-up data, and too little information about providers and interventions.

Since Reddy and Pfeiffer's meta-analysis, several studies have been published that are methodologically stronger and provide clearer results as to the specific practices supporting TFC outcomes. The strongest empirical support for TFC is associated with experimental studies of the Multidimensional Treatment Foster Care (MTFC) model. Originally designed for juvenile offenders, program practices are described in detail in several publications (Chamberlain, 2003; Fisher & Chamberlain, 2000; Fisher, Ellis, & Chamberlain, 1999; Smith, 2004). A total of four articles about the model are included in the research perspective.

Two articles are based on the same study of MTFC and describe outcomes of an experimental five-year study involving 79 (n) randomly assigned male juvenile offenders (Chamberlain & Moore, 1998, R2; Chamberlain & Reid, 1998, R3). While the sample is only of medium size, the study underlying both articles is methodologically sound, and found the model to be a successful, less-costly alternative to residential group placements. One year after measuring baseline data, participants in TFC had significantly fewer arrests than their counterparts in group homes, higher program completion rates, fewer incidents of running away, fewer days in lock-up settings, and higher number of days living with parents or other relatives.

A third relatively strong experimental study of the MTFC model (Smith, 2004, R4) involved 62 delinquent boys and girls randomly assigned to TFC and specifically analyzed gender differences in the likelihood of re-offending 12 months after treatment. Results found the model similarly successful for boys and girls as long as they completed treatment. Yet, about one-third of youth (30.6%) left treatment within the first six months and were considered not having completed the program. Treatment completion in turn was predicted not by gender but by youths' ability to engage in positive behaviors in the first two weeks of TFC as recorded by foster parents.

A fourth, methodologically weaker, study by Fisher and Chamberlain (2000, R5) highlights preliminary outcomes for an adaptation of the MTFC model to provide early intervention for 30 children, ages 3–7, referred by child protective services (details are described also in Fisher et al., 1999). Compared to two comparison groups, results three months after placement support the usefulness of the approach with young maltreated children. Although the small nonrandomized sample must be considered a cautionary factor, the study shows reduction in children's symptomatic behaviors and stress levels. Particularly innovative is the use of a neuro-biological measure (weekly salivary cortisol levels) to gage emotional stress regulation in small children in addition to typical symptom reports by caregivers.

The following studies are methodologically much weaker. However, since they involve TFC programs other than the Oregon MTFC model they serve to broaden the knowledge base and are therefore included in this review. A study by Ownbey, Jones, Judkins, Everidge, and Timbers (2001, R6) focused on the specific effects of TFC on sexual acting out behaviors in a small sample of six children with sexually reactive or offending behaviors. Aside from its rather limited focus, the study is hampered by its small sample, the lack of a control or comparison group, and the use of instruments not yet validated. Using baseline and post-treatment reports of the frequency of unwanted behaviors, and caregivers' estimates of the child's likelihood to re-offend, the author reports a wide variability in outcomes among clients. While the frequency of behaviors reduced quickly, the estimated propensity to re-offend remained quite high after 24 months leading authors to conclude that this population may require extended time in TFC.

Gregory and Phillips (1997, R7) offer the only description of an afro-centered TFC program and its outcomes. The source is focused more on the description of the program than details of outcome evaluations. Nonetheless, authors indicate that this TFC program, designed as a short-term placement of up to two years, led to significant emotional, educational and behavioral improvements. In the absence of detailed information on the evaluation procedures, this source remains seriously limited in its documentation of evidence.

Finally, a large national study conducted by the Child Welfare League of America (CWLA) called the "Odyssey Project" compiled outcomes and characteristics for youth who entered into residential versus TFC programs between 1994 and 2000 (Drais-Parillo, not dated, R8). Nine TFC programs included in the study reported outcomes for a total of 985 (n) children and showed mixed results for improvements in externalizing and internalizing behaviors during youths' time in the program. More than two-thirds of youth went on to live in less restrictive environments with biological or adoptive parents, relatives, or independent living. For available subsamples, follow-up data indicated that a majority continued to live in less restrictive places six months, one year, and two years after discharge. While the size of the sample renders the study rather strong, the study is only descriptive and provides very limited information on the specific practices employed in participating programs.

Research Perspective: Results

From the research perspective, best current practices (those identified by at least four of the eight sources) in TFC programs are theory-based (most often social learning theory), and combine the following components: behavior modification strategies; skill building; individualized treatment plans; targeting multiple dimensions of children's lives (social, academic, recreational, family etc.); recruitment of stable foster parents; extended pre-service training (20–30 hours) for TFC parents; provision of ongoing in-home supports for TFC parents (including crisis intervention, respite care etc.); frequent contacts and communications between TFC families and agency staff; consultation services with schools, early intervention specialists etc.; individual child therapy; regularly scheduled home visits; provision of family therapy, supports, and education to biological families; as well as aftercare support and services for biological families when youth return home. (See also Table 7.4.)

Summary Conclusions of Current Best Practices across Perspectives

Across perspectives, there is limited overlap between practices considered "best" by research, professional, and consumer sources (see Table 7.5).

All sources share a clear emphasis on fostering frequent contacts and visits between the child and his or her biological family, and underscore the need for good communication between TFC staff and TFC families. Four practices can be considered well-supported in that two sources underscored their importance: first, involving biological families in planning and decision-making by fostering a positive relationship between TFC providers and families; second, offering supports for biological families (through therapy, education, advocacy etc.); third, providing ongoing supports for TFC parents, such as crisis intervention, respite care etc.; and, fourth, low caseloads for case managers. Additional practices identified only by consumers essentially specify in more detail how families are best involved and supported. A whole series of practices highly supported in research did not re-appear in professional or consumer perspectives.

Table 7.4 Overview of Practices in TFC from a Research Perspective

Practices	R1	R2	R3	R4	R5	R6	R7	R8
Behavior modification*	X	X	X	X	X	X		X
20+ hours of pre-service training*		X	X	X	X	(X)	X	(X)
Provision of ongoing in-home supports for TFC parents, (e.g. crisis intervention, respite care)*		X	X	X	X	X	X	X
Recruitment of stable foster parents*		X	X	X	X	X	X	
Therapy/education/supports for biological family*	X	X	X	X	X		X	
Theory-based*		X	X	X	X		X	
Low caseloads*		X	X	X	X		X	
Individualized planning*		X	X	X	X	X		
Multidimensional (social, academic, recreational etc.)*		X	X	X	X		X	
School/Early intervention consultation*		X	X	X	X		X	
Individual therapy for each child*	X	X	X	X	X			
Regular visits with family*		X	X	X	X		X	
Aftercare support and services for biological families*		X	X	X	X		X	
Frequent contacts and communication between TFC providers and staff*		X	X	X	X			
Skill building*	X	X	X	X				
Matching children/TFC parents							X	
Activity-based interventions					X			
Group therapy	X							

Notes:
(X)=Length of preservice training not specified.
*=Qualified for best practice from this perspective.

Current State of the Art

Although not univocally established, there is increasing evidence that Therapeutic Foster Care can be an effective form of care for children and youth with SED leading to improved functioning and discharge to less restrictive placements, typically their biological families. Based on this review of research, professional, and consumer sources, two sets of practices emerge as state-of-the-art practices to achieve both outcomes. The first set revolves around facilitating connections to and involvement of the biological family; the second set focuses on the TFC provider families:

1. Facilitating regular contacts and visits between child and parents is an essential component of successful TFC programs endorsed by research,

Table 7.5 Current Best Practices across Perspectives

Best Practices	Research	Professional	Consumer
Facilitating regular contacts and visits between child and parents**	R2, 3, 4, 5, 7	P1, 4, 6	C1, 2, 3, 4
Involvement of biological family: in planning and decision-making, fostering a positive relationship of TFC provider/ agency staff with biological families*		P1, 4, 6	C1, 2, 3, 4, 5
Supports for biological family (therapy, education, advocacy, etc.)*	R1, 2, 3, 4, 5, 7		C1, 2, 5
Aftercare support and services for biological families	R2, 3, 4, 5, 7		
Assistance with transportation			C1, 2, 5
Frequent, clear, and open communication, sharing information w/biological families			C1, 2, 4, 5
Positive staff attitudes toward families: encouragement to participate			C1, 2, 5
Frequent contact, clear communication between TFC families and agency staff (TFC providers included in team)**	R2, 3, 4, 5	P1, 4, 6	C1, 2, 5
Provision of ongoing supports for TFC parents, including crisis intervention, respite care etc.*	R2, 3, 4, 5, 6, 7, 8	P1, 4, 6	
Low caseloads*	R2, 3, 4, 5, 7	P1, 2, 3	
Theory-based	R2, 3, 4, 5, 7		
Individualized planning	R2, 3, 4, 5, 6		
Multidimensional (addressing social, academic, recreational areas etc.)	R2, 3, 4, 5, 7		
School/early intervention consultation	R2, 3, 4, 5, 7		
Individual therapy for each child	R1, 2, 3, 4, 5		
Aftercare support and services for biological families	R2, 3, 4, 5, 7		
Skill building	R1, 2, 3, 4		
Behavior modification	R1, 2, 3, 4, 5, 6, 8		
20+ hours of pre-service training	R2, 3, 4, 5, (6), 7, (8)		
Recruitment of stable foster parents	R2, 3, 4, 5, 6, 7		
Pre-placement: detailed, clear, and complete information in preparation for placement; matching children to foster families		P1, 3, 4	

Notes:
**=Qualified for best practice across perspectives.
*=Qualified for well-supported practice across perspectives.

professional, and consumers alike. Arguably related activities supported by at least two of the groups include involving biological families in planning and decision-making, fostering a positive relationship, and providing supports to biological families.

2. Endorsed by all perspectives, frequent contact and clear communication between TFC parents and agency staff, and including TFC parents as part of the treatment team is the second best practice. Specific activities, supported by two sources, entail provision of ongoing supports for TFC parents including crisis intervention, respite care etc., and low caseloads for TFC caseworkers.

Additional practices received strong empirical support in the research literature but await clear endorsement from consumers and practitioners. These practices include: being theory-based; employing behavior modification; skill building; individualized treatment planning; targeting multiple dimensions of children's lives (social, academic, recreational, family etc.); recruitment of stable foster parents; extended pre-service training for TFC parents; consultation services with schools, early intervention specialists etc.; individual child therapy; and aftercare supports and services for biological families when youth return home.

Critique of Current Best Practices

The Potency of Current Best Practices

The potency of current best practices can be understood in terms of the quality of sources, and the level of agreement within and across perspectives. Overall, the quality of sources for each perspective varies considerably. Consumer sources (see Table 7.1) are quite limited in scope and often do not directly address which practices best increase youths' functioning. Several sources refer not specifically or exclusively to TFC programs but present general practices consumers deem helpful in children's mental health services. Consumer sources tend to address the outcome of "discharge to families" only indirectly by pointing to factors they find important to maintain and/or strengthen involvement of families with their child and their child's care. Within these parameters, consumer sources achieve a moderate level of agreement.

The professional perspective (see Table 7.2) is significantly informed by standards put forth by the FFTA. While the influential position of the FFTA provides great strengths to these standards, related studies suggest that there is only a moderate level of consistency with which those standards are implemented, and no clear evidence as to their effect on outcomes. Direct evidence of professionals' wisdom and insights is limited to a few small-scale, though fairly well designed, qualitative inquiries in which professionals speak mostly to the complexity of the roles TFC parents fulfill and to questions of family involvement. The potency of professional sources is therefore limited in strength, scope, and agreement.

The research perspective supplies the most consistent and qualitatively strong sources (see Table 7.3) which also show a relatively high level of agreement (see Table 7.4). It should be noted though that this strength is largely due to the comparatively good quality of research on one particular model, namely MTFC by the Oregon Social Learning Center. Outside of MTFC, the variability with which TFC is delivered and researched makes it difficult to establish effectiveness (James & Meezan, 2002). In addition, all TFC programs use a combination of intervention components, making it difficult to discern which components are most useful and even more difficult to unpack the processes of TFC. For instance, MTFC researchers themselves have suggested that the main benefit of their model vis-à-vis residential treatment may stem from reducing interactions with anti-social peers rather than from any other particular intervention strategy (Chamberlain, 1996).

Across all three perspectives, two main best practices, namely facilitating contacts of children and their biological families, and clear, frequent communication between TFC families and agency staff, can be considered well established. Several related activities identified by at least two of the perspectives can be considered well supported. Still, the level of agreement across perspectives overall remains somewhat limited, which may in part be due to a relative sparsity of documented knowledge from professional and consumer perspectives. Current discrepancies between sources do not necessarily mean that the three groups are at odds. It is entirely possible that professionals or consumers, for instance, also endorse practices found emphasized only in research, such as individualized treatment plans, or utilizing behavior modification strategies. In any case, the diversity among perspectives highlights different areas of interest pursued by each group. While much of the research is focused on components for intervention and structures of TFC programs, professionals and consumers tend to include a stronger focus on relational practices, such as positive relationships between parties, good communication, etc.

Gaps and Strengths in Current Knowledge and Practices: A Value-Critical Analysis

Through the lens of a value-critical analysis, a variety of gaps and strengths in current TFC practices and knowledge become apparent. One strength of TFC is with respect to the principle of least restrictive environment, since TFC is designed as an alternative to more restrictive, residential treatment. The other values guiding this analysis are borrowed from principles of family-centered practice. Value-based attitudes underlying family-centered practice involve four major elements (Allen & Petr, 1998): 1) recognizing the centrality of families in the lives of individuals and choosing the family as the unit of attention; 2) maximizing families' choices and abilities to make informed decisions; 3) applying a strengths perspective rather than a pathology focus; and 4) ensuring that services are sensitive to diverse populations.

Centrality of Families/Family as Unit of Attention

TFC as an alternative approach to residential or inpatient placements clearly emphasizes the idea of family as a pivotal social structure best suited to meet the needs of children. In addition, the high level of agreement among perspectives on facilitating contacts and visits with biological families also signifies recognition of the centrality of biological families in young people's lives. Less defined, however, is the extent to which TFC programs consider the child's biological family as their main unit of attention. Treatment in most TFC programs seems to revolve around the individual child first, and only second around biological families.

Maximizing Families' Choices and Abilities to Make Informed Decisions

Without successfully involving biological families in TFC treatment and planning, families are deprived of opportunities to make choices and informed decisions about their children. Even though biological families' involvement in treatment is well supported as a best practice, implementation of such involvement varies highly with the attitudes and relationship skills of TFC parents and agency staff. Other than "stability" in TFC parents, very little information is available about the ways in which characteristics and attitudes of TFC providers positively impact family involvement and treatment effectiveness. Perspectives of consumers and professionals provide first important insights into the strategies and factors that increase or hinder families' participation and deserve further attention. Finally, while there is a clear commitment to consider TFC parents "part of the treatment team," no equivalent ideal for the involvement of consumer families was found in this review.

Strengths Perspective

The strengths perspective (Saleebey, 2006) is an approach that acknowledges existing difficulties and problems but emphasizes the need to elicit and build on the resources, hopes, and resiliencies in people and communities. A number of practices and intentions of TFC are compatible with resiliency factors known to contribute to positive development in youth with SED, namely efforts to foster positive parent–child relations, contact with prosocial peers, and development of good social skills (Armstrong et al., 2003; Vance et al., 2002). Still, there is currently little explicit reference to a strengths perspective in TFC, and it remains unclear how programs can specifically foster and harness the resources and capacities of youth and their biological families in service of desired outcomes.

Sensitivity to Diverse Populations

Boys make up the vast majority of samples in empirical studies, however, gender is slowly receiving more attention as a significant factor in TFC (Chamberlain &

Reid, 1994). Studies indicate that girls arrive in TFC with more prior placements than boys, over four times the rate of being sexually abused, are more likely to have attempted suicide, and three times as likely as boys to run away while in TFC (Chamberlain & Reid, 1994; Fasulo, Cross, Mosley, & Leavey, 2002). Girls also seem to take a different path through the TFC program. While boys' behaviors improved or at least did not deteriorate by the time they had spent six months in TFC, girls—after comparatively few problems in the first six months after intake —showed increased behavior problems thereafter (Chamberlain & Reid, 1994). Adolescent girls have by far the highest probability (55%) of disruption in TFC placements (Smith et al., 2001) raising questions about how to make TFC more appropriate and effective for girls.

Ethnicity has received virtually no attention in the literature on TFC (James & Meezan, 2002). The majority of samples in TFC studies is dominated by Caucasian children and youth even though children of color tend to be overrepresented in the SED population overall (James & Meezan, 2002). FFTA standards call for culturally sensitive procedures and efforts to match foster families and youth on cultural variables, yet the absence of research or even conceptual articles on cultural dimensions of therapeutic foster children, their families, and providers points to the relatively low priority granted to the issue.

Recommendations for Improving Current Best Practices

Improving the Potency of Current Best Practices

To improve the potency of current best practices, each perspective could benefit from stronger, more consistent evidence. Equally, the consistency between sources could be strengthened. Given the importance placed on family involvement, it behooves researchers and program administrators to include the voice of biological families in evaluative efforts. Of equal importance are also the insights of young people who are or were consumers of TFC. In addition to highlighting how families are best involved, the field would benefit from knowing which specific practices families and youth find helpful to improve youths' functioning, and which components support the durability of positive developments once children return home. Well suited to publish and represent the experiences of biological families and children are existing consumer organizations, such as the Federation of Families for Children's Mental Health, or other professional advocacy groups such as the Child Welfare League of America who have not yet focused much specifically on TFC.

The professional perspective would benefit from further inquiries as to the actual implementation of FFTA standards and greater fidelity of their implementation. Only then could studies analyze the impact of particular standards on outcomes. Further, the knowledge and experiences of agency staff and TFC families should be granted more systematic attention. Documenting insights in peer-reviewed journals, newsletters, or online publications could increase the distribution of practice wisdom.

While the MTFC model provides excellent guidance for research designs, more experimental or quasi-experimental studies of other TFC programs are needed to expand the research base beyond the MTFC model. In addition, larger sample sizes and replication studies might enable researchers to determine which factors are the most important components of TFC, specifically leading to better functioning and subsequent discharge to biological families.

Finally, the research perspective, on the one hand, and consumer and professional sources, on the other, appear to focus on different factors for best practices in TFC. These discrepancies could be reconciled in two ways toward creating more consistency and thus heightening the potency of current best practices. One, there is a need to explore more directly whether components deemed important in empirical literature are equally meaningful to practitioners and consumers. In other words, it seems worthwhile to explore directly if and to what extent consumers and practitioners find components such as behavior modification, individualized planning etc. important. Second, the emphasis professionals and consumers put on positive relationships between TFC families and biological families calls attention to factors such as attitudes and values of staff and TFC parents, and their respective abilities to build strong therapeutic relationships with youth and biological families. The therapeutic relationship has emerged as a central component in other areas of mental health (Drisko, 2004; Shirk & Karver, 2003). Thus, it seems only fitting for researchers and program designers to attend more to the role of the therapeutic relationship in the highly complex relational networks of TFC.

Toward more Family-Centered TFC Practices

A variety of improvements could make TFC practices more family-centered. Given that a majority of TFC children will return to their families, and are expected to do so, the next conceptual step is to make the biological family the primary unit of attention and to include not only longer-term outcomes for youth but also outcomes for biological families in evaluations of TFC. Toward a more family-centered philosophy, TFC would benefit from a higher and explicit commitment to the child's family as being at the core of treatment and treatment planning, and greater interest in family-centered attitudes, relational skills, and family therapy skills of TFC parents and agency staff.

Similarly, a commitment to consider biological parents "part of the treatment team," akin to philosophies in wraparound (VanDenBerg & Grealish, 1996), would likely increase families' choices and chances for informed decision-making. Existing strengths, hopes, and capacities of biological families and TFC youth deserve much higher conceptual and practical attention than currently reflected in sources informing best practices. TFC administrators and researchers could explore questions of how successful TFC programs already foster the strengths of biological families and youth, and how consumers' resources and knowledge could be employed as an integral part of TFC program design and practice. For instance, consumers could be invited to serve as consultants for program design, training, etc.; former consumers could serve as supports for current consumers, and so forth.

Urgently needed are ideas, strategies, and research to ensure that TFC practices are more sensitive and appropriate for girls and for youth of color. To this end, the ethnic and gender composition of staff and TFC providers should always be noted in studies and by program administrators. In the face of difficulties in recruiting and retaining therapeutic foster parents (Farmer et al., 2002), attention to ethnicity and culture may appear as luxuries in the everyday practice of TFC. However, TFC programs ought to strive to recruit and retain staff and TFC families with diverse cultural backgrounds. As long as it remains difficult to recruit diverse staff and TFC families, cultural consultants from local organizations could serve as assistants and brokers. Cultural and gender sensitivity should be frequently part of TFC trainings, and initiatives to learn from other organizations and programs could also promote ideas for cultural or gender modifications. For instance, MTFC programs could learn from Gregory and Phillips' (1997, R7) afro-centered TFC model, and in return share their expertise on research design and implementation.

Overall, TFC is a promising approach for effectively treating youth with SED and moving them to less restrictive placements. The MTFC model in particular is well-defined and empirically validated. The existence of the FFTA and its guidelines provides constructive conditions to improve current best practices especially through further explorations of consumer and professional perspectives, and by making TFC more family-centered.

Note

1   In the following, the term "biological family" is used to denote the primary caregivers to which children in TFC are typically discharged. The term is meant to include adoptive, or other permanent family constellations fulfilling the same function in a child's life.

References

Allen, R.I., & Petr, C.G. (1998). Rethinking family-centered practice. *American Journal of Orthopsychiatry, 68*(1), 4–16.

Armstrong, K.H., Dedrick, R.F., & Greenbaum, P.E. (2003). Factors associated with community adjustment of young adults with serious emotional disturbance: A longitudinal analysis. *Journal of Emotional and Behavioral Disorders, 11*, 66–76.

Baker, A.J.L., & Curtis, P. (2006). Prior placements of youth admitted to therapeutic foster care and residential treatment centers: The Odyssey Project population. *Child and Adolescent Social Work Journal, 23*(1), 38–60.

Bates, B.C., English, D.J., & Kouidou-Giles, S. (1997). Residential treatment and its alternatives: A review of the literature. *Child and Youth Care Forum, 26*(1), 7–51.

Chamberlain, P. (1996). Community-based residential treatment for adolescents with conduct disorder. In Thomas H. Ollendick & J. Ronald Prinz (Eds.), *Advances in clinical child psychology, Vol. 18. Advances in clinical child psychology* (pp. 63–90). New York: Plenum Press.

Chamberlain, P. (2003). *Treating chronic juvenile offenders.* Washington, DC: APA.

Chamberlain, P., & Moore, K. (1998). A clinical model for parenting juvenile offenders:

A comparison of group care versus family care. *Clinical Child Psychology and Psychiatry, 3*(3), 375–386.

Chamberlain, P., & Reid, J.B. (1991). Using a specialized foster care community treatment model for children and adolescents leaving the state mental hospital. *Journal of Community Psychology, 19*(3), 266–276.

Chamberlain, P., & Reid, J.B. (1994). Differences in risk factors and adjustment for male and female delinquents in treatment foster care. *Journal of Child and Family Studies, 3*(1), 23–39.

Chamberlain, P., & Reid, J.B. (1998). Comparison of two community alternatives to incarceration for chronic juvenile offenders. *Journal of Consulting and Clinical Psychology, 66*(4), 624–633.

Davis, M. (2003). Addressing the needs of youth in transition to adulthood. *Administration and Policy in Mental Health, 30*(6), 495–509.

Davis, M., Banks, S., Fisher, W., & Grudzinskas, A. (2004). Longitudinal patterns of offending during the transition to adulthood in youth from the mental health system. *Journal of Behavioral Health Services and Research, 31*(4), 351–366.

Dore, M.M., & Mullin, D. (2006). Treatment Family Foster Care: Its history and current role in the foster care continuum. *Families in Society, 87*(4), 475–482.

Drais-Parillo, A.A. (not dated). The Odyssey Project: A descriptive and prospective study of children and youth in residential group care and therapeutic foster care, final report. Washington, DC: Child Welfare League of America, retrieved February 10, 2007, from www.cwla.org/programs/research/odysseyfinalreport.pdf.

Drisko, J.W. (2004). Common factors in psychotherapy outcome: Meta-analytic findings and their implications for practice and research. *Families in Society, 85*(1), 81–90.

Farmer, E.M.Z., Burns, B.J., Dubs, M.S., & Thompson, S. (2002). Assessing conformity to standards for treatment foster care. *Journal of Emotional and Behavioral Disorders, 10*(4), 213–222.

Fasulo, S.J., Cross, T.P., Mosley, P., & Leavey, J. (2002). Adolescent runaway behavior in specialized foster care. *Children and Youth Services Review, 24*(8), 623–640.

Federation of Families for Children's Mental Health. (1992). *Principles for Family Involvement.* Rockville, MD; retrieved February 2, 2007, from www.ffcmh.org/pub_facts.htm.

Fisher, P.A., & Chamberlain, P. (2000). Multidimensional treatment foster care: A program for intensive parenting, family support, and skill building. *Journal of Emotional and Behavioral Disorders, 8*(3), 155–164.

Fisher, P.A., Ellis, B.H., & Chamberlain, P. (1999). Early intervention foster care: A model for preventing risk in young children who have been maltreated. *Children's Services: Social Policy, Research, and Practice, 2*(3), 159–182.

Foster Family-Based Treatment Association. (1995). *Program standards for treatment foster care.* New York: Author.

Galaway, B., Nutter, R.W., & Hudson, J. (1995). Relationship between discharge outcomes for treatment foster-care clients and program characteristics. *Journal of Emotional and Behavioral Disorders, 3*(1), 46–54.

Geller, J.L., & Biebel, K. (2006). The premature demise of public child and adolescent inpatient psychiatric beds. *Psychiatry Quarterly, 77*, 251–271.

Gregory, S.D., & Phillips, F.B. (1997). "Of mind, body, and spirit": Therapeutic foster care—An innovative approach to healing from an NTU perspective. *Child Welfare, 76*(1), 127–142.

Hudson, J., Nutter, R.W., & Galaway, B. (1994a). Treatment foster care programs: A review of evaluation research and suggested directions. *Social Work Research, 18*(4), 198–210.

Hudson, J., Nutter, R.W., & Galaway, B. (1994b). Treatment foster family care: Development and current status. *Community Alternatives: International Journal of Family Care, 6*(2), 1–24.

Hussey, D.L., & Guo, S. (2005). Characteristics and trajectories of treatment foster care youth. *Child Welfare, 84*(4), 485–506.

James, S., & Meezan, W. (2002). Refining the evaluation of treatment foster care. *Families in Society, 83*(1), 233–245.

Jivanjee, P. (1999a). Parent perspectives on family involvement in therapeutic foster care. *Journal of Child and Family Studies, 8,* 451–461.

Jivanjee, P. (1999b). Professional and provider perspectives on family involvement in therapeutic foster care. *Journal of Child and Family Studies, 8,* 329–341.

Kruzich, J.M., Jivanjee, P., Robinson, A., & Friesen, B.J. (2003). Family caregivers' perceptions of barriers to and supports of participation in their children's out-of-home treatment. *Psychiatric Services, 54*(11), 1513–1518.

Malloy, J.M., Cheney, D., & Cormier G.M. (1998). Interagency collaboration and the transition to adulthood for students with emotional or behavioral disabilities. *Education and Treatment of Children, 21*(3), 303–320.

Meadowcroft, P., Thomlison, B., & Chamberlain, P. (1994). Treatment foster care services: A research agenda for child welfare. *Child Welfare, 73*(5), 565–581.

Ownbey, M.A., Jones, R.J., Judkins, B.L., Everidge, J.A., & Timbers, G.D. (2001). Tracking the sexual behavior-specific effects of a foster family treatment program for children with serious sexual behavior problems. *Child and Adolescent Social Work Journal, 18*(6), 417–436.

Redding, R.E., Fried, C., & Britner, P.A. (2000). Predictors of placement outcomes in treatment foster care: Implications for foster parent selection and service delivery. *Journal of Child and Family Studies, 9*(4), 425–447.

Reddy, L.A., & Pfeiffer, S. (1997). Effectiveness of treatment foster care with children and adolescents: A review of outcome studies. *Journal of the American Academy of Child and Adolescent Psychiatry, 36*(5), 581–588.

Robinson, A.D., Kruzich, J.M., Friesen, B.J., Jivanjee, P., & Pullmann, M.D. (2005). Preserving family bonds: Examining parent perspectives in the light of practice standards for out-of-home treatment. *American Journal of Orthopsychiatry, 75*(4), 632–643.

Saleebey, D. (Ed.) (2006). The strengths perspective in social work practice (4th ed.). Boston, MA: Allyn & Bacon.

Shirk, S.R., & Karver, M. (2003). Predictions of treatment outcomes from relationship variables in child psychotherapy: A meta-analytic review. *Journal of Consulting and Clinical Psychology, 71*(3), 452–464.

Smith, D.K. (2004). Risk, reinforcement, retention in treatment, and reoffending for boys and girls in multidimensional treatment foster care. *Journal of Emotional and Behavioral Disorders, 12*(1), 38–48.

Smith, D.K., Stormshak, E., Chamberlain, P., & Whaley, R.B. (2001). Placement disruption in treatment foster care. *Journal of Emotional and Behavioral Disorders, 9*(3), 200–205.

U.S. Department of Health and Human Services. (1999). *Mental health: A report of the Surgeon General—executive summary.* Rockville, MD: U.S. Department of Health and Human Services, Substance Abuse and Mental Health Services Administration, Center for Mental Health Services, National Institutes of Health, National Institute of Mental Health.

Vance, J.E., Bowen, N.J., Fernandez, G., & Thompson, S. (2002). Risk and protective factors as predictors of outcome in adolescents with psychiatric disorder and aggression. *Journal of the American Academy of Child and Adolescent Psychiatry, 41*(1), 36–43.

VanDenBerg, J.E., & Grealish, E.M. (1996). Individualized services and supports through the Wraparound process: philosophy and procedures. *Journal of Child and Family Studies, 5*(1), 7–21.

Wagner, M. (1995). Outcomes for youths with serious emotional disturbance in secondary school and early adulthood. *The Future of Children: Critical Issues for Children and Youths, 5*, 90–112.

Wells, K., & D'Angelo, L. (1994). Specialized foster care: Voices from the field. *Social Service Review, 68*(1), 127–144.

Wells, K., Farmer, E.M.Z., Richards, J.T., & Burns, B.J. (2004). The experience of being a treatment foster mother. *Qualitative Social Work, 3*(2), 117–138.

Yampolskaya, S., Brown, E.C., & Greenbaum, P.E. (2002). Early pregnancy among adolescent females with serious emotional disturbances: Risk factors and outcomes. *Journal of Emotional and Behavioral Disorders, 10*(2), 108–115.

8 Best Practices for Achieving Restorative Justice Outcomes for Crime Victims and Offenders in the United States

Jung Jin Choi

Given the importance of assisting victims of crimes and offenders, this chapter attempts to answer the following question: What are the best practices for crime victims and offenders to achieve restorative justice outcomes in the United States? In so doing, this chapter seeks to find the current best practices from multiple points of view, such as consumer, professional, and research perspectives. There are best practices which occur in victim–offender mediation as well as other models including family group conferencing and healing circles: the direct face-to-face human encounter that occurs in a safe environment and is facilitated by trained community volunteer mediators with a staff co-mediator who demonstrates good listening skills and plays a nondirective background role. The programs are expected to maximize the possibility of delivering victim-sensitive services through a noncoercive private agency that works closely with local public venues.

Overview of the Population and Problem of Concern

Any given day, victims suffer tremendous human and financial losses, including physical, psychological, and social costs (The Office of Juvenile Justice and Delinquency Prevention [OJJDP], 1998; The United Nations Office for Drug Control and Crime Prevention [UNODCCP], 1999). In particular, studies identify that the negative psychological impact of victimization includes shock, fear, anger, helplessness, powerlessness, vulnerability, a sense of isolation, disbelief, and guilt, to name a few (Bradshaw & Umbreit, 2003; Zehr, 1990, 2001). However, as the UNODCCP (1999) describes, the victim has been the "forgotten person" in the administration of justice.

Few efforts have worked toward preventing crimes as well as assisting, protecting, and empowering victims (OJJDP, 1998; Schichor & Sechrest, 1998; UNODCCP, 1999; United Nations Office for Drugs and Crime [UNODC], 2006; Wemmers, 2002; Zehr, 1990, 2002). The studies indicate that in the traditional criminal justice system: 1) victims face insensitive treatment; 2) victims have little input into the resolution of their own cases; 3) victims rarely feel heard; and 4) victims often receive no restitution or expression of remorse from the offender. Consequently, not only do the current criminal justice system's processes and procedures not take into account the perspective of victims, but also their needs and dignity often are not respected.

In contrast, the focus of the criminal justice system is mainly on the punishment of offenders (Schichor & Sechrest, 1998; Zehr, 1990, 2002). Elsner (2006) reports that there are more than two million incarcerated people in the United States, which is equivalent to a quarter of the entire world's prisoners. The emphasis on imposing punishment not only escalates expenditures for incarceration, but also takes away the opportunity for offenders to understand the consequences of their actions and further to act on their responsibility to make things right for victims (Lemley, 2001; UNODC, 2006; Zehr, 1990).

Rogers (1989) argues that the long-standing beliefs or myths in the powers of imprisonment lead to punitive reactions to crimes as a solution; however, 1) most of those entering prison eventually return to society and 2) incarceration has not shown to be successful in restoring offenders as "law-abiding citizens" because half of those released from prison return to prison. Similarly, studies indicate that punitive sanctions for offenders, including juvenile delinquents, do not reduce the crime rate (Arrigo & Schehr, 1998; Butts & Mears, 2001; MacKenzie, 2000; Tonry & Petersilia, 1999). Cullen and Gendreau (2000) and MacKenzie (2000) also observe that interventions based on retributive assumptions for juvenile offenders such as boot camps, shock probation, and simple incarceration were not effective. In particular, they also observe that those programs that are based on punitive ideas by utilizing increased control and surveillance in the community and attempting to scare offenders away from criminal activity did not reduce the recidivisim rate of offenders.

Because of dissatisfaction and frustration with the criminal justice system, during the last few decades there have been calls for expanding victim's rights and community-based alternative responses to crime and social disorder (Drowns & Hess, 2000; Roberts, 1997; Sarri, 1995; UNODC, 2006). As an alternative and nontraditional approach to crime, restorative justice has gained support in the field of justice studies (Braithwaite, 2000; Lemley, 2001; Morris & Maxwell, 1993; Umbreit & Coates, 2000; Umbreit, Vos, & Coates, 2005; UNODCCP, 1999; Zehr, 1990). Restorative justice is a justice paradigm. Whereas the traditional criminal justice paradigm or retributive justice emphasizes punishment and stigma imposed on offenders, restorative justice focuses on victims as well as recognition of the centrality of the interpersonal dimension among human relationships based on the belief that crime is a violation of them (Lemley, 2001; Niemeyer & Shichor, 1996; Van Ness, 2004; Zehr, 1990). In implementing restorative justice, the active and direct participation of victims, offenders, and communities is essential to maximize information, dialogue, and mutual agreement among the participants (Lemley, 2001; OJJDP, 1998; Van Ness, 2004; Zehr, 1990). As a collaborative and peacemaking process to conflict or problem-solving in which the victim, the offender, and where appropriate, any other individuals or community members affected by a crime participate together to deal with its aftermath, restorative justice seeks restorative outcomes, including victim's healing and empowerment, offender accountability, reaching agreements on reparation, and reduced recidivism (Bazemore & Schiff, 2005; Boyack, Bowen, & Marshall, 2004; UNODC, 2006).

However, a considerable variability exists in implementing restorative justice. Studies indicate that restorative justice encompasses not only a wide range of policies but also practices in different forms of programs in different communities and countries (Lightfoot & Umbreit, 2004). Therefore, there is no single right way to implement restorative justice in practice (OJJDP, 1998; Zehr, 2002), but the most widely accepted expressions of restorative justice are victim– offender mediation (VOM), family group conferencing (FGC), and healing circle (Bazemore & Umbreit, 2003; Lightfoot & Umbreit, 2004; Umbreit, 1998; Zehr, 2002).

Victim–offender mediation brings a victim(s) and an offender(s) together with a mediator(s) to obtain answers and make amends for the harm inflicted. VOM, also known as the "humanistic model" of mediation as opposed to a settlement-driven model of mediation (Umbreit, Coates, & Roberts, 1998, p. 83), puts an emphasis on victim healing, offender accountability, and restoration of loss, rather than mediating the issues of guilt or innocence (Bradshaw & Umbreit, 1998). It has gained the widest support and popularity particularly in the United States (OJJDP, 1998).

Family group conferencing, rooted in the justice or dispute resolution traditions of Maori people, has been widely accepted in New Zealand and Australia (Morris & Maxwell, 1993). Since the acceptance and growth of the program in the United States is not as extensive as VOM, little research has been done, yet the number of FGC programs is increasing (Bazemore & Umbreit, 2003; Lemley, 2001). In addition to victim and offender, FGC brings family members, friends, and key supports of both parties to the table (OJJDP, 1998).

Another form of restorative justice practice is called the healing circle or circle sentencing or peacemaking circles, which is rooted in the traditional sanctioning and healing practices of Native American cultures (Bazemore & Umbreit, 2003; Lemley, 2001; Zehr, 1990). While, as with FGC, little research has been conducted for empirical verification in the United States, the healing circles bring together not only the victim, offender, and family members but also a number of community members such as justice and social service personnel, and interested community residents (Bazemore & Umbreit, 2003; Schiff, 1998).

Best Practices Inquiry Search Process

Given the importance of assisting victims of crimes and offenders, this chapter attempts to answer the following question: What are the best practices for crime victims and offenders to achieve restorative justice outcomes in the United States? In doing so, this chapter first seeks to find the current best practices from multiple points of view, such as consumer, professional, and research perspectives, to identify the consensus as well as the discrepancies in them. Then, an analysis on the methodological and value-critical issues will be conducted. In providing recommendations for expanding the current best practices, a focus will be given to improving cultural competence in restorative justice.

In order to identify best practices, various search engines such as Web of Science, Social Services Abstracts, Social Work Abstracts, and Dissertation Abstracts Online provided by the University of Kansas Libraries were utilized. In addition, restorative justice online resources Center for Restorative Justice and Peacemaking (http://rjp.umn.edu/) and Restorative Justice Online (www.restorativejustice.org/) were employed. Key search words included "victim-sensitive" or "victim-oriented approaches," "restorative justice," "victim-offender mediation," "family group conference," and "circle sentence" or "healing circles."

Results of Best Practices Inquiry: Three Perspectives

In addition to acquiring a more holistic picture of restorative justice, the multiple points of view including consumer, professional, and research perspectives provide a way to identify the consensus in current best practice in producing restorative outcomes for crime victims and offenders. While research perspectives are expected to provide information on empirical verification of the restorative justice programs, the consumer and professional perspectives will offer "how to do" or "process" of them.

Consumer Perspective: Sources

Consumers know best what works for themselves (Petr & Walter, 2005). As Zehr (2001) argues, it is critical for researchers and practitioners to listen to and respect the voices of the participants of restorative justice programs to improve the current best practices. Consumer perspectives represent the opinions and recommendations of participants such as the victims, offenders, families, and community members. The selection criteria for this perspective were the level of involvement of direct voices of those participants as well as methodology, trustworthiness, and implications for practice, in case of qualitative studies. Information on best practices from this perspective was mainly gathered from qualitative studies that incorporated direct consumers' voices about their experiences in the restorative justice programs.

A case study was conducted to explore the experience of three family members of the two murdered victims and two offenders and in VOM (Umbreit & Vos, 2000, C1). Although the reasons for the participation were not always clear, all three family members wished to meet with the offenders during the trial proceedings. Only one family member explicitly expressed her reasons for seeking to meet the offender in the context of her own healing. Regarding the reasons for meeting with family members, both offenders referred to a process of self-examination in the context of a healing journey and their religious faith as part of living on death row.

White (2001, C2) conducted a case study using observations and open-ended interviews with victims' families, offenders in death row, and mediators in VOM programs in Texas. A total of 13 interviews were conducted over three months. The purpose of the study was to explore the nature of the experiences of VOM and how it impacted all those involved.

The first exploratory study for healing circles in the United States was conducted by Coates, Umbreit, and Vos in 2003 (C3). This study focuses on the peacemaking circles work within the community and schools of South Saint Paul. A total of 62 individuals including victims/family members, offenders/family members, circle keepers, community residents, and people who worked in the formal justice system were interviewed with 13 observations in circles.

Szmania (2005, C4) analyzed offenders' opening statements in VOM based on the assumption that offenders' needs may have often been overlooked based on its strong focus on victims. While focusing on the initial encounters of offenders and victims, the author analyzed the offenders' opening statements in five VOM cases involving crimes of severe violence.

Consumer Perspective: Results

In C1, the five participants described the experience as both powerful and healing. While all three victims reported that their negative feelings had greatly diminished, the offenders were grateful to be able to help them begin to heal. All family members reported that although it was very difficult, the preparation was extremely helpful for them in both preparing and healing. In addition to a capability to be fully present at the mediation, the role of the mediator in this study was character-ized as the "background role" in which mediators did not intervene much and respected silence during the mediation session.

In C2, while several themes were addressed in the study, two dimensions of them were pertinent in identifying best practice components: 1) the training and 2) the process. First of all, the program provided trainings for the prospective volunteer mediators to put them into the same situation of the VOM program beforehand. The training, approximately 100 hours of classroom training, 90 hours per year working closely with a victim and an offender toward mediation, and a two-year minimum commitment to the program, was characterized as being nonlinear, constructivist, transformational. Second, themes that emerged from the interviews were related to the process of the program. Those include a need for creating a safe place for participants. In so doing, a continuing connection to mediators was important not only for building relationship with them but also for fostering empathy, a sense of shared humanity, peace, and reconciliation. The mediator's role was to listen, help redefine lives, engender a freedom to let go in a sense of peace and reconciliation. In addition, the participants highlighted the importance of using reflection and self-awareness particularly in the preparation process.

The findings in C3 indicate that it was important for the participants: 1) to see offenders being responsible as well as held accountable; 2) to maintain the focus on future relationships between victims and offenders; 3) to have an opportunity to express feelings about the incident; and 4) to involve community residents in the process for offering support. In addition, the importance of respectful listening was emphasized in the process. Circle keepers, as with mediators in VOM, were expected to: 1) be able to focus and organize; 2) be open minded and nonjudg-mental; 3) be good listeners; 4) be caring and empathetic; and 5) be respectful, patient, calm, and understanding. However, several negative aspects of the circle were also indicated. Those include the amount of time required for the participation, difficulties in working with family members and close friends because of a lack of privacy and possible embarrassment, lack of professionalism in circle keepers, and religious conflict.

The findings in C4 highlight a need for practitioners to not overlook offenders' needs in VOM. Often, offenders found it very difficult to face the victim's family. They indicated symptoms such as an extreme apprehension and troubled sleeps. Nonetheless, the VOM process also provided the offenders with an opportunity to redefine themselves in a more positive way. While offenders' needs should not be overlooked, the author also suggests a need for offender screening to prevent the revictimization for some victims. The author identifies some criteria that offenders should show to be able to be included in the VOM: 1) to be open to be held accountable; 2) to accept blame; 3) to be honest; 4) to display empathy; 5) to be responsive to the victims' needs; and 6) to be open to emotional dialogue.

Table 8.1 Consumer Perspective

Best Practices	Sources for Consumer Perspectives	C1	C2	C3	C4
Mediator related	Being focused (fully present) and organized	x		x	
	Being nonjudgmental, open-minded, a sense of balance	x	x	x	
	Unobtrusive guidance during the session	x	x	x	
	Being empathetic, and respectful, patient, calm, and understanding (playing background role)	x	x	x	
	Fostering empathy, a sense of shared humanity, peace, and reconciliation	x	x	x	
Program related	A nonlinear, constructivist, transformational training for volunteers		x		
	A need for careful, compassionate preparation for both victims and offenders by using reflection and self-awareness	x	x	x	
	Direct face-to-face human encounter	x	x	x	x
	Maintaining a focus on future 1) relationships between victims and offenders 2) letting go in a sense of peace and reconciliation		x	x	
	Demonstrating a victim sensitivity (e.g., offender screening and continuing connection to mediators)	x	x		x
	Meeting offenders' needs	x	x		x
	The importance of creating a safe place, in which participants can talk about painful stories and express feelings about the incident	x	x	x	x
	An opportunity for community residents being able to involve in the process and offer support		x	x	
	Working closely with local courts and probation department	x	x		x

The consumer perspective highlights the needs of victims and offenders that practitioners should take into account in delivering restorative justice. The victims indicated that experiencing violence is often a devastating experience that affects all areas of their lives, including a wide range of strong emotions. As with Zehr (1990), the consumer perspective also emphasizes that offenders should be seen as who they are rather than what they did.

Two distinctive sets of best practices components, mediator-related and program-related factors, emerged from this perspective. The best practices commonly noted in three or more of the four sources are as following. First, the mediator-related factors are: 1) being nonjudgmental, open-mined, and showing a balance drawn from C1, C2, and C3; 2) guiding during the session in an unobtrusive manner from C1, C2, and C3; 3) playing a background role by being empathetic, respectful, patient, calm, and understanding from C1, C2, and C3; and 4) fostering empathy, a sense of shared humanity, peace, and reconciliation from C1, C2, and C3. The best practices demonstrate the roles of mediators character-ized in the humanistic model of mediation. Second, the program-related factors are: 1) having direct face-to-face human encounter in a safe environment in which participants can talk about painful stories and feelings drawn from C1, C2, C3, and C4; 2) demonstrating the participatory nature of restorative justice in the process of the programs from C1, C2, C3, and C4; 3) emphasizing victim sensitivity (e.g., a need for offender screening, continuing connection to mediators) from C1, C2, and C4; 4) showing capabilities to meet offender's needs from C1, C2, and C4; 5) valuing the importance of in-person preparation from C1, C2, and C3; and 6) working closely with public venues such as local courts and probation department from C1, C2, and C4.

Professional Perspective: Sources

Professional perspectives represent the state-of-the-art approaches endorsed by professionals. The professional perspectives fill the gaps between the consumer and research perspectives (Petr & Walter, 2005). One of the criteria in selecting professional perspectives was how the resources directly speak about the best practices. While three U.S. national surveys were located, those were drawn from practitioners' voices based on their experiences.

Hughes and Schneider (1989, P1) conducted a cross-sectional survey using the juvenile restitution program profiles and directory. Although this study is a bit older than the other two national surveys, it documents the characteristics of earlier programs, which teach important lessons for current programs. With a 70% return rate from representatives of 240 organizations, 79 from 31 states indicated a VOM component in their programs.

Umbreit and Greenwood (1999, P2) conducted a national survey of VOM. While they identified 289 programs, 116 programs participated in the survey. The data were collected through snowball sampling by contacting existing program staff or resource people in addition to utilizing the lists from actual and potential programs.

Bazemore and Schiff (2005, P3) conducted a national survey on the current status of restorative justice programs for youth. By utilizing a general definition of a restorative conference, the authors included four models such as VOM, FGC, circles, and community/neighborhood accountability boards. To collect data, they utilized existing databases and snowball sampling by contacting juvenile justice specialists, state court administrators and other knowledgeable persons in each state.

Professional Perspective: Results

In P1, the professionals, the person most knowledgeable about the mediation or restitution program in each jurisdiction, indicated that holding the offender accountable was the most important mediation goal, followed by providing restitution. In most programs (80%), the authors found that some types of offenses or offenders such as sex offenders, chronic offenders, those with drug, alcohol, and mental health problems, cases of child abuse, and violent offenders with no show of remorse or denying involvement were excluded from the participation. Overly angry victims were also excluded from the target population. Program staff conducted training for citizen volunteer mediators in 59% of the programs. A majority of the programs (70%) allowed parents' participation in the process. The skills that mediators should have were good listening skills, commitment to mediation philosophy, and patience. The support of juvenile court judges was very important, along with assistance from community in the form of volunteer mediators, funding, and staff. Some important program differences were identified; newer programs started since 1980s indicated more importance to the goals of reconciling the victim and offender and meeting the victim's needs. A trend also was found that newer programs were administered more often by private/nonprofit organizations rather than by the court and had a greater inclination to use written policies and procedures.

In P2, the professionals identified that although most programs are operated by private, nonprofit, and community-based agencies, to work closely with public venue has become important because of being funded by either state or local government. Also, an increasing number of probation departments developed VOM programs. Although victim participation was voluntary throughout all programs, 21% of the programs required the offender to participate, if the victim was interested. In 78% of the programs, separate meetings for preparation were held with the victim and offender prior to the mediation. While parents were encouraged to attend, 52% of the surveyed programs indicated that they always had the parents of juvenile offenders present. While in many programs the decision regarding who begins the storytelling was made by mediator and program staff, many programs encouraged victims to speak first to provide an opportunity for victims to be heard fully. In other programs, however, the offender speaks first, but it was to spare the discomfort of the victims. Regarding most important tasks for mediators, the professionals pointed out: 1) facilitating a dialogue between the victim and offender; 2) making the parties feel comfortable and safe; and 3) assisting the parties in negotiating a restitution plan. In addition to the centrality of the in-person preparation to the effectiveness of the process, they indicated that there are important elements of victim sensitivity that are often found in the mediators' style and attitude: 1) patient listening, 2) empathizing, 3) neither pressuring nor pushing, and 4) allowing sufficient time for the process. They also noted the existence of a considerable agreement on the training format to be interactive, participatory, experiential, and utilizing role plays. Many professionals also highlighted the trend in referrals being toward severer level offenses.

The findings drawn from P3 indicate that while currently there are 773 restorative justice programs including a variety of models in the United States, VOM is still dominant. Most programs are located in private agencies staffed mostly by volunteers. While the referrals most likely come from the justice system,

Table 8.2 Professional Perspective

Best Practices	Sources for Professional Perspective	P1	P2	P3
Mediator related	Facilitate dialogue between victim and offender		x	
	Make the parties feel comfortable and safe		x	
	Assist parties in negotiating restitution plan		x	
	Nondirective style of mediation with minimum involvement and respecting silence (e.g., being patient neither pressuring nor pushing and allowing sufficient time for the process)	x	x	
	Good listening skills (e.g., listening patiently with empathy)	x	x	
	Commit to mediation philosophy/principles	x	x	
Program related	Direct face-to-face human encounter following the humanistic model of mediation	x	x	x
	Training format on being interactive, participatory, experiential, and utilizing role plays		x	
	A need to include additional parties (e.g., families)	x	x	x
	Demonstrating victim sensitivity (e.g., victim speaks first, respecting victims' choices throughout the process, a need for offender screening, providing a continued contact with victims for, if necessary, referrals, ongoing support and services)	x	x	x
	Support for the offenders		x	
	A need for victim screening (e.g., overly angry victims)	x		
	The importance of in-person preparation of participants for the mediations		x	x
	A need for follow-up		x	
	Operated by private, nonprofit, community-based agencies	x	x	x
	A need for having support at the top		x	
	The importance of clearly stated goals of the programs regarding restorative justice	x		
	Opportunities for connection and cooperation with public venue	x	x	x
	The assistance from community groups—volunteer mediators, funding, and staff	x	x	x

the most common charges are minor assault, property damage, and personal theft. On average, three additional parties, such as family members (usually from offender's), are increasingly involved in VOM. In VOM-type programs, 38.2% indicated that the offender speaks first in their programs; in 34.5% of programs the victim speaks first. The remainder (24.9%) indicated a variation in terms of who speaks first. Lastly, when offenders fail to complete the restorative justice process, professionals indicated referring them back to court or to probation for action as the most appropriate response.

As with the consumer perspective, the professional sources also demonstrate the importance of the roles of mediators and the distinctive characteristics of the humanistic model of mediation. The professionals pointed out several noticeable trends that demonstrate the increasing acceptance of the restorative justice programs in the justice field: 1) increasing number of restorative justice programs; and 2) increasing numbers of referrals with severer level offenses. In addition, some sources suggest that the restorative justice programs are striving to enhance their programs by: 1) adopting more written policies and procedures; 2) reinforcing victim sensitivity; 3) providing more training on different programs; and 4) involving additional parties particularly in VOM. Several challenging issues were also identified. Professionals in restorative justice find it difficult to work with a conservative juvenile justice system without having support from the top. Other issues included the difficulty in working with participants who come from different cultural backgrounds.

As with the consumer perspective, two distinctive sets of best practices components were identified in the professional perspective: mediator-related and program-related factors. The best practices commonly noted in two or more of the three sources are as following. The mediator-related factors involve: 1) non-directive mediating style to maximize involvement (e.g., respecting silence, neither pressuring nor pushing, and allowing sufficient time for the process) drawn from P1 and P2; 2) good listening skills, demonstrating patience and empathy from P1 and P2; 3) commitment to mediation philosophy and principles rather than adhering to one particular model from P1 and P2. The program-related factors include: 1) direct face-to-face human encounter drawn from P1, P2, and P3; 2) victim sensitivity (e.g., victims/offender speak first but with appropriate rationale) from P1, P2, and P3; 3) the importance of the in-person preparation from P2 and P3; 4) parents or additional parties' participation from P1, P2, and P3; 5) private, nonprofit, community-based agencies' operations from P1, P2, and P3; 6) participation of a community (e.g., involving community volunteers) from P1, P2, and P3; and 7) connection and cooperation with a pubic venue from P1, P2, and P3.

Research Perspective: Sources

Research and evaluations of programs are essential for modifying and improving best practices to victims and offenders by providing the empirical verification (Petr & Walter, 2005). In this section, the results of research regarding the impact

Table 8.3 A Summary Table for the Research Quality Ratings

Criteria	R1	R2	R3	R4	Total
Research design (15)	12	13	14	14	53 (60) 88%
Generalizability (15)	12	11	13	14	50 (60) 83%
Data collection (10)	7	9	8	8	32 (40) 80%
Sample (10)	8	8	9	9	34 (40) 85%
Data analysis (10)	8	8	9	10	35 (40) 87.5%
Theory based (10)	10	10	10	10	40 (40) 100%
Clear research questions (10)	10	9	9	10	38 (40) 95%
Effective communication (10)	10	9	9	10	38 (40) 95%
Uniqueness of the study (5)	5	4	5	5	19 (20) 95%
Utility (5)	4	5	4	5	18 (20) 90%
Total (100)	86	86	90	95	357 (400) 89.3%

of restorative justice will be reviewed. The inclusion criteria for quantitative research includes generalizability, utility, appropriate measurement, research design, sampling method and sample, statistical significance and effect size, uniqueness of the study, effective communication of the findings, clear research question, and effective use of theory. Each has its own weight based on the importance.

In order to identify the factors contributing to the overall satisfaction with mediation from victims' perspective Bradshaw and Umbreit (1998, R1) conducted a study with the programs employing a four-phase process of intake, preparation, mediation, and follow-up following the humanistic model of mediation. The study included the programs across several U.S. sites including Albuquerque, New Mexico; Minneapolis, Minnesota; Oakland, California; and Austin, Texas. While the sample included 215 victims who participated in victim–offender mediation, the data were collected from both pre-mediation and post-mediation victim interviews. The variables included in the predictor model were individual victim characteristics, victimization experience, issues in the process of mediation, the experience of fairness in the criminal justice system, and emotional reactions to the crime. The nature of the study was exploratory.

Umbreit, Vos, and Coates (2005, R2) provide a systematic review of 85 published studies on restorative justice programs, including 53 VOM studies mostly conducted in the U.S. Since the majority of the FGC and healing circles were conducted in New Zealand, Australia, and Canada, this chapter gives more attention to VOM programs. The main themes of the analysis were related to the outcomes of client satisfaction, fairness, restitution, and recidivism, as well as participant rates and reasons.

Two meta-analysis studies were reviewed. These two studies have different components to methodology than R2 particularly by having strict inclusion criteria and providing a quantitative summary of the findings that maybe beyond those a single study can provide (Bonta, Jesseman, Rugge, & Cormier, 2006). Williams-Hayes (2002, R3) conducted a study to compare the outcomes of the two different restorative justice models, VOM and FGC, by reviewing a total of 41 studies. The inclusion criteria were: 1) used either juvenile and/or adult samples; 2) implied the use of either VOM or FGC; 3) experienced a face-to-face meeting rather than indirect negotiation; and 4) involved criminal offenses rather than civil ones. Five variables were identified as potential predictors of magnitude of effect sizes: 1) the type of justice; 2) the age of the offenders; 3) the methodological quality of the studies; 4) the length of time for follow-up to assess recidivism; and 5) the location where the studies occurred.

Bonta et al. (2006, R4) provide another meta-analysis with 39 restorative justice studies. In order to be included, the studies had to have: 1) a comparison group of some type; 2) reported post-program recidivism data to be able to calculate an effect size; and 3) a longitudinal research design for the assessment of recidivism. The researcher coded over 50 variables, then grouped them into three categories: 1) the quality of methodology (e.g., random assignment and length of follow-up, etc.); 2) participant characteristics (e.g., age and race, etc.); and 3) the characteristics of the program (e.g., whether mandatory participation, etc.). Most of the programs were from the United States. Although most of the programs (93.4%) were situated within court, police, or probation/parole settings, 36% of the programs were running through private or public but noncriminal justice agencies. The programs that require a mandatory participation for offenders were up to 35%.

Research Perspective: Results

R1 identifies important contributing factors to victim satisfaction with VOM. In order of relative importance, the attitude toward the mediator, fairness of the restitution agreement, and meeting the offender accounted for 42% of the variance in satisfaction with VOM. In addition to identifying the contributing factors to victim satisfaction, the researchers indicated two important best practice components that include the importance of 1) interpersonal face-to-face encounter and 2) negotiation between victim and offender.

In R2, the VOM studies reported that typically the participation rates ranged from 40–60%. Among victims, variability exists in terms of the reasons to participate in the mediation; while restitution was one of the primary motivations, they also wanted: 1) to hold the offender accountable; 2) to learn more about the reasons that the crime happened to them; 3) to share their pains and impact of the crimes with offenders; 4) to avoid court processing; and 5) to help the offender change behavior or not to commit a repeat offense. Regarding client satisfaction in VOM programs, both victims and offenders in the majority of the studies expressed high satisfaction (80–90%) with the process as well as with the resulting agreement. While participants involved in face-to-face mediation expressed more satisfaction than their counterparts, where comparison groups were involved, those victims and offenders going through mediation were more satisfied than those going through traditional court prosecution. However, the researchers also found that there were some victims not willing to participate because they were fearful of meeting the offender again, and some of them wanted the offender to have a harsher punishment. Regarding fairness, over 80% of VOM participants believed that the process was fair to both sides. Regarding restitution, including apology, monetary and other material compensation, of those cases in VOM that completed a meeting, typically 90% or more reached agreements and approximately 80% to 90% of the contracts were reported as completed, which were greater than their counterparts, where comparison groups were involved. Lastly, in regard to recidivism, while the results were mixed overall, the researchers draw a conclusion that restorative justice programs are at least as viable as traditional approaches.

Three significant findings emerged from R3. First, after controlling for all included explanatory variables, victims participating in both VOM and FGC reported feeling less fearful of revictimization than victims in comparison groups. However, the two models did not show a significant difference in terms of achieving the restorative outcome for victims. Second, both victims and offenders in restorative justice programs were more likely to report feeling satisfied with the justice process than participants in comparison groups. However, neither victims nor offenders in VOM reported greater levels of satisfaction with the justice outcome than their counterparts. Third, participants in restorative justice programs were more likely to negotiate and complete restitution contracts when compared to the comparison groups. However, when it comes to recidivism, the analysis showed that restorative justice programs did not show a significant reduction in recidivism among offenders when compared to their counterparts.

As opposed to the previous two studies, the findings in R4 clearly indicate that restorative justice interventions are associated with significant reductions in recidivism, though it is relatively small (phi = 0.07 or 7% reduction). However, interestingly, the authors found that the more recent the studies, the larger effects were produced: studies after 1995 showed a 25% reduction in recidivism and studies prior to 1996, only 4% reduction. The authors assume that it is because the rationales and models for the recent programs are more clearly formulated in the recent studies. In addition, the restorative justice programs that were contextualized within the coercive criminal justice sanctions showed only 1% reduction in recidivism, whereas the programs delivered within a noncoercive environment showed 10% reduction. Finally, the authors observed that restorative justice programs seemed to be effective with low-risk offenders by showing 8% reduction, whereas higher risk offenders by showing −1% reduction.

The research perspective provides ample evidence in light of the restorative outcomes such as high level of satisfaction; fairness; agreement of restitution and completion rate; empowerment, particularly among victims; and some impacts on decreasing recidivism among offenders. However, the sources in this section rarely identified how restorative justice processes produce restorative justice outcomes. In sum, while findings indicate little or no differences among the models especially

Table 8.4 Research Perspective

Best Practices	Sources for Research Perspective	R1	R2	R3	R4
Mediator related	Attitude toward the mediator	x	x		
	The quality of the mediator	x	x		
	A need to treat the participants fairly to facilitate the dialogue as well as negotiation	x	x	x	
Program related	Direct (interpersonal) face-to-face human encounter	x	x	x	x
	Programs with clearly formulated rationales and models				x
	Programs contextualized within noncoercive environment (private sectors)				x
	A need to screen the attitude of the offender		x		
	A need to screen some victims (some victims want their offenders to have a harsher punishment)		x		
	More effective with low-risk offenders				x

between VOM and FGC of the restorative justice programs in terms of the impacts, restorative justice programs have provided a number of benefits or restorative outcomes. As with the consumer and professional perspectives, best practices commonly noted in three or more of the four sources from the research perspective include the mediator- and program-related factors. The mediator-related factor is that mediators need to treat the participants fairly to facilitate the dialogue as well as negotiation drawn from R1, R2, and R3. The program-related factor is the direct face-to-face human encounter from R1, R2, R3, and R4.

Summary of Current Best Practices

Overall, the three perspectives clearly document that restorative justice programs are likely to provide an opportunity for victims to be heard in the process, to receive restitution and answers, and to be empowered, all opportunities that the retributive justice approaches often are not able to provide, as many comparison studies indicated. For offenders who participated in a restorative program, if they were given the opportunity to do so, the program provided the opportunity to acknowledge responsibility for their behavior by holding themselves accountable. Offenders who participated in the restorative justice programs were significantly more likely to report having experienced fairness and more likely to successfully complete their restitution obligation than the comparison groups. Table 8.5 provides a summary of the current best practice inquiry.

The best practices commonly noted in two or more of the three perspectives are as follows. The mediator-related factors are: 1) exercising nondirective and unobtrusive style to maximize involvement of participants (e.g., neither pressuring nor pushing, and allowing sufficient time for the process drawn from

Table 8.5 Best Practices across Perspectives

	Best Practices	Consumer Perspective	Professional Perspective	Research Perspective
Mediator Related	Being nonjudgmental, open-minded, and keeping a sense of balance	1, 2, 3		
	Unobtrusive guidance during the session (e.g., nondirective style)	1, 2, 3	1, 2	
	Being empathic, respectful, patient, calm, and understanding (e.g., playing background role with good listening skills and treating participants fairly)	1, 2, 3	1, 2	1, 2, 3
	Fostering empathy, a sense of shared humanity, peace, and reconciliation or commit to mediation philosophy/principles	1, 2, 3	1, 2	
Program Related	Direct face-to-face human encounter	1, 2, 3, 4	1, 2, 3	1, 2, 3, 4
	A need for careful, compassionate preparation for both victims and offenders by using reflection and self-awareness	1, 2, 3	2, 3	
	Demonstrating a victim sensitivity	1, 2, 4	1, 2, 3	
	Meeting the offenders' needs	1, 2, 4		
	The importance of creating a safe place, in which participants can talk about painful stories and express feelings about the incident	1, 2, 3, 4		
	Working closely with public venue (e.g., local courts and probation department)	1, 2, 3	1, 2, 3	
	A need to include additional parties (e.g., families)		1, 2, 3	
	Operated by private, nonprofit, community-based agencies		1, 2, 3	
	A need for working with community groups (e.g., for volunteers, funding, and staff)		1, 3	

C and P); 2) playing a background role by being empathetic, respectful, patient, calm, and understanding and showing good listening skills as well as treating participants fairly from C, P, and R; and 3) committing to restorative justice philosophy and principles by fostering empathy, a sense of shared humanity, peace, and reconciliation from C and P. The program-related factors are: 1) the direct face-to-face human encounter drawn from C, P, and R; 2) a need for careful, compassionate preparation for both victims and offenders by using reflection and self-awareness from C and P; 3) a need for victim sensitivity; and 4) a need for working closely with public venue from C and P.

Regarding the mediator-related factors, even though the expressions were different throughout the three perspectives, one of the most important factors was the quality of the volunteer mediator, who often co-mediates with staff mediators. The mediators are expected to play a background or nondirective role by being non-judgmental, respectful, and not pushing the participants. In addition, being empathetic and demonstrating good listening skills were the other skills that they were supposed to have to achieve restorative outcomes.

The best practices based on the program-related factors are the direct face-to-face human encounter that occurs in a safe environment in the forms of especially VOM and FGC. The best practices suggest maximizing the approaches' capability to be victim-sensitive to minimize the possibility of revictimization. For example, victims are expected to continually be connected to mediators and to be able to choose what works for them throughout the processes. Also, the consumers and professionals suggested a need for screening offenders. In order to be fully informed about the expected and/or unexpected situations in the mediation process, the consumers and professionals placed an emphasis on in-person preparation. In addition, the sources from the consumer and professional perspectives suggested that the programs operated by private, nonprofit, community-based agencies in noncoercive environments were more effective in producing restorative outcomes, although they are expected to work closely with public venues such as local courts and probation departments.

Consequently, what are the best practices for crime victims and offenders to achieve restorative outcomes in the United States? There are best practices which occur in VOM as well as other models including FGC and healing circles. The three perspectives clearly suggest that in order to accomplish restorative outcomes such as victims' healing, empowerment, offenders' holding accountable, and reaching agreements on reparation, victims and offenders should be allowed to have direct face-to-face human encounters with proper preparation in a safe environment, where they can share their painful stories, feelings, and emotions to amend wrongdoings. While victims and offenders are needed to be fully informed, a careful and compassionate in-person preparation helps them to achieve more restorative outcomes in the restorative justice programs. In addition, trained community volunteer mediators with a staff co-mediator who demonstrate good listening skills and play a nondirective background role need to deliver the service. In particular, the programs are expected to maximize the possibility of delivering victim-sensitive services through a private agency situated in a noncoercive environment, which is also flexible enough to work closely with the local public venues.

Critique of Current Best Practices

The Potency Factor

The findings from the three perspectives, however, should be taken cautiously as a result of several methodological issues that need to be discussed. Although the qualities of the studies that are included in this inquiry for the research perspective, based on the highly selective nature of this inquiry, are relatively high, the rigor in existing research is one of the major concerns. Studies even within the restorative justice camp (Bradshaw & Umbreit, 1998; Umbreit et al., 1999) identify the issues related to methodological weakness such as the lack of standardized measures of satisfaction and the vulnerability to inflate client reports on levels of satisfaction, which may be true in particularly R1 and R2. In addition, the use of both quasi-experimental study designs with no random assignment that has been used in many VOM studies, which have thus failed to draw causal inferences, and cross-sectional study designs with no possibility of measuring the long-term effect of intervention, have undermined the ability to interpret the data reported on the restorative justice program studies (Umbreit, 1998; UNODC, 2006).

Restorative justice is not only an outcome but is also a process. While the existing studies mainly focus on outcomes with quantitative data, particularly on recidivism, the discussions on what has happened in the process remain under-studied. In fact, the numbers of qualitative research in restorative justice are far lower than their counterparts. In other words, relatively little attention has been given to the issue of process with qualitative data, which fits more to provide an in-depth understanding about how the programs are delivered. Umbreit, Coates, and Vos (2002) even argue that the process of restorative justice is now a "black box" because what constitutes service delivery has not been shown to outsiders. Therefore, what is important is how the program has been developed and delivered (Umbreit et al., 2005; Wemmers, 2002).

As with the research perspective, although the quality of the studies that are included in this inquiry for the consumer perspective are relatively high, many studies that included in R2 and R3 involve the aspects of qualitative research in their designs, in particular among the studies employing mixed-methods designs, the findings of these studies often fail to develop in-depth understandings of the topics under investigation. Therefore, it needs to be acknowledged that the credibility of the qualitative studies has also been damaged because there has been a lack of effort to secure the trustworthiness of inquiry (Lincoln & Guba, 1985).

In addition, the studies that are included for the professional perspective did not include a systematic sampling method, which might have left out many local restorative justice programs including newer and less well-established programs taking place around the country (Bazemore & Schiff, 2005). Therefore, there is a need for a systematic national survey to reflect the state-of-the-art approaches that are endorsed by professionals in improving and modifying the current best practices.

In short, to improve the current best practices, future study should implement more rigorous study designs for both quantitative and qualitative inquiry. Particularly, the qualitative research should focus on describing the processes of the restorative justice programs by involving the voices and opinions of both the consumers and the professionals.

Value-Critical Factors

Zehr (2002) argues that the involvement in their own cases in the justice process can be an important way to return a sense of empowerment to victims. The restorative justice programs reviewed in this chapter have shown a tremendous impact on some victims' empowerment. For example, victims participating in the programs are likely to report that they feel less fearful of revictimization and they view the process as a journey of healing. Also, studies suggest that restorative justice programs have a more positive effect on the sense of closure among victims and their feelings of well-being than the people who were not given the opportunity to do so in those circumstances (Umbreit & Vos, 2000; UNODC, 2006; White, 2001). At the same time, however, some evidence indicates a negative impact on some victims' sense of empowerment involving the restorative justice programs, such as causing fear in victims. Bazemore and Schiff (2005) noted that some victims claim the risk of secondary victimization by saying that they felt pressured to participate, to not express emotions, to forgive, and to be rushed to agree for the reparation, which is also warned by Umbreit (1999) as "fast-food" restorative justice processes. Therefore, in addition to finding the ways to better meet the needs of victims in restorative justice programs, it is also important to find ways to reduce the risk of secondary victimization to take advantage of the benefits of the programs. For example, Wemmers (2002), based on her research on victims' point of view, found that there is a need for restorative justice programs to offer follow-up services such as follow-up counseling and/or more support for victims, which can be a critical modification for the current best practice in light of being more victim-sensitive or meeting the victims' needs.

The UNODC (2006) emphasizes that restorative justice practitioners should focus on a set of restorative justice principles rather than a specific model or process. Although the best practice inquiry of this chapter suggests that the best practices are usually found and documented in VOM, it should be acknowledged that there is a lack of information of the other models of restorative justice and more importantly or admittedly VOM is not yet an ideal interpretation of restorative justice, as many scholars pointed out (Umbreit, 1999; Zehr, 1990). Therefore, what we need to do is to consistently and continually make sure the programs are following the principles of restorative justice to achieve restorative outcomes, rather than stringently following a specific practice or model (UNODC, 2006).

Although it did not make it to the final best practices, an observation made from P1 and R4 suggests that more restorative justice programs adopt written policies and procedures formulated on clearer rationales and models for the programs, which may be associated with decreasing re-offense rate among offenders, and that restorative justice programs move toward being more articulated and one step closer to its ideal expression. Although currently there are 29 states that have VOM or VOM-type statutory authority and numerous local jurisdictions that have adopted restorative justice policies (Lightfoot & Umbreit, 2004; OJJDP, 1998; Umbreit, 1998), the levels of VOM provisions are different in various states, ranging from extremely comprehensive with details on how to run the program to a simple reference to VOM within a long list of sentencing alternatives (Umbreit, Lightfoot, & Fier, 2001). This may suggest that in addition to reinforcing restorative justice principles, we should also have minimum national standards or manuals that not only prescribe acceptable standards of practice (Boyack et al., 2004) but also enhance the current best practices. For instance, one of the most emphasized aspects of restorative justice is the voluntary nature of participation. However, this important aspect did not make it to the final best practices in this chapter because, as shown throughout the three perspectives, in some programs offenders were forced to participate in the process. More importantly, some victims felt pressured to participate. According to Lightfoot and Umbreit (2004), only nine states specify that participation in VOM must be voluntary for the offender as well as the victim. It cannot be overstated, however, that as opposed to retributive justice, restorative justice should place an emphasis on the right that victims and offenders can choose to participate in the process voluntarily.

Restorative justice programs should guarantee a person to participate equally in the process regardless of that person's age, ability, sexual orientation, family status, and diverse cultures and backgrounds (OJJDP, 1998; UNODC, 2006). As Boyack et al. (2004) argue, if it is culturally inaccessible or inappropriate to participants, it is not a restorative justice program.

However, restorative justice programs reviewed in this chapter have shown some gaps when it comes to cultural competence by in general not paying attention to its application within multicultural society. Although ethnic diversity and disproportionate appearance of people of color has been one of the biggest challenges in the criminal justice fields especially in the United States, relatively little work has been done in applying restorative justice in cross-cultural contexts (Zehr, 1990; Umbreit & Coates, 2000). Accordingly, it is largely unknown how culturally competent services are provided in restorative justice programs, although practitioners in the field of restorative justice often identify that cross-cultural challenges, such as misunderstandings among participants based on the different cultural backgrounds among participants, are one of the most difficult situations (Umbreit & Coates, 2000; Umbreit & Greenwood, 1999).

While cultural differences among the parties should be taken into consideration when conducting a restorative process (UNODC, 2006), studies indicate that regardless of victims and offenders, persons of color were less likely to participate in VOM (Williams-Hayes, 2002). In particular Bonta et al. (2006), based on a total of 39 studies, observe that most offenders in the restorative justice programs were Caucasian youth (79.2%). Black youth were only 6.3%. However, it is uncertain if the low participation of people of color in restorative justice is a matter of choice by the participants. Therefore, in future research, the questions should be asked: "Is restorative justice potentially selective in terms of providing services to culturally diverse groups?" "Is choice the issue here or are they being excluded by authorities?" and "Is the same pattern taking place for victims, who happen to be people of color?" At least, at this point, it is obvious that the experiences and needs of diverse people of color have rarely been reflected in empirical studies on restorative justice programs. Although further research is needed by acquiring multi-dimensional perspectives including the consumer, professional, and research perspectives on this issue, since it is beyond the focus of this study, in the following section, several ways to enhance the cultural competence in restorative justice programs will be discussed.

Recommendations for Improving Current Best Practices

Cultural competence is a developmental process aiming at delivering culturally competent services that requires the continual acquisition of knowledge about the specific populations, the development and being equipped with advanced and related skills, and an ongoing self-evaluation about his/her own values, biases, and beliefs (Cross, Bazron, Dennis, & Isaacs, 1989; Mason, Benjamin, & Lewis, 1996; Matthews, 1996; McPhatter, 1997; Ronnau, 1994; Umbreit & Coates, 2000; Weaver, 2004). Here education for practitioners is central.

First, a culturally competent approach for each group should direct practitioners to acquire an understanding of each group and their cultures (UNODC, 2006). In so doing, restorative justice practitioners should try to get to know the participants by acquiring relevant cultural knowledge about them (Umbreit & Coates, 2000; Weaver, 2004). In order to do this, there is a need for considering specific variations to include the cultural characteristics and expectations of particular groups and individuals (Gelman, 2004). The concept of "authentization," coined first by Walton and Abo-El-Nasr (1988, p. 136) and then by Ragab (1990, p. 43) provides a direction to practitioners. The term refers to going back to the cultural roots or searching from within a clients' own indigenized and traditional culture to conceptualize and develop practice models to seek direction for cultural competence (Kee, 2004; Yip, 2005). In a similar sense, Raye (2004) argues that the paths to healing for many victims and offenders of color are found in reclaiming their root values and early cultural practices. While adding important aspects to the existing models of cultural competence, the term "authentization" sheds some light on the need for practitioners to acquire relevant cultural knowledge for the application of restorative justice to culturally and ethnically different groups in the United States. The concept enables practitioners to refocus on the world views and cultures of the local people so that their programs can be more flexible and creative in various cultural contexts (UNODC, 2006).

Second, practitioners need to prepare themselves and the participants by enhancing their skills. In fact, skill enhancement is inseparable with the acquisition of knowledge as addressed above. In order to do this, studies (Umbreit & Coates, 2000; Umbreit & Greenwood, 1999; UNODC, 2006) emphasize the importance of cultural skills training, in which practitioners can interact, participate, and experience particular cultural practices or needs to be accommodated within the restorative justice process. In particular, the cultural skills training could be expanded by including the ways to utilize the following suggestions and strategies by the New Zealand Ministry of Justice to accommodate culturally different communities (cited in UNODC, 2006, pp. 48–49): 1) seeking advice from cultural advisers; 2) working with facilitators of the same ethnicity as the participants; 3) using an interpreter; 4) holding meetings in a culturally significant venue; 5) ensuring that participants are aware of cultural differences and how these may or may not be accommodated; and 6) recruiting volunteers from all segments of the community, with appropriate gender, cultural, and ethnic balance.

Third, in delivering culturally competent restorative justice programs, restorative justice practitioners need not only be aware of but also explore their own values and biases that may or may not be related to racist attitudes, beliefs, and feelings. They should reflect upon and study their own behaviors and communication styles so that they can value and respect differences in culture as well as being comfortable with them (Sue & Sue, 1990, adapted and cited in Umbreit & Coates, 2000).

Conclusions

This chapter has focused on finding the best practices for crime victims and offenders to achieve restorative outcomes, particularly in the United States. The best practices that resulted from the consumer, professional, and research perspectives are the direct face-to-face human encounter between victims and offenders that takes place in a safe space and is mediated by trained community volunteer mediators with a staff co-mediator who demonstrates good listening skills and plays a nondirective background role. At the same time, the programs are also expected to maximize the possibility of delivering victim-sensitive services through a noncoercive private agency that works closely with local public venues. Through these best practices, the crime victims and offenders were more likely to experience satisfaction, fairness, empowerment, restitution negotiation, and completion. Likewise, they were less likely recidivate an offense.

Although the examination of the three perspectives remain partial in scope, the current best inquiry demonstrated that only few efforts have been made to make restorative justice programs more culturally competent services for people of color in the United States. Since the current best practices in restorative justice lack cultural competence, which seems to be an essential element in helping victims and juvenile offenders from different cultural backgrounds, one feasible improvement in restorative justice practice is to move the current practices toward culturally competent practices. In this sense, this chapter has implications for culturally competent restorative justice practice and research for persons of color in the United States. While practitioners, as Weaver (2004) suggests, applying restorative justice to persons of color need to provide informed and quality services by enhancing their cultural competence, researchers should pay attention to the experiences and needs of diverse people of color to improve the current best practices to allow space for cultural differences (Braithwaite, 2000). Eventually, it will help the current best practices to be even more victim- and offender-sensitive, working toward the idealization of restorative justice philosophy by respecting the differences among persons of color in restorative justice programs. Consequently, the dialogue on restorative justice and its cultural competence should continue to promote changes in this approach.

References

Arrigo, B.A., & Schehr, R.C. (1998). Restoring justice for juveniles: A critical analysis of victim-offender mediation. *Justice Quarterly, 15*(4), 629–666.

Bazemore, G., & Schiff, M. (2005). *Juvenile justice reform and restorative justice: Building theory and policy from practice.* Portland, OR: Willan Publishing.

Bazemore, G., & Umbreit, M.S. (2003). A comparison of four restorative conferencing models. In G. Johnstone (Ed.), *A restorative justice reader: Texts, sources, context* (pp. 225–243). Portland, OR: Willan Publishing.

Bonta, J., Jesseman, R., Rugge, T., & Cormier, R. (2006). Restorative justice and recidivism: Promises made, promises kept? In D. Sullivan & L. Tifft (Eds.), *Handbook of restorative justice* (pp. 108–120). New York, NY: Routledge.

Boyack, J., Bowen, H., & Marshall, C. (2004). How does restorative justice ensure good practice? In H. Zehr & B. Toews (Eds.), *Critical issues in restorative justice* (pp. 265–276). Monsey, NY: Criminal Justice Press.

Bradshaw, W., & Umbreit, M.S. (1998). Crime victims meet juvenile offenders: Contributing factors to victim satisfaction with mediated dialogue. *Juvenile & Family Court Journal, 49*(3), 17–25.

Bradshaw, W., & Umbreit, M.S. (2003). Assessing satisfaction with victim services: The development and use of the victim satisfaction with offender dialogue scale (VSODS). *International Review of Victimology, 10*, 71–83.

Braithwaite, J. (2000). *Standards for restorative justice.* Vienna, Austria: United Nations Crime Congress, Ancillary Meetings.

Butts, J.A., & Mears, D.P. (2001). Reviving juvenile justice in a get-tough era. *Youth & Society, 33*(2), 169–198.

Coates, R.B., Umbreit, M.S., & Vos, B. (2003). Restorative justice circles: An exploratory study. *Contemporary Justice Review, 6*(3), 265–278.

Cross, T.L., Bazron, B.J., Dennis, K.W., & Isaacs, M.R. (1989). *Towards a culturally competent system of care.* Washington, DC: Georgetown University Child Development Center.

Cullen, F.T., & Gendreau, P. (2000). Assessing correctional rehabilitation: Policy, practice, and prospects. *Criminal Justice, 3*, 109–175.

Drowns, R.W., & Hess, K.M. (2000). *Juvenile justice.* Belmont, CA: Wadsworth/Thomson Learning.

Elsner, A. (2006). *Gates of injustice.* Upper Saddle River, NJ: Pearson Education, Inc.

Gelman, C.R. (2004). Empirically-based principles for culturally competent practice with Latinos. *Journal of Ethnic & Cultural Diversity in Social Work, 13*(1), 83–108.

Hughes, S.P., & Schneider, A.L. (1989). Victim-offender mediation: A survey of program characteristics and perceptions of effectiveness. *Crime & Delinquency, 35*(2), 217–233.

Kee, L.H. (2004). The search from within: Research issues in relation to developing culturally appropriate social work practice. *International Social Work, 47*(3), 336–345.

Lemley, E.C. (2001). Designing restorative justice policy: An analytical perspective. *Criminal Justice Policy Review, 12*(1), 43–65.

Lightfoot, E., & Umbreit, M.S. (2004). An analysis of state statutory provisions for victim-offender mediation. *Criminal Justice Policy Review, 15*(4), 418–436.

Lincoln, Y. & Guba, E. (1985). *Naturalistic inquiry*. Thousand Oaks, CA: Sage.

MacKenzie, D.L. (2000). Evidence-based corrections: Identifying what works. *Crime & Delinquency, 46*(4), 457–471.

Mason, J.L., Benjamin, M.P., & Lewis, S. (1996). The cultural competence model: Implications for child and family mental health services. In C.A. Heflinger & C.T. Nixon (Eds.), *Families and the mental health system for children and adolescents*. Thousand Oaks, CA: Sage.

Matthews, L. (1996). Culturally competent models in human service organizations. *Journal of Multicultural Social Work, 4*(4), 131–135.

McPhatter, A.R. (1997). Cultural competence in child welfare: What is it? How do we achieve it? What happens without it? *Child Welfare, 76*, 255–278.

Morris, A. (2002). Critiquing the critics: A brief response to critics of restorative justice. *British Journal of Criminology, 42*, 596–615.

Morris, A., & Maxwell, G.M. (1993). Juvenile justice in New Zealand: A new paradigm. *The Australian & New Zealand Journal of Criminology, 26*(1), 72–90.

Niemeyer, M., & Schichor, D. (1996). A preliminary study of a large victim/offender reconciliation program. *Federal Probation, 60*(3), 30–34.

Office of Juvenile Justice and Delinquency Prevention. (1998). *Guide for implementing the balanced and restorative justice model*. Washington, DC: U.S. Department of Justice.

Petr, C.G., & Walter, U.M. (2005). Best practices inquiry: A multidimensional, value-critical framework. *Journal of Social Work Education, 41*(2), 251–267.

Ragab, I. (1990). How social work can take root in developing countries. *Social Development Issues, 12*(3), 38–51.

Raye, B. (2004). How do culture, class and gender affect the practice of restorative justice? (Part 2). In H. Zehr & B. Toews (Eds.), *Critical issues in restorative justice* (pp. 329–340). Monsey, NY: Criminal Justice Press.

Roberts, A. (Ed.). (1997). *Social work in juvenile and criminal justice settings*. Springfield, IL: Charles C Thomas Publisher.

Rogers, J.W. (1989). The greatest correctional myth: Winning the war on crime through incarceration. *Federal Probation, 53*, 21–28.

Ronnau, J.P. (1994). Teaching cultural competence: Practical ideas for social work educators. *Journal of Multicultural Social Work, 3*(1), 29–42.

Sarri, R. (1995). Criminal behavior overview. In R.L. Edwards (Ed.), *Encyclopedia of Social Work*. Washington, DC: NASW Press.

Schichor, D., & Sechrest, D.K. (1998). A comparison of mediated and non-mediated juvenile offender cases in California. *Juvenile & Family Court Journal, 49*(2), 27–39.

Schiff, M.F. (1998). Restorative justice interventions for juvenile offenders: A research agenda for the next decade. *Western Criminology Review, 1*(1). Available: http://wcr. sonoma.edu/v1n1/schiff.html.

Szmania, S.J. (2005). Offenders' communication in victim offender mediation/dialogue: A study of opening statements. *Offender Programs Report, 9*(4), 49–58.

Tonry, M., & Petersilia, J. (1999). American prisons at the beginning of the Twenty-First century. *Crime and Justice, 26*(1), 1–13.

Umbreit, M.S. (1998). Restorative justice through victim-offender mediation: A multi-site assessment. *Western Criminology Review, 1*(1), Available: http://wcr.sonoma.edu/v1n1/umbreit.html.

Umbreit, M.S. (1999). Avoiding the marginalization and McDonaldization of victim offender mediation: A case study in moving toward the mainstream. In G. Bazemore & L. Walgrave (Eds.), *Restorative juvenile justice: Repairing the harm of youth crime*. Monsey, NY: Criminal Justice Press.

Umbreit, M.S., & Coates, R.B. (2000). *Multicultural implications of restorative justice: Potential pitfalls and dangers*. Washington, DC: The Office for Victims of Crime.

Umbreit, M.S., & Greenwood, J. (1999). National survey of victim-offender mediation programs in the United States. *Mediation Quarterly, 16*(3), 235–251.

Umbreit, M.S., & Vos, B. (2000). Homicide survivors meet the offender prior to execution: Restorative justice through dialogue. *Homicide Studies, 4*(1), 63–87.

Umbreit, M.S., Bradshaw, W., & Coates, R.B. (1999). Victims of severe violence meet the offender: Restorative justice through dialogue. *International Review of Victimology, 6*, 321–343.

Umbreit, M.S., Coates, R.B., & Roberts, A.W. (1998). Impact of victim-offender mediation in Canada, England and the United States. *The Crime Victims Report, 1*(6), 83–92.

Umbreit, M.S., Coates, R.B., & Vos, B. (2002). The impact of restorative justice conferencing: A multi-national perspective. *British Journal of Community Justice, 1*(2), 21–48.

Umbreit, M.S., Lightfoot, E., & Fier, J. (2001). *Legislative statutes on victim offender mediation: A national review*. St. Paul, MN: Center for Restorative Justice and Peacemaking, University of Minnesota, 1–115.

Umbreit, M.S., Vos, B., & Coates, R.B. (2005). Restorative justice dialogue: A review of evidence-based practice. *Offender Programs Report, 9*(4), 49–64.

United Nations Office for Drug Control and Crime Prevention. (1999). *Handbook on justice for victims*. New York: Centre for International Crime Prevention.

United Nations Office for Drugs and Crime. (2006). *Handbook on restorative justice programmes*. New York, NY: United Nations.

Van Ness, D.W. (2004). Justice that restores: From impersonal to personal justice. *Journal of Religion & Spirituality in Social Work, 23*(1/2), 93–109.

Walton, R.G., & Abo-El-Nasr, M.M. (1988). Indigenization and authentization in terms of social work in Egypt. *International Social Work, 31*(1), 135–144.

Weaver, H.N. (2004). The elements of cultural competence: Applications with Native American clients. *Journal of Ethnic & Cultural Diversity in Social Work, 13*(1), 19–35.

Wemmers, J. (2002). Restorative justice for victims of crime: A victim-oriented approach to restorative justice. *International Review of Victimology, 9*, 43–59.

White, L.L. (2001). *Hope in process: A qualitative study of victim offender mediation/dialogue in Texas*. Texas A&M University.

Williams-Hayes, M.M. (2002). *The effectiveness of victim-offender mediation and family group conferencing: A meta-analysis.* Knoxville, TN: The University of Tennessee.

Yip, K.S. (2005). A dynamic Asian response to globalization in cross-cultural social work. *International Social Work, 48*(5), 593–607.

Zehr, H. (1990). *Changing lenses.* Scottdale, PA: Herald Press.

Zehr, H. (2001). *Transcending: Reflections of crime victims.* Intercourse, PA: Good Books.

Zehr, H. (2002). *The little book of restorative justice.* Intercourse, PA: Good Books.

9 Best Practices for Helping Clients Diagnosed with a Serious Mental Illness Utilize Spirituality as a Recovery Tool

Vincent R. Starnino

Studies have shown that a high percentage of people diagnosed with a serious mental illness consider spirituality to be an important aspect of their lives. Recently, increased attention has been given to the role of spirituality as a key aspect of mental health recovery. Lacking are clearly established guidelines to direct practitioners who wish to address the topic in practice. As a result, some clients may not be receiving adequate support. The goal of this inquiry is to address this gap by compiling information about best practices for helping clients diagnosed with a serious mental illness utilize spirituality as a recovery tool. A total of eight best practices are identified.

Overview of the Population and Problem of Concern

Studies have shown that a majority of the American population have religious beliefs and consider it to be an important aspect of their lives (Gallup, as cited by Bergin, 1991; Canda & Furman, 1999). Furthermore, in a study of 328 Virginia-licensed clinical social workers, psychologists, and professional counselors, practitioners claimed that approximately one-third of their clients presented such issues in practice (Sheridan, Bullis, Adcock, Berlin, & Miller, 1992). In recent years, the variety of mental health-related professions appear to be taking a closer look at the meaning of religion and spirituality in people's lives, as evidenced by increased publications on the topic in the fields of psychiatry, psychology, social work, and nursing (Canda, 1999; Owen & Khalil, 2007; Sims, 1999; Tepper, Rogers, Coleman, & Maloney, 2001).

There has been increasing evidence that religion and spirituality can be used as positive resources for healing across a number of physical and mental health domains, including hypertension, immune system dysfunction, pain, well-being, and symptoms of anxiety and depression (Canda & Furman, 1999; Corrigan, McCorkle, Schell, & Kidder, 2003; Koenig, McCullough, & Larson, 2001). Until recently, however, research outlining the positive effects of religion and spirituality on mental health focused predominantly on people who experience mild to moderate symptoms, rather than those who are considered to have a serious long-standing mental illness (Corrigan et al., 2003; Fallot, 1998a). A key study that explored the role of spirituality in the lives of people diagnosed with a serious mental illness (SMI) was conducted by Corrigan et al. (2003). The study included a national sample of 1,824 people. Over 89% of respondents described themselves as religious or spiritual, and nearly half considered themselves "very" or "extremely" religious or spiritual. Similar results were found in an earlier study by Tepper et al. (2001), which consisted of a sample of 406 people diagnosed with a mental illness who were receiving treatment at one of 13 Los Angeles mental health facilities. Results indicated that 80% of participants used religion to cope with their psychiatric difficulties.

For those diagnosed with a SMI, spirituality can play an important role in identity, meaning-making, and coping (Fallot, 1998a). Sullivan (1998) pointed out that a relationship with a higher power can function as a significant resource, as it can help people to feel a sense of control over their lives. Also noted was that spirituality can be a helpful coping mechanism for dealing with high levels of stress. In reference to external coping, Sullivan (1992a, 1998) explained that when people are diagnosed with a SMI, their social circle often narrows, and the quality of their social relationships can diminish. Religion and spirituality could provide a key resource, as involvement in a religious/spiritual community has the potential of providing social support, while a relationship with the divine can function as a central personal relationship.

Spirituality has been linked to playing an important role in the recovery process. Sullivan (1992b) conducted a study of people who had been diagnosed with a severe mental illness, but were able to achieve a high level of recovery, as represented by no hospitalizations for at least two years, able to live at least semi-independently, and were engaged in some form of vocational activity. Among the 40 people who participated, 48% reported that spiritual pursuits were central to their success.

Closely linked to the concept of mental health recovery is the growing emphasis on utilizing a strengths-based approach for working with people with SMI (Rapp, 1998; Saleebey, 1996; Sullivan, 1992b). The traditional view of mental illness has been criticized as being too pathologically focused, and is perceived as putting unnecessary artificial limits on people. The strengths perspective, rather, emphasizes the relevance of people's personal and environmental assets—religion and spirituality are recognized as valuable resources.

With increased recognition of the relevance of spirituality in the lives of people diagnosed with SMI, there is a need for clear practice guidelines to help practitioners address the spiritual needs of this population. Although a number of scholars in related fields have worked to developed assessment tools and have introduced differing approaches for integrating spirituality into mental health treatment, practice recommendations more often than not apply to generalist counseling situations, rather than specifically to the needs of the SMI population (Canda & Furman, 1999; McSherry, 2006; Richards & Bergin, 2004; Swinton, 2001). Furthermore, trying to decipher what is appropriate practice can become difficult because of differing and sometimes contradictory opinions.

Among the SMI population, several questions remain unanswered with regards to how to address the topic of spirituality in a manner that fosters recovery. Clearer guidelines are needed for professionals interested in integrating spirituality into practice. This multidimensional evidence based practice (MEBP) inquiry seeks to answer the question: "What are the best practices for helping clients diagnosed with a serious mental illness utilize spirituality as a recovery tool?"

Best Practice Inquiry Search Process

The search process for identifying relevant sources related to best practice question "What are the best practices for helping clients diagnosed with a serious mental illness utilize spirituality as a recovery tool?" began with a detailed exploration of publications listed in the following search engines: Social Services Abstracts; Social Work Abstracts; PsycINFO; ProQuest Nursing Journals; Health and Wellness Resource Center; and Worldcat. Numerous combinations of key words were entered while searching in the named search engines. Examples of combinations of key words included "spirituality and/or mental illness and/or best practice," "spirituality and/or treatment and/or mental illness," "religion and/or mental illness and/or intervention," and "spirituality and/or mental health and/or counseling." The search was limited to the past 15 years. This strategy yielded some success in regards to identifying professional sources. However, it yielded less success for identifying suitable consumer and research sources. Particularly, the author was able to find few relevant studies which focused on the testing of spiritual interventions with people diagnosed with a SMI. Most of the research articles on the topic that appeared in the various search engines included descriptive studies rather than the evaluation of spiritually related treatments. Furthermore, the target population was rarely people diagnosed with a SMI. Regarding the consumer perspective, since consumer information is rarely published, few sources were identified through search engines.

The second search strategy used for identifying sources consisted of searching through library catalogs for books on the topic of spirituality and mental health/ mental illness. The author had moderate success finding books that focused on spirituality in counseling and psychotherapy. However, few books pertained specifically to the target population (SMI). Looking at book reference sections, however, turned out to be a fruitful search strategy, as authors commonly reference research articles to support their ideas. One book in particular, titled *Faith and Mental Health* written by Harold Koenig (2005) was a useful resource for identifying several key studies consisting of research on religious and spiritually related practice interventions in the area of mental health. Two other strategies yielded some success in regards to locating consumer perspectives. First, an internet search of consumer-related sites (i.e., NAMI, consumer organizations etc.) provided some useful leads. Another search strategy included personally contacting scholars who have published on the topic of mental health recovery and possess an interest in both spirituality and the consumer movement. Consumer leaders who have either written or presented on the topic of spirituality were identified and provided some material.

Results of Best Practice Inquiry: Three Perspectives

Consumer Perspective: Sources

The three consumer sources outlined below were chosen based on their ability to meet at least four the following criteria: 1) the source appears as an article in a peer-reviewed journal; 2) represents an authentic consumer voice; 3) the author is an influential leader in the consumer mental health recovery movement; 4) the author has published previously in a refereed journal; 5) the author has presented at conferences on spirituality and/or recovery; and 6) the author is able to describe specific guidelines for practitioners.

C1 (Murphy, 2000) was chosen based on its ability to meet criteria 1, 2, 3, and 4. The article outlines findings from an eight-participant qualitative study of consumers' illness experiences. The consumers in the study had all experienced a psychotic episode, but were able to draw on their spiritual beliefs as a coping tool during the post-illness phase. Several important implications for practitioners (reported below) can be drawn from this article in regards to supporting clients' efforts to utilize their spiritual beliefs to help them heal—especially during the "post-illness" phase.

C2 (Deegan, 2004) met criteria 2, 3, 4, 5, and 6. This source consists of a paper written for a mental health recovery conference in Kansas. The author describes a personal experience in which she experienced meaningful spiritual insights in the midst of a psychotic episode. She was able to draw on this spiritual teaching during both the active psychotic and the post-psychotic phases of her illness. In both cases, the author's spiritual experience provided her with hope and an avenue for healing. The author gives direct recommendations for practitioners.

C3 (Leibrich, 2002) met criteria 1, 2 3, 5, and 6. This paper was originally written for a national conference in Vancouver, Canada. The author shares how she has used spirituality in her personal journey. An emphasis is put on listening to people's stories and their interpretations of what spirituality means to them, regardless of how it may differ from our own world view. Recommendations are given for practitioners who have failed to recognize the whole person, namely the spiritual aspect of human service consumers.

Consumer Perspective: Results

Table 9.1 provides a list of 15 practice themes identified by consumers from the three articles summarized above. Because consumers did not write specifically for professionals as their target audience, guidelines for best practice were sometimes explicitly stated, while at other times they were implied. Both are included as qualifiers for best practice from a consumer perspective, because both explicitly stated and implied themes offer powerful insights for professionals interested in addressing spiritual issues with mental health consumers. All three consumers agreed on seven practice themes while each of the other eight themes was mentioned by only one consumer. Therefore, only the seven themes that were agreed upon by all three consumers are discussed as best practices from a consumer perspective. (Numbers correspond to numbers in Table 9.1.)

1) Honor and encourage consumers' own interpretations of their spiritual experiences and beliefs

A theme that was common to all three consumer writers was that consumers' interpretations of their spiritual experiences and beliefs need to be valued and encouraged. C3 commented that by defining their spirituality for themselves, clients can prevent others from having the authority to validate or invalidate their experiences.

2) Recognize clients' need for meaning-making, and make room for clients' exploration of spirituality as a potential meaning-making tool

A second theme that was agreed upon by all three consumers is that mental health consumers often draw upon their spiritual beliefs to make meaning. Clients can experience a period of meaninglessness and/or depression following an episode of psychiatric illness. Practitioners need to allow clients to find answers to profound questions about the meaning of their lives and of their illness experience through exploration of their spirituality.

3) Promote clients' spirituality as a potential source of strength/explore and encourage clients' spiritual resources

All consumer writers spoke about spirituality as an overall potential positive resource for people recovering from SMI. Some of positive ways in which spirituality can be a strength or resource include providing necessary hope during difficult periods and involvement in a faith-based community.

4) Recognize that clients' spiritual beliefs can manifest differently during different phases of illness

All three consumers spoke about how one's spiritual beliefs can manifest differently according to phase of illness. Consumers in C1's article spoke about their delusions containing negative or unpleasant religious or spiritual themes, while during their post-psychotic phase of illness they were able to utilize their spiritual resources in a positive way. C3 spoke about sometimes having difficulty connecting to her spirituality during periods of severe depression.

5) Recognize and encourage the transformative potential of illness experience

C1 pointed out that mental illness can lead to spiritual growth or transformation. Both C1 and C3 linked spiritual growth to becoming an improved person with greater capacity for compassion for others and a deeper sense of self.

7) Be able to distinguish between illness- and nonillness-related spiritual beliefs/recognize and validate the authentic aspects of clients' spiritual experiences

All consumers expressed concern that some practitioners, especially adherents to a strict medical-based model, are at risk of dismissing too easily mental health consumers' spiritual experiences. Practitioners are guided to listen more closely to clients' experiences before assuming pathology. Consumer authors all spoke about the need to have their spiritual experiences valued, even when they happen in the midst of the active symptom phase of psychiatric illness.

9) A client-centered approach

All three consumers advocated a client-centered approach to addressing consumers' spirituality in practice. Listening, validating and respecting were common themes.

Table 9.1 Consumer Perspectives on Best Practice

Best Practice	C1	C2	C3
1. Honor and encourage consumers' own interpretations of their spiritual experiences and beliefs	X	X	X
2. Recognize clients' need for meaning-making, and make room for clients' exploration of spirituality as a potential meaning-making tool	X	I	I
3. Promote clients' spirituality as a potential source of strength/ explore and encourage clients' spiritual resources	X	X	X
4. Recognize that clients' spiritual beliefs can manifest differently during different phases of illness	X	X	X
5. Recognize and encourage the transformative potential of illness experience	X	X	X
6. Spirituality in conjunction with medication is ideal	X		
7. Be able to distinguish between illness- and nonillness-related spiritual beliefs/recognize and validate the authentic aspects of clients' spiritual experiences	X	X	X
8. Professionals should recognize their own limitations and biases regarding spirituality		X	
9. A client-centered approach	I	X	X
10. Remind clients of their identified spiritual teaching (or resource) when it can be a helpful resource or coping tool		X	
11. Practitioners need to explore their own spirituality in order to be able to connect with clients' spirituality		X	
12. Creativity as a form of spirituality (poetry)			X
13. Treat the whole person, not just the illness			X
14. Spirituality is a wordless concept			X
15. Tolerate ambiguity			X

Note:
*X=explicitly stated; I=implied

Professional Perspective: Sources

The five professional sources outlined below were chosen based on their ability to meet at least five the following criteria: 1) the chosen article is published in a peer-reviewed journal; 2) the author has many years of direct practice experience; 3) clear and specific practice guidelines are offered; 4) guidelines are applicable to generalist human service provision as opposed to religion-specific; 5) practice recommendations are targeted at the SMI population specifically; 6) the author's proposed practice recommendations are supported by a well-established theoretical foundation; 7) the author is an influential figure on the topic; and 8) the author has presented practice recommendations to a major mental health board.

P1 (Puchalaski, Larson, & Lu, 2001) was chosen based on its ability to meet criteria 1, 3, 4, 5, and 8. In the mid-1990s a committee of psychiatrists formed with the purpose of creating a curriculum for training psychiatry residents to address the spiritual dimensions of their clients' lives. The article outlines practice guidelines, which includes a set of knowledge, skills, and attitudes that psychiatrists are expected to acquire in order to be able to address spirituality effectively in practice.

Criteria 1, 2, 3, 4, 5, and 7 were met by P2 (Kehoe, 1998). The article is a description of the author's 16 years of experience facilitating a "Spiritual Issues and Values" group with people who have been diagnosed with a SMI. The group was born out of a recognized gap in services for SMI clients who identified spirituality and/or religion to be important. In the article the author describes group content and processes, and provides several examples of clients' responses to the group intervention.

Criteria met by P3 (Fallot, 1998b) include 1, 2, 4, 5, and 7. This work was published simultaneously as a book chapter and in a special edition of the *New Directions for Mental Health Services* journal. The article is the last chapter of both the book and the journal edition and summarizes both theoretical and practical guidelines for professionals looking to incorporate spirituality into mental health treatment.

P4 (Swinton, 2001) met criteria 2, 3, 4, 5, and 6. Practice guidelines for spiritual care in the mental health field based on a hermeneutical/phenomenological theoretical approach are introduced. A strong emphasis is placed on valuing client's interpretations and meaning-making. The deepest levels of listening, understanding and empathy are emphasized. The author's practice guidelines are based on a qualitative research study that he conducted on the topic, which includes the consumer voice.

Criteria met by P5 (Lukoff, 2005) include 2, 4, 5, 7, and 8. The particular book chapter was chosen because it addresses important issues related to distinguishing between different types of altered states of consciousness, namely, spiritual emergencies and pathological-based psychotic episodes. The author offers guidelines for practitioners for treating spiritual issues of both those who have experienced psychotic spiritual emergencies and those who have experienced psychosis stemming from mental illness. The author draws on transpersonal theory.

Professional Perspective: Results

Table 9.2 provides a list of 20 practice themes identified by professionals from the five articles summarized above. Among professionals, practice guidelines were more often than not explicitly stated, rather than simply implied. In Table 9.2, explicitly stated guidelines are identified with an "X," while implied guidelines are labeled with an "I." To be included as a best practice in this category, a practice theme needed to be: 1) identified by at least four out of the five authors either explicitly or implicitly, or 2) identified explicitly by at least three of the five authors. Out of a total of 20 practice themes listed in Table 9.2, 12 qualified as best practices. (Numbers correspond to numbers in Table 9.2.)

1) Respect the whole person by including the spiritual aspect of clients
Four out of five professionals expressed a need for professionals to understand and address clients more holistically, namely, paying attention to clients' spiritual/religious beliefs is a necessary component for a more holistic approach to mental health.

2) A client-centered approach
All five authors advocated the use of client-centered strategies for addressing clients' spirituality in practice. Practitioner skills and attitude such as empathy, compassion, respect, nonjudgmentalism and collaborative decision-making were emphasized.

3) Recognize clients' need for meaning-making/make room for clients' exploration of spirituality as a potential meaning-making tool
Meaning making was touched upon by all five authors. Authors spoke about clients' need to find meaning related to their illness experience. For example, some clients may ask questions such as "Why me?" or "Am I being punished by God?" Other clients may want to discuss the meaning of life in general, unrelated to their psychiatric illness.

4) Refer/collaboration with religious professionals
Four authors suggested or implied that practitioners should either refer to or collaborate with clergy.

5) Spiritual assessment
Three professionals spoke about the need to include questions about clients' spiritual or religious beliefs as part of the mental health assessment process. Also recommended was utilizing information gained from the assessment for treatment planning.

7) Understand and discuss the ways in which clients' spirituality and mental illness interact
Authors pointed out that spirituality has the potential to affect symptoms (as would be the case when a client draws on their spiritual resources to relieve

depression); while symptoms can affect a person's spirituality (e.g., a person believes they are a prominent religious figure when they are experiencing psychosis).

8) Be able to distinguish between illness- and nonillness-related spiritual beliefs/recognize and validate the authentic aspects of clients' spiritual experiences
Four out of five authors addressed the potential for clients to experience delusions containing spiritual or religious content. Authors warned that practitioners need to correctly distinguish between illness- and nonillness-related spiritual beliefs. P5 addressed the topic of spiritual emergencies, which refer to sudden and intense spiritual experiences. For some people, spiritual emergencies can be dramatic, leading to a temporary feeling of losing oneself. According to the author, spiritual emergencies are often an important step leading toward authentic spiritual growth, and therefore need to be distinguished from experiences related to mental illness. P4 and P5 strongly advised that regardless of a client's level of pathology, spiritual experiences still carry a certain level of authenticity, and therefore should be explored and validated by professionals.

9) Practitioners need to educate themselves in the area of spirituality
Three of the five authors felt that in order for practitioners to be able to address clients' spirituality, a certain level of understanding of the topic is essential. Since all of the professional sources were nondenominationally oriented, authors promoted a universal understanding of spirituality, which includes gaining knowledge of a variety of spiritual and religious belief systems.

10) Address both helpful and unhelpful beliefs with clients
Four out of five authors acknowledged that clients sometimes struggle with negative beliefs. Authors recommend that practitioners discuss openly with clients how both positive and negative spiritual beliefs impact them (e.g., client may have the negative belief that they are being punished by God).

15) Explore spiritual themes with clients
Spiritual themes such as hope, courage, and forgiveness were mentioned by professionals as important topics to discuss with clients in the context of addressing clients' spirituality and recovery journey.

16) Promote clients' spirituality as a potential source of strength/explore and encourage clients' spiritual resources
Authors discussed the importance of acknowledging and promoting clients' strengths, which include clients' spiritual resources. This relates to a sense that the mental health profession has traditionally either ignored clients' spirituality or viewed it as pathological.

19) Honor and encourage consumers' own interpretations of their spiritual experiences and beliefs
Authors suggested that practitioners should consider clients' interpretations of their spiritual experiences and beliefs. P4 and P5 recommended using a narrative approach to helping clients reframe their spiritual experiences in a positive way, rather than viewing their experiences as pathological.

Table 9.2 Professional Perspectives on Best Practice

	Best Practice	*P1*	*P2*	*P3*	*P4*	*P5*
1.	Respect the whole person by including the spiritual aspect of clients	X		X	X	X
2.	A client-centered approach	X	X	X	X	I
3.	Recognize clients' need for meaning-making/make room for clients' exploration of spirituality as a potential meaning-making tool	I	X	I	X	X
4.	Refer/collaboration with religious professionals	I		X	X	I
5.	Spiritual assessment	X		X	X	
6.	Understand impact of spirituality on development	X				
7.	Understand and discuss the ways in which clients' spirituality and mental illness interact	X	X		I	I
8.	Be able to distinguish between illness- and nonillness-related spiritual beliefs/recognize and validate the authentic aspects of clients' spiritual experiences	X	X		X	X
9.	Practitioners need to educate themselves in the area of spirituality	X		X	X	
10.	Address both helpful and unhelpful beliefs with clients	X	X		X	X
11.	Practitioners need to be aware of their own biases and its impact on treatment	X			X	
12.	Help clients develop tolerance and understanding of religious and spiritual diversity		X	I		
13.	Do not proselytize		X			
14.	Discuss spiritual values		X	X	I	
15.	Explore spiritual themes with clients		X	I	I	I
16.	Promote clients' spirituality as a potential source of strength/explore and encourage clients' spiritual resources		X	I	X	X
17.	Utilize a hermeneutical–phenomenological approach			X		
18.	Consider the role of language and cultural context			X		
19.	Honor and encourage consumers' own interpretations of their spiritual experiences and beliefs			X	X	X
20.	Mind–body practices (meditation)					X

Note:
*X=explicitly stated; I=implied

Research Perspective: Sources

It is important to point out that there is a dearth of research on spiritual interventions for people diagnosed with SMI (see the later Potency Critique section for
a more detailed explanation of the status of current research.) In total, the author
located ten intervention studies which included people with some type of mental
illness as part of the sample. Priority was given to those studies which focused on
people diagnosed with serious mental disorders. Ultimately, sources were chosen
according to the scores they received on quality rating scales created specifically
for this best practice inquiry. Separate scales were created for the quantitative and
qualitative sources. Nine criteria are included in each scale, along with the
maximum number of points that can be allotted according to the ability of a source
to meet each criterion. Tables 9.3 and 9.4 present the quality rating scale scores
for the seven research-based sources that were chosen to represent best practices
from the research perspective. Five of the chosen sources are based on quantitative
studies, while two are of a qualitative nature.

R1 (Lindgren & Coursey, 1995) was one of the earliest studies to publish on the
effects of spirituality group treatment for people diagnosed with SMI. The study
used a pre-test/post-test research design, which included treatment and waitlist
groups. A highly structured four-session psychoeducational spirituality group was
devised. Thirty clients from three mental health sites participated, as six different
spirituality groups were formed for the study. The proposed spirituality group
treatment was open to people of all faiths. Topics addressed included self-
awareness, understanding the impact of one's spiritual values, meanings given to
one's illness, the effects of negative interpretations, forgiveness, and general
discussion of people's spiritual experiences. Researchers examined the effects of
the spirituality group on measures of depression, hopelessness, spiritual support,

Table 9.3 Summary of Quality Criteria Scoring for Quantitative Research Sources

Criteria	Max # of Points	R1	R2	R5	R6	R7	Total
1. Matches topic area	(10)	10	6	4	5	4	29 (50)
2. Contributes useful knowledge/ implications for practice	(20)	15	10	8	8	7	48 (100)
3. Conceptual/theoretical base	(10)	6	7	6	4	4	27 (50)
4. Data collection/measurement	(10)	8	7	9	5	6	35 (50)
5. Research design	(15)	10	6	12	9	10	47 (75)
6. Sample	(10)	5	5	4	6	6	26 (50)
7. Data analysis/results	(10)	4	6	5	5	6	26 (50)
8. Intervention clearly described/ fidelity of implementation	(10)	6	10	6	5	4	31 (50)
9. Clearly written/limitations explained	(5)	5	5	4	2	2	18 (25)
Total (100)		69	62	58	49	49	287 (500)

Table 9.4 Summary of Quality Criteria Scoring for Qualitative Research Sources

Criteria	Max # of Points	R3	R4	Total
1. Relevance to topic	(10)	10	9	19 (20)
2. Contributes useful knowledge/Implications for practice	(20)	16	12	28 (40)
3. Historical/theoretical context	(10)	6	7	13 (20)
4. Methods	(10)	4	4	8 (20)
5. Sample	(10)	4	5	9 (20)
6. Data analysis	(10)	3	5	8 (20)
7. Trustworthiness	(10)	5	4	9 (20)
8. Communicating findings/Voice	(15)	6	10	16 (30)
9. Reputable source	(5)	4	3	7 (10)
Total (100)		58	59	117 (200)

self-esteem, and purpose of life. Results showed significant change only for the spiritual support measure from pre-test to post-test. The authors also conducted interviews with each participant and included the combined findings from these interviews with the statistical results to make a strong argument that a spirituality group treatment model is an effective approach for helping enhance clients' recovery. A limitation of the study is that the duration of the group treatment may not have been long enough to be able to yield significant results on some of the measures other than spiritual support. The authors considered the study to be exploratory.

R2 (Kabat-Zinn et al., 1992) used a repeated measures design to test the effectiveness of participating in a meditation-based outpatient stress reduction program. The treatment was eight weeks long and was in a course format, as participants attended weekly classes. Also included was a day-long meditation retreat at the sixth session. Finally, participants were expected to practice meditation at home on a regular basis. A total of 22 people that met the criteria for generalized anxiety and/or panic disorder comprised the sample. The authors used a variety of measures, which mainly assessed levels of depression and anxiety. The results indicated improvement in both anxiety and depression from pre-test to post-test. The authors concluded that a mindfulness meditation program can help to reduce anxiety and panic symptoms for people diagnosed with an anxiety disorder. A strength of the article is that the treatment program appeared to be well designed and implemented. A limitation is that there lacked a comparison group.

R3 (Phillips, Lakin, & Pargament, 2002) offered a preliminary report on a semi-structured spirituality group treatment approach which was designed to offer participants information as well as creating opportunity for discussion about a variety of spiritual themes including spiritual struggles, spiritual resources, forgiveness, and hope. Authors concluded that a group format is a safe and effective strategy for helping people diagnosed with a SMI to explore their spiritual resources. This article offers a relevant contribution to the knowledge base on spiritual interventions for people diagnosed with SMI. A limitation is that it does not appear to follow the standard format of a qualitative study. The authors mentioned that they plan to publish a follow-up study with quantitative results in the future.

R4 (O'Rourke, 1997) presents the findings from a qualitative study which evaluates the effectiveness of a group psychotherapy approach for people diagnosed with SMI. The group treatment was designed to assist clients in examining their spiritual beliefs, with an emphasis on identifying one's spiritual resources, as well as exploring spiritual or religious conflicts. The author, guided by object relations theory, concluded that a spiritual psychotherapy approach can provide a transitional space for clients as they resolve emotional and spiritual crises, essentially allowing movement toward higher levels of functioning. A limitation of the study is that it included only one treatment group. All 12 participants were from the same mental health center. Nevertheless, the study is key in that it shares relevant insights related to spiritual interventions for people with mental illness.

R5 (Propst, Ostrom, Watkins, Dean, & Mashburn, 1992) looked at the effectiveness of an adapted cognitive–behavioral therapy approach for treating clinical depression in highly religious clients. Standard cognitive–behavioral therapy was adapted to include religious rationales and arguments for refuting irrational thoughts. The study compared three forms of therapy (religious cognitive therapy, standard cognitive therapy, and pastoral counseling) and a waitlist group. The sample comprised of 59 participants who were randomly assigned to one of the groups. All groups showed a higher rate of improvement than the waitlist group at post-test, as well as at three-month and two-year follow-ups. Specifically, those who participated in religious cognitive therapy and pastoral counseling showed a quicker rate of improvement than standard cognitive therapy amongst highly religious clients. However, at three month follow-up those who had participated in standard cognitive therapy showed similar gains to the other two treatment groups. In conclusion, the authors argued that adapting standard cognitive–behavioral therapy to make it more relevant for highly religious clients could lead to quicker symptom alleviation. Also, the authors were surprised to discover that nonreligious therapists were actually more successful at administering religious cognitive therapy than were religious therapists. A limitation of the study is that some of the results are mixed and need to be interpreted cautiously. Implications are offered for nonreligious therapists working with religious clients.

R6 (Azhar, Varma, & Dharap, 1994) evaluated the effectiveness of supplanting standard treatment approaches for anxiety disorders with an additional religious component. The study was conducted in Malaysia and the sample consisted of 62 highly religious Muslim clients who met the Diagnostic and Statistical Manual for Mental Disorders (DSM) criteria for an anxiety disorder. The sample was randomly assigned to a treatment group and control group. The control group received supportive psychotherapy, along with anxiety medication. The experimental graph received the same treatment as the control group but were given additional religious psychotherapy, which included discussing religious issues, reading the Koran, and encouraging prayer. The results indicated that the group that received the additional religious psychotherapy responded faster than the group that received standard therapy. At six-month follow-up, however, both groups showed similar improvement. The authors conclude that supplementing standard therapy with religious content could make treatment more relevant to religious clients, which can lead to quicker improvements. A limitation of the study is that the sample was homogeneous. It consisted entirely of highly religious Muslim clients from one area in Malaysia. Nevertheless, the findings have important implications for highly religious clients.

R7 (Razali, Hasanah, Aminah, & Subramaniam, 1998) is basically a replication of Azhar et al.'s (1994) study. Both studies are conducted in Malaysia with religious Muslim participants and both look at the effectiveness of supplementing standard therapy with religious content for treating anxiety. This study yielded similar results but with a larger sample (n = 106 in the experimental group and n = 97 in the control group).

Research Perspective: Results

Table 9.5 provides a list of 22 practice themes identified by researchers from the seven studies summarized above. Among researchers, all practice guidelines were explicitly stated. To qualify as a best practice, a practice theme needed to be identified by at least three out of seven researchers. A total of nine practice guidelines met this criterion and are discussed below as best practices from researchers' perspectives. (Numbers correspond to numbers in Table 9.5.)

1) Recognize clients' need for meaning-making/make room for clients' exploration of spirituality as a potential meaning-making tool
Three of the researcher sources concluded that clients benefit from finding spiritual meaning related to their psychiatric illness and other life experiences.

6) A client-centered approach
Four research sources emphasized the need for practitioners to use a client-centered approach for addressing clients' spiritual beliefs. Attitudes and skills that were mentioned include valuing and respecting clients' beliefs, listening, being nonjudgmental, providing a safe environment and establishing therapeutic rapport.

8) Address both helpful and unhelpful beliefs with clients
Three researchers discussed the need for practitioners to address both positive and negative spiritual beliefs that clients may have. R3 used the terms "positive" and "negative" religious coping to help practitioners distinguish between healthy and unhealthy use of spirituality and/or religion. Negative belief styles are thought to be counterproductive for clients who are striving to recover.

9) Spirituality group is an ideal model for addressing spirituality
Four out of the seven studies chosen outlined some form of group treatment for dealing with spiritual-related issues. Three of these four studies were of a qualitative nature.

10) Explore spiritual themes with clients
Three research sources recommended discussing spiritual themes such as hope and forgiveness with clients.

13) Explore and encourage clients' spiritual resources
Four sources emphasized the need for practitioners to encourage clients in identifying and utilizing personal and community spiritual resources. A variety of potential resources were mentioned including prayer, meditation, nature, church, and scripture.

15) Avoid coercion or proselytizing
Three sources spoke about the need to avoid coercion or proselytizing when clients' spiritual beliefs are addressed.

16) Honor and encourage consumers' own interpretations of their spiritual experiences and beliefs
Four research sources outlined the importance of allowing clients to define their own spiritual issues.

20) Adapt standard therapies when working with highly religious clients
Three sources presented standard treatment approaches that were either adapted or supplemented to include religious content. In each of the three studies the population was very homogeneous and the treatment was geared toward people from a specific religion. Regardless, the three studies combined to make a strong point about the benefits of adapting standard therapy in order make it more relevant for highly religious clients.

Summary Conclusions of Current Best Practices

Thus far, seven best practices have been identified from a consumer perspective, while 12 were identified from a professional perspective, and nine were identified from a researcher perspective. In order to accurately reflect current understanding of what the best practices are for helping clients utilize their spiritual propensities to enhance mental health recovery, best practice recommendations that were in common among the perspectives have been identified in efforts to present a "finalized" or "overall" list. Only best practice recommendations that were in common to at least two out of three perspectives are considered as representative of overall best practices. In total, eight overall best practices have been identified, as outlined in Table 9.6.

Table 9.5 Research Perspectives on Best Practice

Best Practice	R1	R2	R3	R4	R5	R6	R7
1. Recognize clients' need for meaning-making/ make room for clients' exploration of spirituality as a potential meaning-making tool	X		X	X			
2. Proceed cautiously in discussing spiritual issues	X						
3. Obtain mutual consent from client	X						
4. Practitioners should possess an understanding of diverse religious and spiritual perspectives	X						
5. Practitioners should have an understanding of ethical issues involved in addressing spirituality	X		X				
6. A client-centered approach	X		X	X			X
7. Have a list of religious or spiritual referrals available	X			X			
8. Address both helpful and unhelpful beliefs with clients	X		X	X			
9. Spirituality group is an ideal model for addressing spirituality	X	X	X	X			
10. Explore spiritual themes with clients	X		X	X			
11. Mindfulness meditation		X					
12. Explore impact of childhood trauma on spiritual development				X			
13. Explore and encourage clients' spiritual resources			X	X		X	X
14. Emphasize tolerance of different viewpoints			X	X			
15. Avoid coercion or proselytizing			X	X			X
16. Honor and encourage consumers' own interpretations of their spiritual experiences and beliefs				X	X	X	X
17. Discuss how psychiatric symptoms affect one's spirituality				X			
18. Assessment				X			
19. Draw on object relations theory				X			
20. Adapt standard therapies when working with highly religious clients					X	X	X
21. Pastoral counseling					X		
22. Explore clients' values						X	X

Table 9.6 Overall Best Practices (best practices that are common to at least two out of three perspectives)

"Overall" Best Practices	Consumer	Professional	Researcher
1. Recognize clients' need for meaning-making/make room for clients' exploration of spirituality as a potential meaning-making tool	BP #2 (C1-X, C2-I, C3-I)	BP #3 (P1-I, P2-X, P3-I, P4-X, P5 X)	BP #1 (R1-X, R3-X, R4-X)
2. Honor and encourage consumers' own interpretations of their spiritual experiences and beliefs	BP #1 (C1-X, C2-X, C3-X)	BP #19 (P3-X, P4-X, P5-X)	BP #16 (R4-X, R5-X, R6-X, R7-X)
3. Promote clients' spirituality as a potential source of strength/explore and encourage clients' spiritual resources	BP #3 (C1-X, C2-X, C3-X)	BP #16 (P2-X, P3-I, P4-X, P5-X)	BP #13 (R3-X, R4-X, R6-X, R7-X)
4. A client-centered approach	BP #9 (C1-I, C2-X, C3-X)	BP #2 (P1-X, P2-X, P3-X, P4-X, P5-I)	BP #6 (R1-X, R3-X, R4-X, R7-X)
5. Understand and discuss the various ways in which clients' spirituality and mental illness can interact/ clients'spiritual beliefs can manifest differently during different phases of illness*	BP #4 *(Combined C#4 with P#7) (C1-X, C2-X, C3-X)	BP #7 (P1-X, P2-X, P4-I, P5-I)	
6. Be able to distinguish between illness- and nonillness-related spiritual beliefs/recognize and validate the authentic aspects of clients' spiritual experience	BP #7 (C1-X, C2-X, C3-X)	BP #8 (P1-X, P2-X, P4-X, P5-X)	
7. Address both helpful and unhelpful beliefs with clients		BP #10 (P1-X, P2-X, P4-X, P5-X)	BP #8 (R1-X, R3-X, R4-X)
8. Explore spiritual themes with clients		BP #15 (P2-X, P3-I, P4-I, P5-I)	BP #10 (R1-X, R3-X, R4-X)

Note:

*Best practice #5 is a new category that was made from combining best practice # 4 from the consumer perspective list (*Clients' spiritual beliefs can manifest differently during different phases of illness*) with best practice #7 from the professional perspective list (*Understand and discuss the various ways in which clients' spirituality and mental illness can interact*). These were combined because they focus on a similar theme.

**X=explicitly stated; I=implied.

From this point on, whenever the term "best practice" is used, it will refer only to those practices that have been identified as overall best practices listed in Table 9.6. Although the three perspectives differed on some aspects, there was a high degree of similarity with regards to attitudes and strategies related to validating clients' spirituality. In total, four best practices were agreed upon by all three perspectives, while four others were agreed upon by two out of the three perspectives.

Best practice #1 outlines an expectation for practitioners to recognize clients' need for meaning-making. All three perspectives acknowledged that the illness experience often necessitates the need to re-evaluate the meaning of one's life. Practitioners are expected to play a role in aiding clients to explore meaning. A second best practice agreed upon by all three perspectives was that practitioners should honor clients' own interpretations of their spiritual experiences and beliefs. Namely, it was felt that practitioners who do not make efforts to emphasize clients' interpretations are at risk of disregarding and misinterpreting what deeply matters to clients. Two professionals described a narrative approach as an ideal strategy for eliciting clients' interpretations, while three researchers mentioned the importance of honoring highly religious clients' interpretations of psychiatric illness, which may be markedly different than standard psychological/biological-based interpretations. A third best practice that was agreed upon unanimously was related to exploring, affirming and promoting spiritual-related strengths and resources available to clients. Practitioners are expected to recognize clients' capacity to utilize spirituality to induce things such as hope and courage, which are important factors in advancing one's recovery. Some personal and community-related resources that were identified among the three perspectives include prayer, meditation, nature, scripture, and involvement in a faith community. A fourth best practice—also identified across all three perspectives—is that practitioners are expected to utilize a client-centered approach when addressing spirituality with clients. Namely, attitudes and skills such as listening, respect, validation, nonjudgmentalism, collaborative decision-making, and providing a safe therapeutic environment were emphasized.

A fifth best practice was agreed upon by consumers and professionals. Both perspectives outlined the need for practitioners to understand and discuss with clients the various ways in which spirituality and mental illness can interact. It was suggested that some clients with SMI may experience spirituality differently according to their illness phase (consumers were most strong in making this point). Practitioners need to understand and openly discuss both how illness symptoms can affect one's spirituality (e.g. as in the case where a person with "normal" spiritual beliefs suddenly becomes delusional and believes they are Jesus), and also how spirituality can affect one's course of illness (e.g. as in the case when the same person is able to experience relief from post-psychotic depressive symptoms by drawing on their "regular" spirituality). This best practice is especially relevant to the SMI population because many experience several cycles of symptom phases. A sixth best practice—also agreed upon by consumers and professionals—is related to practitioners being able to distinguish between illness- and nonillness-related spiritual beliefs. This, in turn, is related to practitioners' ability to recognize and validate the authentic aspects of clients' spiritual experiences. Concerns were expressed that practitioners sometimes have difficulty distinguishing between different types of spiritual experiences. It is believed that practitioners need to be trained to be better able to discern. This being said, even in cases in which a client's spirituality is understood as being meshed within psychotic processes, practitioners are nevertheless expected to recognize that aspects of the client's spiritual experiences can be authentic and meaningful to the person experiencing them.

Best practices #7 and # 8 were agreed upon by professionals and researchers. Best practice #7 states that practitioners should address both helpful and unhelpful spiritual beliefs with clients. It was pointed out that some clients may hold spiritual beliefs that can negatively impact their recovery (e.g. "God is punishing me"). Some authors presented a group treatment approach as an ideal format for clients to explore the impact of both helpful and unhelpful beliefs. Finally, best practice #8 suggests that practitioners should explore spiritual themes with clients. Some of the themes mentioned include hope, courage, and forgiveness. Once again, authors who presented a group format were most likely to encourage the exploration of spiritual themes.

Note that there are eight practices that had been identified as best practices within at least one perspective (consumer, professional, or researcher), but did not make the finalized list of best practices outlined in Table 9.6. These practices include the following: 1) recognize and encourage the transformative potential of illness experience (consumer); 2) respect the whole person by including the spiritual aspect of clients (professional); 3) refer/collaboration with religious professionals (professional); 4) spiritual assessment (professional); 5) practitioners need to educate themselves in the area of spirituality (professional); 6) spirituality group is an ideal model for addressing spirituality (researcher); 7) avoid coercion or proselytizing (researcher); and 8) adapt standard therapies when working with highly religious clients (researcher). This list is included in efforts to illustrate in which manner the three perspectives differ in regards to opinions on best practices. Although there are some differences among the three perspectives, there does not appear to be a high degree of disagreement or contradiction. Rather, each perspective appears to differ mainly in that each adds to the knowledge base by emphasizing different elements of practice. For example, conducting a proper spiritual assessment was emphasized primarily by the professional perspective, but other perspectives did not advocate against this practice. Overall, the consumer perspective was most focused on validating clients' experiences (although, as stated above, all perspectives emphasized this point to some extent). The professional perspective was the most comprehensive of the three perspectives. Practitioners' attitudes and use of the therapeutic relationship was most pronounced. Researchers were most apt to focus on the effectiveness of packaged treatment models rather than isolated practice themes or concepts.

Critique and Recommendations

Potency Critique

Although much has been written about spirituality and religion in the human services in the past few years, best practices are at the very early stage of development. No articles or books on the topic of spirituality and mental health referred to the term "best practice." Furthermore, although some have written about strategies for incorporating spirituality into practice, few have focused their attention on the SMI population specifically. It is worth noting that there was considerably more available information on the topic from the professional perspective than the other two perspectives. For this reason, some difficult decisions needed to be made in choosing professional sources. This writer made efforts to choose the highest quality sources that were most relevant in answering the best practice question outlined for this chapter. The fact that there was an adequate level of agreement within the chosen professional sources, and all eight of the "overall" best practices included the professional perspective, indicates that the chosen sources provided a fair representation of what professionals are saying about how practitioners should address spirituality. However, had more than five professional sources been included, professional practice recommendations might well have contributed more strongly to our current understanding of best practices.

In reference to the consumer and research perspectives, there appears to be shortage of available knowledge in regard to answering our best practice question. Most consumers writing about spirituality are interested primarily in sharing their personal recovery journeys—guidelines for practice are implied rather than explicitly stated. The sources chosen for this chapter were of high quality in that they represent the voices of influential consumer leaders. Consumer sources were the most likely to have unanimous agreement about how spirituality should be approached, as all three consumers agreed on seven practice recommendations, six of which made it into the overall list. The fact that many of these consumer ideas were reified in the other perspectives speaks to the quality of consumer wisdom, and supports confidence in the validity of the sources.

Koenig (2005) reviewed hundreds of studies on spirituality/religion and mental health-related indicators such as well-being, substance use, anxiety, depression, and eating disorders. However, the results from the majority of the reviewed studies were based on correlations. Koenig noted that there is a scarcity of quality research on spiritual interventions. This is especially evident for spiritual intervention research geared toward people with SMI, in which only a handful of studies exist. A summary of the quality criteria scale scoring for the included research sources are presented in Tables 9.3 and 9.4. Note that some of the research studies included have a relatively low quality rating scale score. A decision was made to include these studies precisely because they represent the research that is currently available.

The qualitative research sources were most likely to have strong relevance to the best practice question and were more thorough in offering implications for practice. The quantitative research sources were strongest in research design, using an intervention that was clearly defined and well implemented, and the use of quality measurement instruments. Samples were somewhat weak across all of the research sources—most used a sample that was either small or did not adequately represent the SMI target population. Another weakness across research sources is related to data analysis/results. The chosen qualitative studies did not include enough information about data analysis procedures, while the results produced in the quantitative sources were not always conclusive. In general, research appears to be at the early stages in its ability to contribute to our understanding of how to best help SMI clients utilize their spiritual resources toward recovery.

Value Critique

An important next step in assessing the quality or "strength" of conclusions made about current best practices is to determine how well professional values are represented. The chosen values criterion is comprised of commonly accepted values in social work and related professions. These include: 1) utilizing a client-centered approach; 2) encouraging strengths and resources; 3) recognizing the whole person; 4) embracing diversity and inclusivity; 5) promoting self-determination; 6) noncoercion of clients; 7) ensuring client safety; 8) practitioner competence; and 9) practitioner self-awareness.

Two highly emphasized values in the social work profession—utilizing a client-centered approach, and encouraging clients' strengths and resources—were well represented among the list of best practices. Namely, both of these values were also included as best practice categories (BP #3 and #4 in Table 9.6). Overall, there appears to be a strong degree of support for the inclusion of a client-centered approach, and the promotion of clients' strengths and resources as best practices for helping clients utilize spirituality to enhance recovery.

Several of the best practices listed in Table 9.6 reflect the social work profession's value of considering the whole person. This value entails an expansion of the commonly accepted bio-psycho-social model to include the spiritual aspect of the person. The best practice of promoting spiritual-related strengths and resources (BP# 3), which considers environmental resources (faith communities), as well as psychological resources (hope), and resources that transcend everyday reality (belief in God or ultimate reality), is a prime example of valuing the whole person.

Two other values—embracing diversity and inclusivity, and promoting self-determination—are implied by various best practices. For example, helping clients to make meaning (BP#1) and encouraging clients' interpretations of their spiritual experiences (BP #2) are best practices that imply openness to a diverse range of views and beliefs. Also implied is that clients determine their own meanings and are expected to make decisions about how they wish to define their experiences, rather than having their experiences defined for them—congruent with the value of self-determination. Closely related is the value of noncoercion. Some authors have expressed concern that there is potential for some practitioners to proselytize when they attempt to address clients' spirituality (Canda and Furman, 1999). Many of the best practices listed in Table 9.6 present strategies that help minimize the potential of coercing clients.

Some of the values underrepresented by our current understanding of best practices (as outlined in this chapter) include the following: ensuring safety; practitioner competence; and practitioner self-awareness. The insufficient representation of these values will be explored in more detail, as they function as key contributors toward making recommendations for improving our understanding about how to best help clients utilize spirituality toward recovery enhancement.

Current best practices express little concern about client safety. Only one source (R1) suggested that practitioners may need to proceed cautiously in discussing spiritual issues. Sullivan (1992a) acknowledged that the SMI population can be considered vulnerable when compared to the general population. Also, it has been noted that, traditionally, mental health practitioners have been wary of discussing religion with clients in fear that such discussions may exacerbate symptoms. Although several authors have debated the validity of such beliefs (Fallot, 1998a; Kehoe, 1998), best practice #5 makes it clear that practitioners should recognize that a person's spirituality may manifest differently according to one's phase of illness. It is problematic that there are currently no specific guidelines that outline how practitioners should respond to clients' spirituality in a way that takes vulnerability level into consideration. Because clients may be more vulnerable when experiencing more intense symptoms, practitioners may need to be more cautious about engaging in deeper level exploration of spirituality when clients are experiencing higher levels of symptoms, or certain types of symptoms. Therefore, until there is a better understanding about how spirituality and symptoms interact, it is important that practitioners continue to emphasize the value of client safety, especially during times when clients appear most vulnerable.

Practitioner competence is highly valued within social work and related professions. Although the value of professional "competence" was strongly mentioned within the professional perspective (BP #9 was "Practitioners need to educate themselves in the area of spirituality—see Table 9.2), it was not as well represented in the "overall" best practice list. Two "overall" best practices (BP# 6 and #7) imply that social workers need to possess greater knowledge about spirituality. Best practice #6 states that practitioners should be able to discern between spirituality that is illness-based versus nonillness-based. Also, best practice #7 indicates that practitioners should help clients explore both helpful and unhelpful spiritual beliefs. However, in order to be able to effectively implement these best practices, practitioners would need to have more than just a superficial understanding. Opportunities for more in-depth training on the topic of spirituality and mental health are needed.

Current best practices do not explicitly emphasize the need for practitioners to be aware of their own biases around religion and spirituality. In total, only one consumer and two professional sources stated that practitioner bias can be a problem when addressing clients' spirituality. However, scholars who write about spirituality have expressed concern that some practitioners may carry unresolved issues related to their childhood religion, which can make it difficult to deal with the topic objectively in practice (Canda and Furman, 1999). Best practices can be improved by placing a stronger emphasis on practitioner self-awareness.

Finally, it was mentioned above that best practices for addressing spirituality give emphasis to an inclusive approach that respects the diverse range of spiritual perspectives that exist. However, further discussion is warranted, especially considering that three research sources promoted the adaptation of standard therapies to include religion-specific content when working with highly religious clients. Examples given by the research sources were geared specifically toward either Christian or Muslim clients. An improvement would be to develop multiple versions of these adapted standard therapies to make them applicable to people from diverse religious perspectives. For example, cognitive–behavioral therapy (CBT) could be adapted to include Christian content for use with Christian clients, and also adapted to include Muslim or Judaic content for use with clients from the Muslim or Jewish faiths.

Conclusion

The goal of this best practice investigation has been to more clearly identify current guidelines for helping clients diagnosed with a SMI utilize spirituality as a recovery tool. Eight best practices were identified as representing our current understanding (Table 9.6). These eight are: 1) recognize clients' need for meaning-making/make room for clients' exploration of spirituality as a potential meaning-making tool; 2) honor and encourage consumers' own interpretations of their spiritual experiences and beliefs; 3) promote clients' spirituality as a potential source of strength/ explore and encourage clients' spiritual resources; 4) a client-centered approach; 5) understand and discuss the various ways in which clients' spirituality and mental illness can interact/clients' spiritual beliefs can manifest differently during different phases of illness; 6) be able to distinguish between illness- and nonillness-related spiritual beliefs/recognize and validate the authentic aspects of clients' spiritual experience; 7) address both helpful and unhelpful beliefs with clients; and 8) explore spiritual themes with clients.

It is important to keep in mind that the professional knowledge base related to spiritual intervention strategies for working with people with SMI remains underdeveloped. This best practice inquiry can be viewed as a preliminary attempt at synthesizing current understanding on the topic. It is reassuring that the best practices outlined in this inquiry measure up well against key professional values including: 1) client-centeredness; 2) encouraging strengths and resources; 3) recognizing the whole person; 4) embracing diversity and inclusivity; 5) promoting self-determination; and 6) noncoercion of clients.

To improve current best practices, several recommendations are offered. First, there needs to be a better understanding of the impact of discussing spirituality with clients who may be experiencing symptoms, namely psychosis. Until knowledge is further developed in this area, it is recommended that practitioners continue to emphasize the value of client safety in situations in which they suspect that clients are especially vulnerable. Second, in order to effectively integrate spirituality into practice, increased opportunities are needed for professional training on the topic. Third, best practices need to place a stronger emphasis on practitioner self-awareness. Practitioners who make efforts to address their personal biases around spirituality will be in a better position to support clients' spiritual viewpoints. Finally, there have been some recent studies related to adapting standard therapies to include religion-specific content. This approach may have a particular appeal to a subpopulation of religious clients. In adherence with the value of inclusivity, it is recommended that such adaptations of standard therapy are developed in a manner that considers the wide range of spiritual and religious orientations that exist.

References

Azhar, M., Varma, S., & Dharap, A. (1994). Religious psychotherapy in anxiety disorder patients. *Acta Psychiatrica Scandinavic, 90*, 1–3.

Bergin, A. (1991). Values and religious issues in psychotherapy and mental health. *American Psychologist, 46*, 393–403.

Canda, E. (1999). Spiritually sensitive social work: Key concepts and ideals. *Journal of Social Work Theory and Practice, 1*(1), 1–15.

Canda, E., & Furman, L. (1999). *Spiritual diversity in social work practice.* New York: The Free Press.

Corrigan, P., McCorkle, B., Schell, B., & Kidder, K. (2003). Religion and spirituality in the lives of people with serious mental illness. *Community Mental Health Journal, 39*(6), 487–499.

Deegan, P. (2004). *Recovery journal: Spiritual lessons in recovery.* Retrieved April 1, 2008 from www.patdeegan.com.

Fallot, R. (1998a). *Spirituality and religion in recovery from mental illness.* San Francisco: Jossey-Bass Publishers.

Fallot, R. (1998b). Recommendations for integrating spirituality into mental health services. *New Directions for Mental Health Services, 80*, 97–100.

Kabat-Zinn, J., Massion, A., Kristeller, J., Peterson, L., Fletcher, K., Pbert, L., Lenderking, W., & Santorelli, S. (1992). Effectiveness of a meditation-based stress reduction program in the treatment of anxiety disorders. *American Journal of Psychiatry, 149*(7), 936–943.

Kehoe, N. (1998). Religious-issues group therapy. *New Directions for Mental Health Services, 80*, 45–55.

Koenig, H. (2005). *Faith and mental health: Religious resources for healing.* Philadelphia: Templeton Foundation Press.

Koenig, H., McCullough, M., & Larson, D. (2001). *Handbook of religion and health.* New York: Oxford University Press.

Leibrich, J. (2002). Making space: spirituality and mental health. *Mental Health, Religion and Culture, 5*(2), 143–162.

Lindgren, K., & Coursey, R. (1995). Spirituality and serious mental illness: A two part study. *Psychosocial Rehabilitation Journal, 18*(3), 93–111.

Lukoff, D. (2005). Spiritual and transpersonal approaches to psychotic disorders. In S.G. Mijares & G.S. Khalsa (Eds.), *The psychospiritual clinician's handbook* (pp. 233–257). New York: Haworth Press.

McSherry, W. (2006). *Making sense of spirituality in nursing and health care practice: an interactive approach.* Philadelphia: Jessica Kingsley Publishers.

Murphy, M. (2000). Coping with the spiritual meaning of psychosis. *Psychiatric Rehabilitation Journal, 24*(2), 179–183.

O'Rourke, C. (1997). Listening for the sacred: Addressing spiritual issues in the group treatment of adults with mental illness. *Smith College Studies in Social Work, 67*(2), 177–196.

Owen, S., & Khalil, E. (2007). Addressing diversity in mental health care: A review of guidance documents. *International Journal of Nursing Studies, 44*(3), 467–478.

Phillips, R., Lakin, R., & Pargament, K. (2002). Brief report: Development and implementation of a spiritual issues psychoeducational group for those with serious mental illness. *Community Mental Health Journal, 38*(6), 487–495.

Propst, R., Ostrom, R., Watkins, P., Dean, T., & Mashburn, D. (1992). Comparative efficacy of religious and nonreligious cognitive-behavioral therapy for the treatment of clinical depression in religious individuals. *Journal of Consulting and Clinical Psychology, 60*(1), 94–103.

Puchalaski, C., Larson, D., & Lu, F. (2001). Spirituality in psychiatry residency training programs. *International Review of Psychiatry, 13*(2), 132–138.

Rapp, C. (1998). *The strengths model: Case management with people suffering from severe and persistent mental illness.* New York: Oxford University Press.

Razali, S., Hasanah, C., Aminah, K., & Subramaniam, M. (1998). Religious-sociocultural psychotherapy in patients with anxiety and depression. *Australian and New Zealand Journal of Psychiatry, 32*(6), 867–872.

Richards, S., & Bergin A. (2004). *Casebook for a spiritual strategy in counseling and psychotherapy.* Washington, DC: American Psychological Association.

Saleebey, D. (1996). The strengths perspective in social work practice: extensions and cautions. *Social Work, 41*(3), 296–305.

Sheridan, M., Bullis, R., Adcock, C., Berlin, S., & Miller, P. (1992). Practitioners' personal and professional attitudes toward religion and spirituality: Issues for education and practice. *Journal of Social Work Education, 28*(2), 190–203.

Sims, A. (1999). The cure of souls: Psychiatric dilemmas. *International Review of Psychiatry, 11*(2/3), 97–102.

Sullivan, W. (1992a). Spirituality as social support for individuals with severe mental illness. *Spirituality and Social Work Journal, 1*(3), 7–13.

Sullivan, W. (1992b). Reclaiming the community: The strengths perspective and Deinstitutionalization. *Social Work, 37*(3), 204–209.

Sullivan, W. (1998). Recoiling, regrouping, and recovering: First-person accounts of the role of spirituality in the course of serious mental illness. In R. D. Fallot (Ed.), *Spirituality and religion in recovery from mental illness* (pp. 25–44). San Francisco: Jossey-Bass.

Swinton, J. (2001). *Spirituality and mental health care: Rediscovering a forgotten dimension.* London: Jessica Kingsley.

Tepper, L., Rogers, S., Coleman, E., & Maloney, H. (2001). The prevalence of religious coping among persons with persistent mental illness. *Psychiatric Services, 52*(5), 660–665.

Postscript

Christopher G. Petr

As a method to ascertain best practices, MEBP offers a broader, more nuanced view than other approaches. The examples presented in Chapters 3–9 demonstrate the utility and strengths of MEBP to synthesize knowledge from consumer, professional, and research (both qualitative and quantitative) sources toward a complex, and ultimately more realistic, view of the current state-of-the-art practices. With the added practicality of the potency and value critiques, MEBP offers clear, though not always simple, guidelines for potential implementation that decision-makers can use to improve local responses to perplexing social issues.

At the same time, it is important to acknowledge that there are limitations to the MEBP approach. All systematic reviews, including MEBP, are limited in that they may or may not apply to individual clients and settings. With MEBP and other systematic reviews, practice-based research, in which local data is collected about the implementation of best practices, is an essential component of state-of-the art best practices. Because it is so comprehensive and inclusive in scope, MEBP may sacrifice some depth, especially with respect to the research perspective. MEBP is not meant to be, itself, a systematic meta-analysis of the empirical literature. MEBP investigators have neither the time nor the resources and expertise to conduct such exhaustive reviews of the empirical literature. Although existing meta-analyses are valued and incorporated, in the event that these are nonexistent, the MEBP process requires only that a handful of the highest rated individual studies be included. In reality, this is often sufficient because of the paucity of research about the service effectiveness for many, if not most, MEBP questions in the social services arena. This general lack of intervention research is a compelling reason to add professional and consumer perspectives to the inquiry.

Yet, for many MEBP questions, there may also be a dearth of sources informing the consumer and professional perspectives, thus limiting the potency of the analysis. In order for the full effect of MEBP to be realized, the general discourse about best practices needs to more fully honor and validate these perspectives. MEBP compels researchers and administrators and policymakers to acknowledge the limits of evidence-based practice, and support alternative ways of knowing, while at the same time advocating for more and better intervention research. This process would improve the general potency of best practices across topics.

Ultimately, MEBP is not merely a method, it is a way of thinking about and dialoging what best practices really are. Unlike other approaches, MEBP insists not only that knowledge be broadened beyond intervention research, but also that values be central to the analysis of best practices. Instead of pretending that values are irrelevant or somehow toxic to the process, the discourse about best practices needs to address this thorny issue head on. More widespread discussion at policy conferences and professional meetings about what values are universal and, most important, would provide support and direction for the values critique in the last step of MEBP. Values enter the discourse at all stages, not just at the critique stage as they primarily do in MEBP. Qualitative researchers have long required that researchers be transparent about their agendas, their biases, and their relationships. Quantitative researchers would be well served to follow that lead, so that potential conflicts of interest and hidden agendas can be examined. Research is not value free.

The MEBP process values diversity, inclusiveness, empowerment of subjugated voices, and progressive change. Regarding the latter, MEBP influences the best practices discourse by exposing the myth that best practices are immutable. Like everything else in life, best practices are, and thus should be reified as, dynamic processes. It is expected that the MEBP process itself will change once more experience is gained and more discourse ensues about its essential merit.

Contributors

Jung Jin Choi is a doctoral student at the University of Kansas, where he is a research assistant on projects studying the interface of juvenile justice and children's mental health. He holds MSW degrees from both the University of Wisconsin—Milwaukee and the Kyong-Gi University in Korea. In Korea, he worked at the Brief Family Therapy Center of Seoul as a research associate and developed an interest in Solution-focused Brief Therapy. Currently, he is conducting research for his doctoral dissertation focused on experiences of actors in victim–offender mediation. His professional passion is to make a difference in the juvenile justice system, especially in helping the system be more culturally sensitive for Asian Americans.

Jacqueline M. Counts is associate director at The Institute for Educational Research and Public Service, a unit in the School of Education at the University of Kansas. She is a doctoral student at the KU School of Social Welfare, and holds an MSW from the University of California at Berkeley. Ms. Counts is the author of the Kansas Early Childhood Systems Plan and is the evaluator for the Kansas Community-Based Child Abuse and Neglect Prevention programs. Current projects include the development of a Kansas Strengthening Families Plan, a Protective Factors Survey to measure the effects of prevention programs, and an accountability framework to determine the impact of tobacco settlement dollars awarded to Kansas.

Emily McCave is a doctoral student at the University of Kansas, School of Social Welfare. She received her MSW at Washington University, in St. Louis. Her prior professional experience has been in community mental health, specifically working with children with trauma. While completing her doctorate, she continues to do research in children's mental health, as well as teach social work practice, and has co-taught a human sexuality course. Her current areas of interest include women's sexual health, children's mental health, and lesbian, gay, bisexual and transgender (LGBT) issues.

Tara McLendon received bachelor and master's degrees in social work from the University of Kansas. She is a licensed specialist clinical social worker and has worked in Community Mental Health since 1993. Her clinical and research interests include children's mental health and family therapy. She is currently a doctoral student in the School of Social Welfare at the University of Kansas, where she is involved in training and evaluation of Family Directed Structural Therapy.

Christopher G. Petr is professor at the University of Kansas, School of Social Welfare, where he received both his MSW and Ph.D. degrees. He is author or co-author of more than 20 journal publications and the book, *Social Work with Children and Their Families*, in its second edition, published by Oxford University Press. He serves as co-chair of Douglas County Success by Six Coalition Board of Directors and is a member of a local foster care citizen review board. For a number of years, he has collaborated with the state mental health authority on numerous research and training projects related to children's mental health.

Vincent R. Starnino is trained as a licensed therapist. He specializes in treating adults diagnosed with mental illness, children and families, and inmates. Vincent obtained his MSW degree from McGill University in Montreal, Canada and is presently pursuing a Ph.D. at the University of Kansas, School of Social Welfare. Vincent's main area of interest is exploring the role of spirituality in mental health recovery. He is preparing to write a doctoral dissertation on the topic.

Karen Flint Stipp has worked as a clinical social worker in public schools and in a private clinical setting serving children and families. Karen's practice put her in touch with dozens of children without access to health care. Her first-hand encounters with the confounding effects of lacking access to health care energize her work as a social welfare doctoral student at the University of Kansas. Karen holds a bachelor's degree in psychology and social welfare from Olivet Nazarene University and an MSW from the University of Illinois.

Uta M. Walter came to the United States as a Fulbright Scholar from Germany in 1995. After receiving her MSW (1996) from the University of Kansas, School of Social Welfare, she served as a post-master's fellow for clinical social work at the Menninger Clinic. Subsequently, she returned to the University of Kansas for doctoral work and completed her Ph.D. in 2006. She currently works as a lecturer at the Catholic University of Applied Sciences as well as the Alice-Salomon-University of Applied Sciences in Berlin, Germany, and continues to serve as a research consultant for the School of Social Welfare at KU.

Index